Lecture Notes in Computer Science 2704
Edited by G. Goos, J. Hartmanis, and J. van Leeuwen

Springer

Berlin
Heidelberg
New York
Barcelona
Hong Kong
London
Milan
Paris
Tokyo

Shing-Tsaan Huang   Ted Herman (Eds.)

Self-Stabilizing Systems

6th International Symposium, SSS 2003
San Francisco, CA, USA, June 24-25, 2003
Proceedings

Springer

Series Editors

Gerhard Goos, Karlsruhe University, Germany
Juris Hartmanis, Cornell University, NY, USA
Jan van Leeuwen, Utrecht University, The Netherlands

Volume Editors

Shing-Tsaan Huang
National Central University
College of Electrical Engineering and Computer Science
Chung-Li (32054),Taiwan
E-mail: sthuang@csie.ncu.edu.tw

Ted Herman
University of Iowa, Dept. of Computer Science
Iowa City, IA 52242, USA
E-mail: herman@cs.uiowa.edu

Cataloging-in-Publication Data applied for

A catalog record for this book is available from the Library of Congress

Bibliographic information published by Die Deutsche Bibliothek
Die Deutsche Bibliothek lists this publication in the Deutsche Nationalbibliografie;
detailed bibliographic data is available in the Internet at <http://dnb.ddb.de>.

CR Subject Classification (1998): C.2.4, C.2, C.3, F.1, F.2.2, K.6

ISSN 0302-9743
ISBN 3-540-40453-8 Springer-Verlag Berlin Heidelberg New York

Springer-Verlag Berlin Heidelberg New York
a member of BertelsmannSpringer Science+Business Media GmbH

http://www.springer.de

© Springer-Verlag Berlin Heidelberg 2003
Printed in Germany

Typesetting: Camera-ready by author, data conversion by DA-TeX Gerd Blumenstein
Printed on acid-free paper   SPIN 10928691   06/3142   5 4 3 2 1 0

Preface

Self-stabilization is an established principle of modern distributed system design. The advantages of systems that self-recover from transient failures, temporary security attacks, and spontaneous reconfiguration are obvious. Less well understood are the inherent costs and design tradeoffs that accompany self-stabilization. The need for autonomous recovery, not just of entire systems, but also of individual components, algorithms, and communication protocols, is becoming more apparent because distributed systems of immense scale are presently emerging.

The Symposium on Self-Stabilizing Systems (SSS) is the main forum for research in the area of self-stabilization. This year's meeting changed the name from *workshop* to *symposium*, in recognition of some maturity in the area, which is increasingly also represented by papers at the best conferences on distributed systems. The previous Workshops on Self-Stabilizing Systems (WSS) were held in 1989, 1995, 1997, 1999, and 2001. This year's symposium was organized on short notice, leaving researchers far less time to prepare submissions than in past workshops (it becomes ever more challenging to fit our conference into the very active schedules of the research community). Nonetheless, we received 27 submitted papers, which is equal to the number submitted to the workshop of 2001. Out of the submitted papers, the program committee chose 15 for inclusion in these proceedings.

A presentation at the symposium which is not represented in these proceedings was the invited talk by Anish Arora. The title of his presentation was "Taking Stabilization to the Masses: Problems, Opportunities and Progress." Professor Arora discussed recent computing trends that derive benefit from self-stabilization principles, as well as some perceived and some real problems that have thus far prevented wide spread deployment of self-stabilization techniques. In particular, he focused on wireless sensor networks, which are a promising platform for stabilization due to thair lightweight model of hardware and software, their error-prone measurement of sensory information, and the suitability of the forward recovery semantics of many self-stabilizing protocols for their applications. The first paper in these proceedings deals with one of these applications, namely tracking of mobile objects, and is illustrative of some of the research problems and opportunities in this area.

Futurists of applied computing technology dream of a time when computing devices with attached sensors and actuators can be manufactured in microscale (MEMS) to nanoscale dimensions; such devices could be deployed in enormous networks, consisting of millions of nodes with varying levels of computing and communication resource. In this new regime, issues of fault tolerance, power conservation, and adaptivity will be crucial (see, for example, LNCS 2634). Self-stabilization and techniques derived from stabilization will no doubt become routine, and research on these challenging issues will motivate our field. Not entirely by coincidence, at the same time as researchers investigate nanoscale technology, other scientists are looking at the mechanisms of life on an even smaller scale. Computer science is essential to the mapping of genetic codes, the modeling of protein folding, and the extraction of patterns from vast genomic databases. In coping with the scale of the Internet and imagined sensor networks, it is natural to find parallels in biological systems (the third paper in these proceedings is an example of this motif).

The symposium of 2003 was held in collaboration with DSN 2003, the International Conference on Dependable Systems and Networks, in San Francisco, June 24th and June 25th. We thank Charles B. Weinstock, the general chair of DSN 2003, for the opportunity to hold the symposium at that venue. We gratefully acknowledge the efforts of the SSS program committee members and the reviewers, who provided thorough reviews on a rather short schedule. In particular, we thank Anish Arora, Ajoy Datta, and Neeraj Suri for their work with conference arrangements and many other details to support the symposium.

April 2003   Shing-Tsaan Huang
                                                        Ted Herman

Program Committee

Referees

Table of Contents

A Pursuer-Evader Game for Sensor Networks[*]

Murat Demirbas[1], Anish Arora[1], and Mohamed G. Gouda[2]

[1] Department of Computer & Information Science, The Ohio State University
Columbus, Ohio 43210 USA
[2] Department of Computer Sciences, The University of Texas at Austin
Austin, TX 78712 USA

Abstract. In this paper a self-stabilizing program for solving a pursuer-evader problem in sensor networks is presented. The program can be tuned for tracking speed or energy efficiency. In the program, sensor motes close to the evader dynamically maintain a "tracking" tree of depth R that is always rooted at the evader. The pursuer, on the other hand, searches the sensor network until it reaches the tracking tree, and then follows the tree to its root in order to catch the evader.

1 Introduction

Due to its importance in military contexts, pursuer-evader tracking has received significant attention [3, 16, 17, 4] and has been posed by the DARPA network embedded software technology (NEST) program as a challenge problem. Here, we consider the problem in the context of wireless sensor networks. Such networks comprising potentially many thousands of low-cost and low-power wireless sensor nodes have recently became feasible, thanks to advances in microelectromechanical systems technology, and are being regarded as a realistic basis for deploying large-scale pursuer evader tracking.

Previous work on the pursuer-evader problem is not directly applicable to tracking in sensor networks, since these networks introduce the following challenges: Firstly, sensor nodes have very limited computational resources (e.g., 8K RAM and 128K flash memory); thus, centralized algorithms are not suitable for sensor networks due to their larger computational requirements. Secondly, sensor nodes are energy constrained; thus, algorithms that impose an excessive communication burden on nodes are not acceptable since they drain the battery power quickly. Thirdly, sensor networks are fault-prone: message losses and corruptions (due to fading, collusion, and hidden node effect), and node failures (due to crash and energy exhaustion) are the norm rather than the exception. Thus, sensor nodes can lose synchrony and their programs can reach arbitrary states [14]. Finally, on-site maintenance is not feasible; thus, sensor networks should be self-healing. Indeed, one of the emphases of the NEST program is to

---

[*] This work was partially sponsored by DARPA contract OSU-RF #F33615-01-C-1901, NSF grant NSF-CCR-9972368, an Ameritech Faculty Fellowship, and two grants from Microsoft Research.

design low-cost fault-tolerant, and more specifically self-stabilizing, services for the sensor network domain.

In this paper we present a tunable and self-stabilizing program for solving a pursuer-evader problem in sensor networks. The goal of the pursuer is to catch the evader (despite the occurrence of faults) by means of information gathered by the sensor network. The pursuer can move faster than the evader. However, the evader is omniscient —it can see the state of the entire network— whereas the pursuer can only see the state of one sensor node (say the nearest one). Note that this model captures a simple, abstract version of problems that arise in tracking via sensor networks.

Tunability. We achieve tunability of our program by constructing it to be a hybrid between two orthogonal programs: an evader-centric program and a pursuer-centric program.

In the evader-centric program, nodes communicate periodically with neighbors and dynamically maintain a "tracking" tree structure that is always rooted at the evader. The pursuer eventually catches the evader by following this tree structure to the root: the pursuer asks the closest sensor node who its parent is, then proceeds to that node, and thus, reaches the root node (and hence the evader) eventually.

In the pursuer-centric program, nodes communicate with neighbors only at the request of the pursuer: When the pursuer reaches a node, the node resets its recorded time of a detection of an evader to zero and directs the pursuer to a neighboring node with the highest recorded time.

The evader-centric program converges and tracks the evader faster, whereas the pursuer-centric program is more energy-efficient. In the hybrid program we combine the evader-centric and pursuer-centric programs:

1. We modify the evader-centric program to limit the tracking tree to a bounded depth R to save energy.
2. We modify the pursuer-centric program to exploit the tracking tree structure.

The hybrid program is tuned for tracking speed or energy efficiency by selecting R appropriately. In particular, for the extended hybrid program in Section 6, the tracking time is $3 * (D - R) + R * \alpha/(1 - \alpha)$ steps, and at most n communications take place at each program step, where D denotes the diameter of the network, α is the ratio of the speed of the evader to that of the pursuer, and n is the number of sensor nodes included in the tracking tree.

Self-Stabilization. In the presence of faults, our program recovers from arbitrary states to states from where it correctly tracks the evader; this sort of fault-tolerance is commonly referred to as stabilizing fault-tolerance. In particular, starting from any arbitrary state, the tracking time is $2R + 3 * (D - R) + R * \alpha/(1 - \alpha)$ steps for our extended hybrid program.

Organization of the Paper. After presenting the system and fault model in the next section, we present an evader-centric program in Section 3 and a pursuer-centric program in Section 4. In Section 5, we present the tunable, hybrid program combining the previous two programs. We present an efficient version of the hybrid program in Section 6. Finally, we discuss related work and make concluding remarks in Section 7.

2   The Problem

System Model. A sensor network consists of a (potentially large) number of sensor nodes (called motes). Each mote is capable of receiving/transmitting messages within its field of communication. All motes within this communication field are its neighbors; we denote this set for mote j as $nbr.j$. We assume the nbr relation is symmetric and induces a connected graph. (Protocols for maintaining biconnectivity in sensor networks are known [8].)

Problem Statement. Given are two distinguished processes, the pursuer and the evader, that each reside at some mote in the sensor network. Each mote can immediately detect whether the pursuer and/or the evader are resident at that mote.

Both the pursuer and the evader are mobile: each can atomically move from one mote to another, but the speed of evader movement is less than the speed of the pursuer movement.

The strategy of evader movement is unknown to the network. The strategy could in particular be intelligent, with the evader omnisciently inspecting the entire network to decide whether and where to move. By way of contrast, the pursuer strategy is based only on the state of the mote at which it resides.

Required is to design a program for the motes and the pursuer so that the pursuer can "catch" the evader, i.e., guarantee in every computation of the network that eventually both the pursuer and the evader reside at the same mote.

Programming Model. A program consists of a set of variables, mote actions, pursuer actions, and evader actions.

Each variable and each action resides at some mote. Variables of a mote j can be updated only by j's mote actions. Mote actions can only read the variables of their mote and the neighboring motes. Pursuer actions can only read the variables of their mote. The evader actions can read the variables of the entire program, however, they cannot update any of these variables.

Each action has the form:

$$\langle guard \rangle \longrightarrow \langle assignment\ statement \rangle$$

A guard is a boolean expression over variables. An assignment statement updates one or more variables.

A state is defined by a value for every variable in the program, chosen from the predefined domain of that variable. An action whose guard is true at some state is said to be *enabled* at that state.

We assume maximal parallelism in the execution of mote actions. At each state, each mote executes all actions that are enabled in that state. (Execution of multiple enabled actions in a mote is treated as executing them in some sequential order.) Maximal parallelism is not assumed for the execution of the pursuer and evader actions. Recall, however, that the speed of execution of the former exceeds that of the latter. For ease of exposition, we assume that evader and pursuer actions do not occur strictly in parallel with mote actions.

A computation of the program is a maximal sequence of program steps: in each step, actions that are enabled at the current state is executed according to the above operational semantics, thereby yielding the next state in the computation. The maximality of a computation implies that no computation is a proper prefix of another computation.

We assume that each mote has a clock, that is synchronized with the clocks of other motes. (Real time advances with each program step, in a non-Zeno sense.) This assumption is reasonably implemented at least for Mica motes [12]. Later, in Section 7, we show how our programs can be modified to work without the synchronized clocks assumption.

Notation. In this paper, we use j, k, and l to denote motes. We use $var.j$ to denote the variable var residing at j. We use ▯ to separate the actions in a program and $x :\in A$ to denote that x is assigned to an element of set A.

Each **parameter** in a program ranges over the nbr set of a mote. The function of a parameter is to define a set of actions as one parameterized action. For example, let k be a parameter whose value is 0, 1, or 2; then an action act of mote j parameterized over k abbreviates the following set of actions:

$$act\backslash(k = 0) \quad ▯ \quad act\backslash(k = 1) \quad ▯ \quad act\backslash(k = 2)$$

where $act\backslash(k = i)$ is act with every occurrence of k substituted with i.

We describe certain conjuncts in a guard in English: {Evader resides at j} and {Evader detected at j}. The former expression evaluates to true at all states where the evader is at j whereas the latter evaluates to true only at the state immediately following any step where the evader moves to mote j, and evaluates to false in the subsequent states even if the evader is still at j.

We use N to denote the number of motes in the sensor network, D the diameter of the network, and M the distance between the pursuer and evader. Finally, we use α to denote the ratio of the speed of the evader to that of the pursuer.

Evader Action. In each of the programs that we present in this paper, we use the following evader action.

{ Evader resides at j } $\longrightarrow$ Evader moves to l, $l :\in \{k \mid k \in nbr.j \cup \{j\}\}$

When this action is executed, the evader moves to an arbitrary neighbor of j or skips a move. This notion of nondeterministic moves suffices to capture the strategy of an omniscient evader.

Recall from the discussion in the problem statement that, when the evader moves to a mote, the mote immediately detects this fact (i.e., the detection actions have priority over normal mote actions and are fired instantaneously).

Fault Model. Transient faults may corrupt the program state. Transient faults may also fail-stop or restart motes (in a manner that is detectable to their neighbors); we assume that the connectivity of the graph is maintained despite these faults.

A program P is **stabilizing fault-tolerant** iff starting from an arbitrary state P eventually recovers to a state from where its specification is satisfied.

3 An Evader-Centric Program

In this section we present an evader-centric solution to the pursuer-evader problem in sensor networks. In our program every sensor mote, j, maintains a value, $ts.j$, that denotes the latest timestamp that j knows for the detection of the evader. Initially, for all j, $ts.j = 0$. If j detects the evader, it sets $ts.j$ to its clock's value. Every mote j periodically updates its $ts.j$ value based on the ts values of its neighbors: j assigns the maximum timestamp value it is aware of as $ts.j$. We use $p.j$ (read parent of j) to record the mote that j received the maximum timestamp value. Note that the parent relation embeds a tree rooted at the evader on the sensor network. We refer to this tree as the *tracking tree*.

In addition to above variables, we maintain a variable $d.j$ at each mote j to denote the distance of j from the evader. In the case where $ts.j$ is equal to ts values of j's neighbors, j uses the d values of the neighbors to elect its parent to be the one offering the shortest distance to the evader. Thus, the actions for mote j (parameterized with respect to neighbor k) in the evader-centric program is as follows.

$$
\begin{array}{l}
\{\ \text{Evader resides at } j\ \} \longrightarrow p.j := j;\ ts.j := clock.j;\ d.j := 0 \\
[] \\
ts.k > ts.j\ \lor\ (ts.k = ts.j\ \land\ d.k + 1 < d.j) \\
\qquad\qquad \longrightarrow p.j := k;\ ts.j\ :=\ ts.(p.j); \\
\qquad\qquad\qquad\quad d.j := d.(p.j) + 1
\end{array}
$$

Once a tracking tree is formed, the pursuer follows this tree to reach the evader simply by querying its closest mote for its parent and proceeding to the parent mote. Thus, the pursuer action is as follows.

$$
\{\text{Pursuer resides at } j\} \longrightarrow \quad \text{Pursuer moves to } p.j
$$

3.1   Proof of Correctness

As the following example illustrates, if the evader is moving it may not be possible to maintain a minimum distance spanning tree.

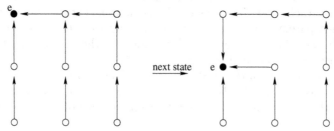

However, we can still prove the following theorem.

Theorem 1 The tracking tree is a spanning tree rooted at the mote where the evader resides.

Proof From the synchronized clocks assumption and the privileged detection action, {Evader resides at j}, it follows that the mote j where the evader resides has the highest timestamp value in the network. Observe from the second mote action that the $p.k$ variable at every mote k embed a logical tree structure over the sensor network. Cycles cannot occur since $(\forall k : ts.k > 0 : d.(p.k) < d.k)$[1]. Since $(\forall k : ts.k > 0 : ts.(p.k) > ts.k)$, the network is connected, and the mote j where the evader resides has the highest timestamp value in the network, it follows that there exists only one tree in the network and it is rooted at j.   □

Corollary 2 The tracking tree is fully constructed in at most D steps.

Proof Within at most D steps all the motes in the network receives a message from a mote that is already included in the tracking tree (due to the maximal parallelism model and the second mote action). From Theorem 1 it follows that a tracking tree covering the entire network is constructed.   □

Lemma 3 The distance between the pursuer and evader does not increase once the constructed tree includes the mote where the pursuer resides.

---

[1] A formula $(op\ i : R.i : X.i)$ denotes the value obtained by performing the (commutative and associative) op on the $X.i$ values for all i that satisfy $R.i$. Where $R.i$ is true, we omit $R.i$. As a special case, where op is conjunction, we write $(\forall i : R.i : X.i)$ which may be read as "if $R.i$ is true then so is $X.i$".

Proof Once the constructed tree includes the mote k_x where the pursuer resides, there exists a path $k_1, k_2, \ldots, k_x$ such that $(\forall i : 1 < i \le x : p.k_i = k_{i-1})$ and the evader resides at k_1. At each program step, any mote k_i in this path may choose to change its parent, rendering a different path between the pursuer and the evader. However, observe from the second mote action that, k_i changes its parent only if the new parent has a shorter path to the evader (higher timestamp implies shorter path since the mote where evader resides has the highest timestamp and motes execute under maximal parallelism model).

At any program step, if the evader moves to a neighboring mote, the pursuer, being faster than the evader, also moves to the next mote in the path. Thus, the net effect is that the path length can only decrease but not increase.   □

Theorem 4 The pursuer catches the evader in at most $M + 2M * \lceil \alpha/(1-\alpha) \rceil$ steps.

Proof Since the initial distance between the evader and the pursuer is M, after M program steps the tracking tree includes the mote at which the pursuer resides. Within this period, the evader can move to at most M hops away, potentially increasing the distance between the evader and pursuer to $2M$. From Lemma 3, it follows that this distance cannot increase in the subsequent program steps. Since the pursuer is faster than the evader, it catches the evader in at most $2M * \lceil \alpha/(1-\alpha) \rceil$ steps (follows from solving $\alpha = X/(X+2M)$ for X).   □

3.2   Proof of Stabilization

In the presence of faults variables of a mote j can be arbitrarily corrupted. However, for the sake of simplicity we assume that even in the presence of faults the following two conditions hold:

1. always $ts.j \le clock.j$
2. always $\{p.j \in \{nbr.j \cup \{j\} \cup \{\bot\}\}$

The first condition states that the timestamp for the detection of evader at mote j is always less than the local clock at j (i.e., $ts.j$ cannot be in the future). The second condition states that the domain of $p.j$ is restricted to the set $\{nbr.j \cup \{j\} \cup \{\bot\}\}$ where $p.j = \bot$ denotes that j does not have any parent. These are both locally checkable and enforceable conditions; in order to keep the program simple we will not include the corresponding correction actions in our presentation.

Lemma 5 The tracking tree stabilizes in at most D steps.

Proof Since we have always $ts.j \leq clock.j$, even at an arbitrary state (which might be reached due to transient faults) the mote where the evader resides has the highest timestamp value in the network. From Corollary 2 and Theorem 1 it follows that a fresh tracking tree is constructed within at most D steps and this tracking tree is a spanning tree rooted at the mote where the evader currently resides.   □

Theorem 6 Starting from an arbitrarily corrupted state, the pursuer catches the evader in at most $D + 2D * \alpha/(1 - \alpha)$.

Proof The proof follows from the proofs of Lemma 5 and Theorem 4.   □

3.3 Performance Metrics

The evader-centric program is not energy efficient since every mote communicates with its neighbor at each step of the program. That is, $\omega * N$ communications occur each step, where ω denotes the average degree of a mote. The communications can be treated as broadcasts, and hence, the number of total communications per step is effectively N.

On the other hand, the tracking time and the convergence time of the evader-centric program is fast: starting from an arbitrarily corrupted state it takes at most $D + 2D * \alpha/(1 - \alpha)$ steps for the pursuer to catch the evader.

4 A Pursuer-Centric Program

In this section we present a pursuer-centric solution to the pursuer-evader problem in sensor networks. Here, similar to the evader-centric program, every sensor mote, j, maintains a value, $ts.j$, that denotes the latest timestamp that j knows for the detection of the evader. Initially, for all j, $ts.j = 0$. If j detects the evader, it sets $ts.j$ to its clock's value.

In this program, motes communicate with neighbors only at the request of the pursuer: When the pursuer reaches a mote j, j resets $ts.j$ to zero and directs the pursuer to a neighboring mote with the highest recorded time (we use $next.j$ to denote this neighbor). Note that if all ts values of the neighbors are the same (e.g., zero), the pursuer is sent to an arbitrary neighbor. Also, if there is no pursuer at j, $next.j$ is set to $\bot$ (i.e., *undefined*).

Thus, the actions for mote j in the pursuer-centric program is as follows:

$$
\begin{array}{l}
\{ \text{ Evader detected at } j \ \} \longrightarrow ts.j := clock.j \\[4pt]
[] \\
\{ \text{ Pursuer detected at } j \ \} \longmapsto next.j :\in \{k \mid k \in nbr.j \ \wedge \\
\qquad\qquad\qquad\qquad\qquad ts.k = max(\{ \ ts.l \mid l \in nbr.j \ \}) \}; \\
\qquad\qquad\qquad ts.j := 0
\end{array}
$$

The pursuer's action is as follows.

$$\{\text{Pursuer resides at } j\} \longrightarrow \quad \text{Pursuer moves to } next.j$$

4.1 Proof of Correctness

Lemma 7 If the pursuer reaches a mote j where $ts.j > 0$, the pursuer catches the evader in at most $N * \alpha/(1 - \alpha)$ steps.

Proof If the pursuer reaches a mote j where $ts.j > 0$, then there exists a path between the pursuer and the evader that is at most of length N. This distance does not increase in the following program steps (due to maximal parallel execution semantics and the program actions).   □

In [6], it is proven that during a random walk on a graph the expected time to find N distinct vertices is $O(N^3)$. However, a recent result [13] shows that by using a local topology information (i.e., degree information of neighbor vertices) it is possible to achieve the cover time $O(N^2 logN)$ for random walk on any graph. Thus, we have:

Lemma 8 The pursuer reaches a mote j where $ts.j > 0$ within $O(N^2 logN)$ steps.   □

Theorem 9 The pursuer catches the evader within $O(N^2 logN)$ steps.   □

4.2 Proof of Stabilization

Since each mote j resets $ts.j$ to zero upon a detection of the pursuer, arbitrary $ts.j$ values eventually disappear, and hence, the pursuer-centric program is self-stabilizing.

Theorem 10 Starting from an arbitrary state, the pursuer catches the evader within $O(N^2 logN)$ steps.   □

4.3 Performance Metrics

The pursuer-centric program is energy efficient. At each step of the program only the mote where the pursuer resides communicates with its neighbors. That is, ω communications occur at each step.

On the other hand, the tracking and the convergence time of the pursuer-centric program is slow: $O(N^2 logN)$ steps.

5   A Hybrid Pursuer-Evader Program

In the hybrid program we combine the evader-centric and pursuer-centric approaches:

1. We modify the evader-centric program to limit the tracking tree to a bounded depth R to save energy.
2. We modify the pursuer-centric program to exploit the tracking tree structure.

We limit the depth of the tracking tree to R by means of the distance, d, variable.

$$
\{ \text{ Evader resides at } j \} \longmapsto p.j := j; \ ts.j := clock.j; \ d.j := 0
$$

$$
\square
$$

$$
d.k + 1 \leq R \ \wedge \ (ts.k > ts.j \ \vee \ (ts.k = ts.j \ \wedge \ d.k{+}1 < d.j))
$$
$$
\longrightarrow \ p.j := k; \ ts.j := \ ts.(p.j);
$$
$$
d.j := d.(p.j) + 1
$$

By limiting the tree to a depth R we lose the advantages of soft-state stabilization: there is no more a flow of fresh information to correct the state of the motes that are outside the tracking tree. To achieve stabilization, we add explicit stabilization actions. Next we describe these two actions.

For the case where the initial graph has cycles, each cycle is detected and removed by using the bound on the length of the path from each process to its root process in the tree. To this end, we exploit the way that we maintain the d variable: j sets $d.j$ to be $d.(p.j) + 1$ whenever $p.j \in nbr.j$ and $d.(p.j) + 1 \leq R$. The net effect of executing this action is that if a cycle exists then the $d.j$ value of each process j in the cycle gets "bumped up" repeatedly. Within at most R steps, some $d.(p.j)$ reaches R, and since the length of each path in the adjacency graph is bounded by R, the cycle is detected. To remove a cycle that it has detected, j sets $p.j$ to $\perp$ (undefined) and $d.j$ to ∞, from whereon the cycle is completely cleaned within the next R steps. Note that this action also takes care of pruning the tracking tree to height R (e.g., when the evader moves and as a result a mote j with $d.j = R$ becomes $R + 1$ away from the evader).

Mote j also sets $p.j$ to $\perp$ (undefined) and $d.j$ to ∞ if $p.j$ is not a valid parent (e.g. $d.j \neq d.(p.j) + 1$ or $ts.j > ts.(p.j)$ or $(p.j = j \ \wedge \ d.j \neq 0)$).

We add another action to correct the fake tree roots. If a mote j is spuriously corrupted to $p.j = j \ \wedge \ d.j = 0$, this is detected by explicitly asking for a proof of the evader at j.

Thus the stabilization actions for the bounded length tracking tree is as follows.

$$
p.j \neq \perp \ \wedge \ ((p.j = j \ \wedge \ d.j \neq 0) \ \vee \ ts.j > ts.(p.j)
$$
$$
\vee \ d.j \neq d.(p.j) + 1 \ \vee \ d.(p.j) \geq R - 1)
$$
$$
\longrightarrow \ p.j := \perp; \ d.j := \infty
$$

$$
\square
$$

$$
p.j = j \ \wedge \ d.j = 0 \ \wedge \ \neg\{ \text{ Evader resides at } j \ \}
$$
$$
\longrightarrow \ p.j := \perp; \ d.j := \infty
$$

We modify the mote action in the pursuer-centric program only slightly so as to exploit the tracking tree structure.

```
{ Pursuer detected at j } ⟶
        if (p.j ≠ ⊥) then next.j := p.j
        else
            next.j :∈ {k | k ∈ nbr.j ∧ ts.k = max({ts.l | l ∈ nbr.j})};
            ts.j := 0
```

Finally, the pursuer action is the same as that in Section 4.

5.1 Proof of Correctness

The following lemmas and theorem follow from their counterparts in Sections 3 and 4.

Lemma 11 The tracking tree is fully constructed in at most R steps. □

Below n denotes the number of motes included in the tracking tree.

Lemma 12 The pursuer reaches the tracking tree within $O((N-n)^2 log(N-n))$ steps. □

Theorem 13 The pursuer catches the evader within $O((N-n)^2 log(N-n))$ steps. □

5.2 Proof of Stabilization

Lemma 14 The tracking tree structure stabilizes in at most $2R$ steps.

Proof Follows from Lemma 5 and the discussion above about the stabilization actions of the hybrid program. □

Theorem 15 Starting from an arbitrary state, the pursuer catches the evader within $O((N-n)^2 log(N-n))$ steps. □

5.3 Performance Metrics

The hybrid program for the motes can be tuned to be energy efficient. At each step of the program at most $n + \omega$ communications take place.

The hybrid program can also be tuned to track and converge faster. The random walk now takes $O((N-n)^2 log(N-n))$ steps to find the tracking tree. From that point on it takes $R * \alpha/(1 - \alpha)$ steps for the pursuer to catch the evader.

6   An Efficient Version of the Hybrid Program

In this section we present an efficient version of the hybrid program. To this end, we first present an extended version of the pursuer-centric program, and then show how this extended pursuer-centric program can be incorporated into the hybrid program.

Extended Pursuer-Centric Program. In the extended version of the pursuer-centric program, instead of the random walk prescribed in Section 4, the pursuer uses *agents* to search the network for a trace of the evader. The pursuer agents idea can be implemented by constructing a (depth-first or bread-first) tree rooted at the mote where the pursuer resides. If a mote j with $ts.j > 0$ is included in this *pursuer tree*, the pursuer is notified of this result along with a path to j. The pursuer then follows this path to reach j. From this point on, due to Lemma 7, it will take at most $N * \alpha/(1 - \alpha)$ steps for the pursuer to catch the evader.

This program can be seen as an extension of the original pursuer-centric program in that instead of a 1-hop tree construction (i.e., the mote k where the pursuer resides contacts $nbr.k$) embedded in the original pursuer-centric program, we now employ a D-hop tree construction. To this end we change the original pursuer program as follows. The mote k where the pursuer resides sets $next.j$ to $\perp$ if none of its neighbors has a timestamp value greater than 0, instead of setting $next.j$ to point to a random neighbor of j. The pursuer upon reading a $\perp$ value for the $next$ variable, starts a tree construction to search for a trace of the evader. Note that by using a depth D, the pursuer tree is guaranteed to encounter a mote j with $ts.j > 0$.

Several extant self-stabilizing tree construction programs [1, 7, 9] suffice for constructing the pursuer tree in D steps and to complete the information feedback within another D steps. Also since the root of the pursuer tree is static (root does not change dynamically unlike the root of the tracking tree), it is possible to achieve self-stabilization of pursuer tree within D steps in an energy efficient manner. That is, in contrast to the evader-centric tracking tree program where all motes communicate at each program step, in the pursuer tree program only the motes propagating a (tree construction or information feedback) wave need to communicate with their immediate neighbors.

Extended Hybrid Program. It is straightforward to incorporate the extended version of the pursuer-centric program into the hybrid program. The only modification required is to set the depth of pursuer tree to be $D - R$ hops instead of D hops. Note that $D - R$ hops is enough for ensuring that the pursuer will encounter a trace of the evader (i.e., pursuer tree will reach a mote included in the tracking tree).

6.1 Performance Metrics

The extension improves the tracking and the convergence time of the pursuer-centric program from $O(N^2 log N)$ steps to $3D + N * \alpha/(1 - \alpha)$ steps ($2D$ steps for the pursuer tree construction and information feedback, and D steps for the pursuer to follow the path returned by the pursuer tree program). The extended pursuer-centric program remains energy efficient; the only overhead incurred is the one-time invocation of the pursuer tree construction.

In the extended hybrid program, it takes at most $3 * (D - R)$ steps for the pursuer to reach the tracking tree. (Compare this to $O((N - n)^2 log(N - n))$ steps in the original hybrid program.) From that point on it takes $R * \alpha/(1 - \alpha)$ steps for the pursuer to catch the evader. At each step of the extended hybrid program at most n communications take place, however, due to the pursuer tree computation, a one time cost of $2 * (D - R)$ is incurred.

1-Pursuer 0-Evader Scenario. The evader-centric program is energy efficient in a scenario where there is no evader but there is a pursuer in the system: no energy is spent since no communication is needed. On the other hand, the pursuer-centric program performs poorly in this case: at each step the pursuer queries the neighboring motes incurring a communication cost of w. The hybrid program, since it borrows the pursuer action from the pursuer-centric program, also performs badly in this scenario.

The extended pursuer-centric program fixes this problem by modifying the pursuer tree construction to require that an answer is returned only if the evader tree is encountered. That is, if there is no evader in the network, the pursuer tree program continues to wait for the information feedback wave to be triggered, and hence, it does not waste energy.

0-Pursuer 1-Evader Scenario. By enforcing that pursuers authenticate themselves when they join the network and notify the network when they leave, a similar improvement in the energy-efficiency is obtained.

7 Discussion and Related Work

In this paper we have investigated a pursuer-evader game for sensor networks. More specifically, we have presented a hybrid, tunable, and self-stabilizing program to solve this problem. We proved that the pursuer catches the evader even in the presence of faults.

For the sake of simplicity, we have adopted a shared-memory model; our results are still valid for message passing memory model. Note that the semantics of the message-passing program would be event-based execution (e.g., upon receiving a message or detecting the evader), rather than maximal parallelism.

Asynchronous Program. Even though we assumed an underlying clock synchronization service, it is possible to modify the evader-centric program slightly to obtain an asynchronous version. The modification is to use, at every mote j, a counter variable $val.j$ that denotes the number of detections of the evader that j is aware of, instead of $ts.j$ that denotes the latest timestamp that j knows for the detection of the evader. When j detects the evader, instead of setting $ts.j$ to $clock.j$, j increases $val.j$ by one.

The extended pursuer program is also made asynchronous in a straightforward manner, since the idea of pursuer agents (a tree rooted at the pursuer) is readily implemented in the asynchronous model.

Implementation. We have implemented the asynchronous version of the evader-centric program on the Berkeley's Mica mote platform [12] for a demonstration at the June 2002 DARPA–NEST retreat held in Bar Harbor, Maine. In our demonstration, a Lego Mindstorms^{TM} robot serving as a pursuer used our program to catch another Lego Mindstorms robot serving as an evader, in a 4 by 4 grid of motes subject to a variety of faults. We have recently ported the code to nesC [10]; the source code is available at www.cis.ohio-state.edu/~demirbas/peDemo.

Energy Efficiency. We have demonstrated that our program is tunable for tracking speed or energy efficiency. Our program is also be tunable for stabilization speed or energy efficiency. The periodicity of soft-state updates for stabilization should be kept low if the faults are relatively rare in the network. For example, in the absence of faults, the first action (i.e., {Evader resides at j} action) need not be executed unless the evader moves to a different mote. Similarly, the stabilization actions (actions 3 and 4 of the hybrid program) can be executed with low frequency to conserve energy.

Another way to improve the energy-efficiency is to maintain the tracking tree over a small number of motes. For example, hierarchical structuring can be employed to maintain tracking information with accuracy proportional to the distance from the evader. Also maintaining the tracking tree in a directional manner and only up to the location of the pursuer will help conserve energy.

Related Work. Several self-stabilizing programs exist for tree construction ([1, 7, 9] to name a few). However, our evader-centric program is unique in the sense that a dynamic spanning tree is maintained even though the root changes continuously.

A self-stabilizing distributed directory protocol based on path reversal on a network-wide, fixed spanning tree is presented in [11]. The spanning tree is initialized to guarantee a reachability condition: following the links from any node leads to the evader. When the evader moves from a node j to another node k, all the links along the path from j to k in the spanning tree are reversed. This way, the tree always guarantees the reachability condition. This protocol suffers from a nonlocal update problem because it is possible to find at least two adjacent nodes j, k in the network such that the distance between j and k in the overlayed spanning tree structure is twice the height of the tree (i.e., equal to the diameter of the network). An evader that is dithering between these two nodes may cause the protocol to perform nonlocal updates for each small move, and would result in a scenario where the pursuer is never able to catch the evader. In contrast, our protocol maintains a dynamic tree and does not suffer from the nonlocal update problem.

In our program, we choose to update the location of the evader immediately. In [5], three strategies for when to update the location the evader (time-based, number of movements-based, and distance-based) are evaluated with respect to their energy efficiency.

Relating to the idea of achieving energy efficiency by using a small number of nodes, Awerbuch and Peleg [3] present a local scheme that maintains tracking information with accuracy proportional to the distance from the evader[2]. They achieve this goal by maintaining a hierarchy of $logD$ regional directories (using the graph-theoretic concept of *regional matching*) where the purpose of the i'th level regional directory is to enable a pursuer to track the evader residing within 2^i distance from it. They show that the communication overhead of their program is within a polylogarithmic factor of the lower bound. Loosely speaking, their regional matching idea is an efficient realization of our pursuer-centric program and their forwarding pointer structure is analogous to our tracking tree structure.

By way of contrast, their focus is on optimizing the complexity during the initialized case, whereas we focus on optimizing complexity during stabilization as well. That is, we are interested in (a) tracking that occurs while initialization is occuring; in other words, soon after the evader joins the system, and (b) tracking that occurs from inconsistent states; in other words, if the evader moves in an undetectable/unannounced manner for some period of time yielding inconsistent tracks. Their complexity of initialization is $O(E\ log^4N)$ where E is the number of edges in the graph and N is the number of nodes. Thus, brute force stabilization of their structure completes in $O(E\ log^4N)$ time as compared with the $2R$ steps it takes in our extended hybrid program.

We have recently found that [15] if we restrict the problem domain to tracking in planar graphs, it is possible to optimize the tracking time in the presence of faults as well as the communication cost and tracking time in the absence of faults. A topology change triggers a global initialization in Awerbuch and Peleg's program since their m-regional matching structure depends on a non-local algorithm that constructs sparse covers [2]. Assuming that the graph is planar (neither [3] nor this paper assumes planarity), we present in [15] a local and self-stabilizing clustering algorithm for constructing the m-regional matching structure, and hence, we are able to deal with topology changes locally.

---

[2] We thank Nancy Lynch for bringing this paper to our attention.

Future Work. We have found several variations of the pursuer-evader problem to be worthy of study, where we change for instance the communication time between motes, the communication model to be message broadcast instead of shared memory, the numbers of pursuers and evaders, the range of a move, and the semantics of computation to be interleaving instead of maximal parallelism.

Especially of interest to us are general forms of the tracking problem where efficient solutions can be devised by hybrid control involving traditional control theory and self-stabilizing distributed data structures (such as tracking trees and regional directories).

References

[1] A. Arora and M. G. Gouda. Distributed reset. *IEEE Transactions on Computers*, 43(9):1026–1038, 1994. 12, 14
[2] B. Awerbuch and D. Peleg. Sparse partitions (extended abstract). In *IEEE Symposium on Foundations of Computer Science*, pages 503–513, 1990. 15
[3] B. Awerbuch and D. Peleg. Online tracking of mobile user. *Journal of the Association for Computing Machinery*, 42:1021–1058, 1995. 1, 15
[4] A. Bar-Noy and I. Kessler. Tracking mobile users in wireless communication networks. In *INFOCOM*, pages 1232–1239, 1993. 1
[5] A. Bar-Noy, I. Kessler, and M. Sidi. Mobile users: To update or not to update? In *INFOCOM*, pages 570–576, 1994. 15
[6] G. Barnes and U. Feige. Short random walks on graphs. *SIAM Journal on Discrete Mathematics*, 9(1):19–28, 1996. 9
[7] N. S. Chen and S. T. Huang. A self-stabilizing algorithm for constructing spanning trees. *Information Processing Letters (IPL)*, 39:147–151, 1991. 12, 14
[8] Y. Choi, M. Gouda, M. C. Kim, and A. Arora. The mote connectivity protocol. Technical Report TR03-08, Department of Computer Sciences, The University of Texas at Austin, 2003. 3
[9] A. Cournier, A. K. Datta, F. Petit, and V. Villain. Self-stabilizing PIF algorithms in arbitrary networks. *International Conference on Distributed Computing Systems (ICDCS)*, pages 91–98, 2001. 12, 14
[10] D. Gay, P. Levis, R. von Behren, M. Welsh, E. Brewer, and D. Culler. The NESC language: A holistic approach to network embedded systems. Submitted to the ACM SIGPLAN(PLDI), June 2003. 14
[11] M. P. Herlihy and S. Tirthapura. Self-Stabilizing Distributed Queuing. *Proceedings of the th International Symposium on Distributed Computing* , 2001. 14
[12] J. Hill, R. Szewczyk, A. Woo, S. Hollar, D. Culler, and K. Pister. System architecture directions for network sensors. *ASPLOS*, 2000. 4, 14
[13] S. Ikeda, I. Kubo, N. Okumoto, and M. Yamashita. Local topological information and cover time. Research manuscript, 2002. 9
[14] M. Jayaram and G. Varghese. Crash failures can drive protocols to arbitrary states. *ACM Symposium on Principles of Distributed Computing*, 1996. 1
[15] V. Mittal, M. Demirbas, and A. Arora. LOCI: Local clustering in large scale wireless networks. Technical Report OSU-CISRC-2/03-TR07, The Ohio State University, February 2003. 15
[16] E. Pitoura and G. Samaras. Locating objects in mobile computing. *Koledge and Data Engineering*, 13(4):571–592, 2001. 1
[17] A. P. Sistla, O. Wolfson, S. Chamberlain, and S. Dao. Modeling and querying moving objects. In *ICDE*, pages 422–432, 1997. 1

Collision-Free Communication in Sensor Networks*

Sandeep S. Kulkarni and Umamaheswaran Arumugam

Software Engineering and Networks Laboratory, Department of Computer Science
and Engineering
Michigan State University, East Lansing MI 48824 USA
{sandeep,arumugam}@cse.msu.edu
http://www.cse.msu.edu/ {sandeep,arumugam}

Abstract. In this paper, we provide a stabilizing solution for collision-free diffusion in sensor networks. Such diffusions are often necessary in sensor networks when information from one sensor needs to be communicated to other sensors that satisfy certain geographic properties. Our solution deals with several difficulties, e.g., unidirectional links, unreliable links, long links, failed sensors, and sensors that are sleeping in order to save energy, that occur in sensor networks. It also ensures that there are no collisions during the diffusion and that the time required for the diffusion is $O(D)$ where D is the diameter of the network. Moreover, while the solution can be applied to an arbitrary topology, it is more suitable for a commonly occurring topology, a two-dimensional grid.
We show how our solution for collision-free diffusion can be used for time-division multiplexing (TDM) in sensor networks. TDM ensures that the message communication (other than the messages sent by diffusion) among sensors is also collision-free. While collision-free diffusion and time-division multiplexing are interdependent, we show how both these properties can be achieved simultaneously. Our algorithms are stabilizing fault-tolerant, i.e., collision-free diffusion and time-division multiplexing are restored even if the system reaches an arbitrary state where the sensors are corrupted or improperly initialized.

1 Introduction

In recent years, sensor networks have become popular in the academic and industrial environment due to their application in data gathering, active and passive tracking of unexpected/undesirable objects, environment monitoring and unattended hazard detection. Due to their low cost and small size, it is possible to rapidly deploy them in large numbers. These sensors are resource constrained and can typically communicate with other (neighboring) sensors over a wireless

---

* This work was partially sponsored by NSF CAREER CCR-0092724, DARPA Grant OSURS01-C-1901, ONR Grant N00014-01-1-0744, and a grant from Michigan State University.

network. However, due to limited power and communication range, they need to collaborate to achieve the required task.

One of the important issues in sensor networks is message collision: Due to the shared wireless medium, if a sensor simultaneously receives two messages then they collide and, hence, both messages become incomprehensible. Such collision is undesirable as it results in wastage of power to transmit the message that resulted in a collision.

Collision among messages is especially problematic in the context of *system-wide computations* where some sensor needs to communicate some information to the entire network (respectively, a subset of the network that satisfies the geographic properties of interest). Such computations arise when a sensor needs to communicate the observed value to the *base station* or when we want to organize these sensors in a suitable topology (e.g., tree). In such diffusion, every sensor that receives a message transmits it to its neighbors (in the given direction). It follows that at any time multiple sensors may be forwarding the sensor values to their respective neighbors. Therefore, the possibility of a collision increases.

Challenges in Sensor Networks. One of the important issues in sensor networks is the scenario where two sensors can communicate with each other only with a very low probability. Also, sensor networks suffer from unidirectional links where one sensor can communicate with another with a high probability although the probability of the reverse communication is very low. In a situation where sensor j can only communicate occasionally with sensor k, it is expected that the signal strength received by k is so small that k cannot correctly determine all the bits in that message. However, the signal strength that k receives is often strong enough that it can corrupt another message that was sent to k at the same time. The above discussion suggests that we need to consider the situation where two sensors cannot effectively *communicate* with each other although they can effectively *interfere* with each other.

A collision-free diffusion is advantageous in obtaining clock synchronization and time-division multiplexing. More specifically, when a sensor receives the diffusion message, it can uniquely determine its clock by considering the clock value when the diffusion was initiated and the path that the diffusion took to reach that sensor. If clocks are synchronized, we can assign slots to each sensor such that simultaneous message transmissions by two sensors do not collide.

A closer inspection of diffusion and time-division multiplexing shows that these two problems are interdependent. More specifically, if clocks are not synchronized then the diffusion may fail in the following scenario: the clock values of two sensors differ, one of these sensors transmits the diffusion message and the other sensor transmits an unrelated message at the same time. It follows that a collision in this situation will prevent the diffusion message from reaching all the desired destinations. Moreover, if the diffusion does not complete successfully then the clocks may remain unsynchronized forever. It is therefore necessary that diffusion be stabilizing fault-tolerant [1], i.e., starting from an arbitrary state, the system should recover to states from where subsequent diffusing computation is collision-free. A stabilizing fault-tolerant solution also deals with the case where the sensors are inactive for a long time and subsequently become active, although at slightly different times.

Contributions of the Paper. With the above motivation, in this paper, we focus on stabilizing collision-free algorithm for diffusing computations in sensor networks. The main contributions of this paper are as follows.

1. We present an algorithm (with 4 versions) for collision-free diffusion in sensor networks. The first version focuses on an ideal sensor network where a sensor communicates perfectly with the neighbors in its grid and does not interfere with any other sensors in the network. Our second version improves the performance of the first version for the case where a sensor can communicate with other non-neighboring sensors at some distance, say x. The third version extends the first version to deal with the case where a sensor interferes with other sensors at some distance, say y. Finally, the fourth version combines the second and the third versions to deal with the case where a sensor may communicate with other sensors at distance, say x, and interfere with sensors at a larger distance, say y.
2. We show how the algorithm for collision-free diffusion enables us to obtain time-division multiplexing in sensor networks. In a two-dimensional grid, we show that messages of two sensors that transmit simultaneously do not collide with each other.
3. We show how collision-free diffusion can be obtained if some sensors have failed or have been shut off to save power.
4. We show how stabilizing fault-tolerance can be added to our algorithms. Thus, starting from an arbitrary state, each of our algorithms recovers to states from where collision-free diffusion and time-division multiplexing are achieved. Finally, these algorithms can also be tailored to deal with the case where communication between (even the neighboring) sensors is unreliable.

Organization of the Paper. The rest of the paper is organized as follows: In Section 2, we discuss the model of the sensor network. Then, in Section 3, we present our algorithm for collision-free diffusion. In Section 4, we extend our algorithm to provide time-division multiplexing and show how both these properties can be achieved even if one begins in a state where the sensor clocks are not synchronized. Subsequently, in Section 5, we discuss extensions of our algorithms. Finally, in Section 6, we discuss the related work and make concluding remarks in Section 7.

2   Model and Assumptions

In this section, we present the system model and identify the assumptions made in this paper. We assume that sensors are arranged in a grid where each sensor knows its location in the network (geometric position). Each message sent by a sensor includes this geometric position. Thus, a sensor can determine the position, direction and distance (with respect to itself) of the sensors that send messages to it. Also, we assume that each sensor is aware of its communication range and an interference range. Note that, interference range is greater than or equal to the communication range.

Additionally, we assume that one clock tick of the sensor corresponds to the propagation time of a message. Though the sensors can have high-precision clocks, for communication, we use only the higher-order bits that correspond to the propagation time of a message.

We assume that there is exactly one initiator that initiates the diffusion. For simplicity, initially, we assume that the sensor at the left-top (at location $\langle 0, 0 \rangle$) is the initiator. This assumption is made since we can view the diffusion as propagating from this sensor to all the sensors in the network in one single (south-east) quadrant. We remove this assumption in Section 3.5 and provide an algorithm where the initiator is not at the left-top position.

We assume that the sensor network has a perfect grid topology and no sensors have failed or are in sleeping state. By making these assumptions, we can design algorithms for perfect grid-based sensor networks. Then, we extend the algorithms to deal with the case where sensors (other than the initiator) have failed.

3   Collision-Free Diffusion

In this section, we provide an algorithm for collision-free diffusion for sensors arranged in a two-dimensional grid. As mentioned in the Introduction, whenever a sensor receives a diffusion message for the first time, it retransmits the message to its neighbors. However, if two (nearby) sensors transmit the diffusion message at the same time then the messages collide. The collision becomes even more problematic in sensor networks where it is often not possible to detect whether collision has occurred or not. Also, it is possible that message sent by one sensor collides at one receiver whereas another receiver correctly receives it.

To deal with these problems, we define the problem of collision-free diffusion as follows. The first requirement for collision-free diffusion is that the diffusion message should reach every sensor. The second requirement is that collisions should not occur. More specifically, when sensor j transmits a message, it is necessary that a collision should not occur at any sensor that is expected to receive the message from j, i.e., a sensor in the communication range of j. Thus, if sensor k transmits concurrently then the set of sensors in the communication range of j should be disjoint from the set of sensors in the interference range of k. Thus, the problem statement is defined as follows:

Problem Statement: Collision-free Diffusion

Given a sensor grid; if a sensor initiates diffusion then the following properties should be satisfied:

    1. Diffusion message should reach every sensor.

    2. If two sensors j and k transmit at the same time,

        (Sensors in communication range of j) $\bigcap$

        (Sensors in interference range of k) $= \emptyset$.

We present four versions of our collision-free diffusion algorithm. For simplicity, in Sections 3.1-3.4, we assume that the sensor at $\langle 0, 0 \rangle$ initiates the diffusion. In Section 3.1, we discuss the algorithm for diffusion in networks where a sensor can communicate only with its distance 1 neighbors. In Section 3.2, we extend this version for diffusion in networks where a sensor can communicate with its distance $x, x \geq 1$, neighbors. In both these algorithms, we assume that the interference range of a sensor is same as its communication range. We weaken this requirement in Sections 3.3, and 3.4. Specifically, in Section 3.3, we extend the first version (cf. Section 3.1) to deal with the case where a sensor can communicate with its distance 1 neighbors and interfere with its distance $y, y \geq 1$, neighbors. And, in Section 3.4, we extend the third version (cf. Section 3.3) to deal with the case where a sensor can communicate with its distance $x, x \geq 1$, neighbors and interfere with its distance $y, y \geq x$, neighbors. In Section 3.5, we provide an algorithm for collision-free diffusion initiated by an arbitrary sensor. Although in Sections 3.1-3.5 we assume that the communication range (respectively, interference range) of all sensors are identical, observations made in Section 3.6 show that the algorithm can be applied even if they are different.

3.1   Version 1: Communicate 1, Interfere 1

Consider a simple grid network where a sensor can communicate with sensors that are distance 1 away (cf. Figure 1)[1].

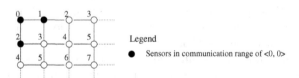

Fig. 1. Sample diffusion in networks where a sensor communicates with its distance 1 neighbors. The number associated with a sensor shows the slot in which it should transmit

---

[1] In these examples we have used the manhattan distance between sensors. Our algorithms can be applied even if we consider the geographic distance between sensors. See the first observation in Section 3.6.

Fig. 2. Sample diffusion in networks where a sensor communicates with its distance 2 neighbors. The number associated with a sensor shows the slot in which it should transmit

From this figure, we observe that sensors $\langle 1, 0 \rangle$ and $\langle 0, 1 \rangle$ should not transmit at the same time as their messages will collide at sensor $\langle 1, 1 \rangle$. The following algorithm provides a collision-free diffusion in networks where sensors can communicate only with their distance 1 neighbors.

---
when sensor j receives a diffusion message from sensor k
    if (k is west neighbor at distance 1)
        transmit after 1 clock tick.
    else if (k is north neighbor at distance 1)
        transmit after 2 clock ticks.
    else // duplicate message received from east/south neighbor
        ignore

Theorem 3.1 The above algorithm satisfies the problem specification of collision-free diffusion.
Proof. The proof is similar to that of Theorem 3.3where $y = 1$.   □

3.2 Version 2: Communicate x, Interfere x

Consider a grid network where a sensor can communicate with sensors that are distance $x, x \geq 1$ away (cf. Figure 2, where $x = 2$).

From Figure 2, we observe that sensors $\langle 2, 0 \rangle$ and $\langle 0, 2 \rangle$ should not transmit at the same time as these messages will collide at $\langle 2, 2 \rangle$. Since the sensor $\langle 0, 0 \rangle$ can communicate at a larger distance and the sensors $\langle 0, 2 \rangle$, $\langle 2, 0 \rangle$ propagate the diffusion, sensors $\langle 0, 1 \rangle$, $\langle 1, 0 \rangle$ and $\langle 1, 1 \rangle$ need not transmit. The following algorithm provides a collision-free diffusion in networks where sensors can communicate with their distance $x, x \geq 1$, neighbors.

---
when sensor j receives a diffusion message from sensor k
    if (k is west neighbor at distance x)
        transmit after 1 clock tick.
    else if (k is north neighbor at distance x)
        transmit after 2 clock ticks.
    else //duplicate message from east/south neighbor or too close to source
        ignore

Theorem 3.2 The above algorithm satisfies the problem specification of collision-free diffusion.   □

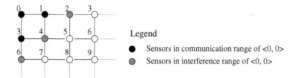

Fig. 3. Sample diffusion in networks where a sensor communicates with its distance 1 neighbors and interferes with its distance 2 neighbors. The number associated with a sensor shows the slot in which it should transmit

3.3   Version 3: Communicate 1, Interfere y

Consider a grid network where a sensor can communicate with sensors that are distance 1 away and interfere with sensors that are distance $y, y \geq 1$ away (cf. Figure 3, where $y = 2$).

Once again, we observe that sensors $\langle 1, 0 \rangle$ and $\langle 0, 1 \rangle$ should not transmit at the same time. Also, sensors $\langle 2, 0 \rangle$ and $\langle 0, 1 \rangle$ should not transmit at the same time as their messages will collide at $\langle 1, 1 \rangle$ and $\langle 2, 1 \rangle$. The third version of the algorithm is as follows:

---

when sensor j receives a diffusion message from sensor k
    if (k is west neighbor at distance 1)
       transmit after 1 clock tick.
    else if (k is north neighbor at distance 1)
       transmit after $y + 1$ clock ticks.
    else // duplicate message received from east/south neighbor
       ignore

Theorem 3.3   The above algorithm satisfies the problem specification of collision-free diffusion.

Proof. Let us assume that the source sensor $\langle 0, 0 \rangle$ starts transmitting at time $t = 0$. By induction, we observe that sensor $\langle i, j \rangle$ will transmit at time $t = i + (y + 1)j$. Now, we show that collisions will not occur in this algorithm. Consider two sensors $\langle i_1, j_1 \rangle$ and $\langle i_2, j_2 \rangle$. Sensor $\langle i_1, j_1 \rangle$ will transmit at time $t_1 = i_1 + (y+1)j_1$ and $\langle i_2, j_2 \rangle$ will transmit at time $t_2 = i_2 + (y + 1)j_2$. Collision is possible only if the following conditions hold:

- $t_1 = t_2$, i.e., $(i_1 - i_2) + (y + 1)(j_1 - j_2) = 0$.
- $|i_1 - i_2| + |j_1 - j_2| \leq y + 1$.
- $|i_1 - i_2| + |j_1 - j_2| \geq 1$.

From the first condition, we conclude that $(i_1 - i_2)$ is a multiple of $(y + 1)$. Combining this with the second condition, we have $|i_1 - i_2| = 0$ or $|j_1 - j_2| = 0$. However, if $|i_1 - i_2| = 0$ (respectively, $|j_1 - j_2| = 0$) then from the first condition $(j_1 - j_2)$ (respectively, $(i_1 - i_2)$) must be zero. If both $(i_1 - i_2)$ and $(j_1 - j_2)$ are zero then the third condition is violated. Thus, collision cannot occur in this algorithm.   □

3.4   Version 4: Communicate x, Interfere y

Consider a grid network where a sensor can communicate with sensors that are distance $x, x \geq 1$ away and interfere with sensors that are distance $y, y \geq x$ away. This network can be viewed as a modified network where the intermediate sensors are removed. Hence, in this modified network, a sensor can communicate with its distance 1 neighbors and interfere with its distance $\lceil \frac{y}{x} \rceil$ neighbors. Now, we apply the version 3 of our algorithm with parameters *communicate* 1, *interfere* $\lceil \frac{y}{x} \rceil$.

3.5   Diffusion by an Arbitrary Sensor

If sensor k (other than, $\langle 0, 0 \rangle$) initiates the diffusion, we split the network into four quadrants with sensor k at the intersection of x and y axes. For each quadrant, we can use the algorithm similar to that in Sections 3.1-3.4; We simply need to ensure that messages in different quadrants do not collide (on x and y axes). For the case where communication range = interference range = 1, we can achieve this as follows: (Extensions for other values of communication and interference range are also similar.)

Sensors in south-east quadrant transmit the diffusion message as before (i.e., a sensor $\langle i, j \rangle$ will transmit the diffusion at $|i| + 2|j|$). Sensors in the north-east and south-west quadrants (including the $-$ve x-axis and $+$ve y-axis but excluding the $+$ve x-axis and $-$ve y-axis) transmit the diffusion similar to the south-east quadrant, but with 2 clock ticks delay. This is to ensure the diffusion messages do not collide at the x and y axes. Specifically, a sensor $\langle i, j \rangle$ in the north-east quadrant or in the south-west quadrant transmits the diffusion at $|i| + 2|j| + 2$. Sensors in the north-west quadrant (excluding the axes) transmits the diffusion similar to the other quadrants except that the delay here is 4 clock ticks. In other words, a sensor $\langle i, j \rangle$ in the north-west quadrant transmits the diffusion at $|i| + 2|j| + 4$. We leave it to the reader to verify that with this modification, diffusion initiated by an arbitrary sensor is collision-free.

3.6   Observations about Our Algorithm

We make the following observations about our algorithm:

1. In Sections 3.1-3.5, we considered the manhattan distance between sensors, i.e., if the interference range is y then we said that sensors $\langle i_1, j_1 \rangle$ and $\langle i_2, j_2 \rangle$ interfered with each other only if $|i_1 - i_2| + |j_1 - j_2| \leq y$. We note that our algorithm works correctly even if we say that sensors $\langle i_1, j_1 \rangle$ and $\langle i_2, j_2 \rangle$ interfere only if $|i_1 - i_2| \leq y$ and $|j_1 - j_2| \leq y$. It follows that our algorithm works correctly even if we consider the geographic distance between sensors and say that two sensors $\langle i_1, j_1 \rangle$ and $\langle i_2, j_2 \rangle$ interfere with each other if the geographic distance between them, $\sqrt{|i_1 - i_2|^2 + |j_1 - j_2|^2}$, is less than or equal to y.
2. Even if the interference range is overestimated, our algorithm works correctly.
3. Even if the communication range is underestimated, as long as it is at least 1, our algorithm works correctly.

4. We can apply our algorithm even if the communication and interference ranges of different sensors vary. We can use the minimum of the communication range of each sensor (underestimate) and the maximum of the interference range of each sensor (overestimate).

4   Application to Time-Division Multiplexing (TDM)

In this section, we present an algorithm for time-division multiplexing in sensor networks using the collision-free diffusion algorithm discussed earlier. Time-division multiplexing is the problem of assigning time slots to each sensor. Two sensors j and k can transmit in the same time slot if j does not interfere with the communication of k and k does not interfere with the communication of j. In this context, we define the notion of *collision-group*. The *collision-group* of sensor j includes the sensors that are in the communication range of j and the sensors that interfere with the sensors in the communication range of j. Hence, if two sensors j and k are alloted the same time slot then j should not be present in the collision-group of k and k should not be present in the collision-group of j. Thus, the problem of time-division multiplexing is defined as follows:

> **Problem Statement: Time-division Multiplexing**
> Assign time slots to each sensor such that,
>   If two sensors j and k transmit at the same time then
>   ($j \notin$ collision-group of sensor k).

Now, we present the algorithm for allotting time slots to the sensors. In Section 4.1, we present the algorithm for TDM in perfect grids. In Section 4.2, we discuss how stabilization is achieved starting from an improperly initialized state.

4.1   Simple TDM Algorithm

In this section, we present our simple TDM algorithm that uses the third version of the diffusion algorithm (cf. Section 3.3) where communication range is 1 and interference range is y. Let j and k be two sensors such that j is in the collision group of k. Let t_j (respectively, t_k) be the slots in which j (respectively, k) transmits its diffusion message. We propose an algorithm where the slots assigned for j are $t_j + c * MCG$ where $c \geq 0$ and MCG captures information about the maximum collision group in the system.

From the correctness of the diffusion computation, we know that $t_j \neq t_k$. Now, future messages sent by j and k can collide if $t_j + c_1 * MCG = t_k + c_2 * MCG$, where $c_1, c_2 \geq 0$. In other words, future messages from j and k can collide iff $|t_j - t_k|$ is a multiple of MCG. More specifically, to ensure collision-freedom, it suffices that for any two sensors j and k such that j is in the collision group of k, MCG does not divide $|t_j - t_k|$. We can achieve this by choosing MCG to be $max(|t_j - t_k| : j$ is in the collision group of $k) + 1$.

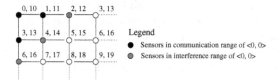

Fig. 4. Sample TDM in networks where a sensor communicates with its distance 1 neighbors and interferes with its distance 2 neighbors. The numbers associated with a sensor shows the slots in which it could transmit

In the third version of our algorithm, if j is in the collision group of k then $|t_j - t_k|$ is at most $(y+1)^2$; such a situation occurs if j is at distance of $y+1$ in north/south of k. Hence, the algorithm for time division multiplexing is as follows:

> If sensor j transmits a diffusion message at time slot t_j,
> j can transmit at time slots, $\forall c, c \geq 0, t_j + c * ((y+1)^2 + 1)$.

The algorithm assigns time slots for each sensor based on the time at which it transmits the diffusion. Thus, a sensor (say, j) can transmit in slots: t_j, $t_j + ((y+1)^2 + 1)$, $t_j + 2((y+1)^2 + 1)$, ..., etc. Figure 4 shows a sample allocation of slots to the sensors.

Theorem 4.1 The above algorithm satisfies the problem specification of TDM.

$\square$

4.2   Stabilization of TDM and Diffusion

We now add stabilization to the TDM algorithm discussed in Section 4.1, i.e., if the network is initialized with arbitrary clock values (including the case where there is a phase offset among clocks), we ensure that it recovers to states from where collision-free communication is achieved. The simple TDM algorithm relies on the collision-free diffusion algorithm discussed earlier (cf. Section 3.3). Whenever a sensor does not get the diffusion message for certain consecutive number of times, the sensor shuts down, i.e., it will not transmit any message until it receives a diffusion message. The network will eventually reach a state where the diffusion message can be received by all sensors. From then on, the sensors can use the simple TDM algorithm to transmit messages across different sensors. Moreover, if there are no faults in the network and the links are reliable then no sensor will ever shut down.

Dealing with Unreliable Links. Now, we show that in the absence of faults, a sensor rarely shuts down even if the link between the neighboring sensors are unreliable. Let p be the probability that a sensor receives a message from its neighbor. Also, let n be the number of diffusion periods a sensor waits before shutting down. Now, consider a sensor j that receives a diffusion message after l

intermediate transmissions. The probability that this sensor does not receive the diffusion message is $1 - p^l$ and the probability that this sensor shuts down in the absence of faults is $(1 - p^l)^n$. Note that this is an overestimate since a sensor receives the diffusion message from more than one sensor. If we consider $p = 0.90$, $l = 10$ and $n = 10$, the probability that the sensor j will incorrectly shut down is 0.0137.

Observations about Our Stabilizing Fault-Tolerant Algorithms. We make the following observations about our stabilizing fault-tolerant algorithms:

1. If there are no failures in the network and the links are reliable then no sensor will ever shut down.
2. If there are no failures in the network and the links are unreliable then sensors may shut down rarely. However, the probability that a sensor shuts down incorrectly due to unreliable links can be made as small as possible.

5   Extensions: Dealing with Failed/Sleeping Sensors and Arbitrary Topology

In this section, we discuss extensions that remove some of the assumptions made in Section 2. In Section 5.1, we extend the algorithm to deal with the case where sensors are subject to fail-stop faults. In Section 5.2, we provide an algorithm for collision-free diffusion in the case where the underlying graph is not a two-dimensional grid.

5.1   Diffusion in Imperfect Grids or Grids with Failed Sensors/Links

In this section, we consider the case where sensors can fail, links between sensors can fail, or the grid can be improperly configured (with some sensors missing).

Based on the extension in Section 3.5, without loss of generality, assume that the left-top sensor initiates the diffusion. In the absence of failure of sensors or links between them, the sensors receive the diffusion messages from their north or west neighbors before receiving duplicate messages from their east or south neighbors. Hence, if a sensor receives the diffusion message for the first time from its east or south neighbor, it can conclude that some of the sensors in the network are missing or failed. When a sensor receives such a message from the south/east neighbor, it updates its clock based on the time information in the diffusion message. Based on its geographic location, it then determines the slot in which it would have transmitted the diffusion if no sensor had failed. Finally, it uses the time-division multiplexing algorithm (cf. Section 4) to find the next slot when it can transmit a message; this slot would be used for retransmitting the diffusion message.

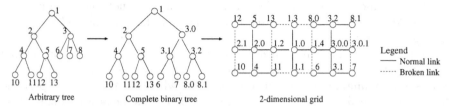

Fig. 5. Mapping an arbitrary tree into a 2-dimensional grid

5.2   Diffusion to Other Graphs

Collision-free diffusion in other graphs can be achieved by embedding a (partial) grid in that graph. (Note that the goal of this solution is to show the feasibility of such extension. If additional information about the topology is available then it is possible to improve the efficiency of the diffusion on the transformed graph [2].) To show one approach for embedding such a partial grid, we begin with the observation that, an arbitrary tree can be mapped into a (complete) binary tree. Also, a complete binary tree can be mapped on a 2-dimensional grid with *dilation* $\lceil (k-1)/2 \rceil$ where k is the depth of the tree [3]. If the degree of a node is more than 3, we split that node to construct a binary tree (cf. Figure 5).

We can observe from Figure 5 that node 1 is split into 5 nodes, $1.0 \ldots 1.4$. Hence, node 1 will get 5 different time slots for communication. Also, nodes in the 2-dimensional grid can communicate with the nodes that are at distance 1 (except in the case where the link drawn is a broken link). Some of the nodes in the 2-dimensional grid can communicate with nodes that are at a larger distance. For the purpose of collision-free diffusion, we can treat this communication as interference (e.g., in Figure 5, the communication between 1.1 and 3.1 can be treated as interference). It follows that given an arbitrary tree, we can embed a partial grid in it; in this partial grid, the communication range is 1. And, the interference range is determined based on the way in which nodes of degree more than 3 are split.

Finally, for an arbitrary graph, we can use its spanning tree, and embed a partial grid in it. Then, we can add the remaining edges to this partial grid and treat them as interference-only. With such approach, it is possible to apply the collision-free diffusion algorithm to arbitrary graphs.

6   Related Work

Related work that deals with communication issues in radio/wireless/sensor networks includes [4, 5, 6]. In [4], the authors provide a fault-tolerant broadcasting algorithm in radio networks. The model proposed in this paper assumes that the upper bound on the number of faulty nodes is known at start. They also assume that the faults are permanent. The authors do not consider the notion of interference range for nodes. Our paper differs considerably from that in [4]. The assumption about knowledge of the number of faults is not made in our algorithms. Also, unlike [4], we allow sensors (other than the initiator) to fail/recover during computation.

In [5, 6], new time synchronization services are proposed. In [5], the authors propose a time synchronization service for tiny sensor devices like *motes* [7]. This service maintains a tree structure of motes where the root sends a periodic beacon message about its time. Each non-root node gets the best-approximation of the root's time from the neighbor which is closest to the root. In [6], the authors propose a time synchronization service which rely on a third-party node. The nodes normalize their local-time based on the synchronization pulse sent by the third-party node. Based on our observations with motes, collision-freedom is important in these system-wide computations. For this reason, in this paper, we developed a collision-free communication algorithm. Our algorithm can be used for collision-free transmission of the time synchronization messages, thereby enhancing the proposed time synchronization services.

In [8], the authors provide algorithms for completely connected graphs where they consider the difference between a globally synchronous (global clock) and a locally synchronous (local clock with same rate of increase) model with known or unknown network size. In [9], the authors provide algorithms for mobile/ad hoc networks. They provide broadcasting algorithms for a model without collision detection and a model with collision detection. Unlike our algorithms, in [8, 9], the authors assume that the network is fully connected. Also, the algorithms in [8, 9] are not stabilizing fault-tolerant.

Our algorithms differ from Code-division Multiple Access (CDMA) [10]. CDMA requires that the codes used in the system should be orthogonal to ensure minimal interference. Also, it requires expensive operations to encode/decode a message. Our algorithms do not need any specialized codes. Further, to ensure collision-freedom, our algorithm requires only very limited resources, e.g., an addition and a comparison unit.

In [11], the authors have proposed a randomized startup algorithm for TDM. Whenever a collision occurs during startup, exponential backoff is used for determining the time to transmit next. In our approach, we use a deterministic startup algorithm which guarantees collision-freedom and stabilization in case of fail-stop failures. Further, the complexity of the algorithm proposed in [11] is $O(N)$ where N is the number of system nodes, whereas the complexity of our diffusion algorithm is $O(D)$ where D is the diameter of the network. Moreover, the algorithm in [11] optimizes time and communication overhead with increased computation overhead, while our diffusion algorithm optimizes all the three overheads. The disadvantage of our algorithm is that it has a single point of failure (i.e., initiator of diffusion). In situations where the initiator fails, we can use the startup algorithm from [11] to assign TDM slots.

7   Conclusion and Future Work

In this paper, we presented a stabilizing algorithm for collision-free diffusion in sensor networks and showed how it can be used to provide time-division multiplexing. We presented four versions of our collision-free diffusion algorithm based on the ability of sensors to communicate with each other and their ability to interfere with each other. While the solutions were designed for a grid network, we showed how they could be modified to deal with failed sensors as well as with arbitrary topologies. With these modifications, our solutions deal with commonly occurring difficulties, e.g., failed sensors, sleeping sensors, unidirectional links, and unreliable links, in sensor networks.

Our algorithms permit sensors to save power by turning off the radio completely as long as the remaining sensors remain connected. These sleeping sensors can periodically wake up, wait for one diffusion message from one of its neighbors and return to sleeping state. This will allow the sensors to save power as well as keep the clock synchronized with their neighbors. Moreover, our algorithm is stabilizing fault-tolerant [1]. Thus, even if all sensors are deactivated for a long time causing arbitrary clock drift, our algorithm ensures that starting from such an arbitrary state, eventually the diffusion will complete successfully and the time-division multiplexing would be restored.

One of the important issues in our algorithms is to determine the communication and interference range of a sensor. Initially, we can start with the manufacture specification about the ability of sensors to communicate with each other. Then, we can use the biconnectivity experiments by Choi et al [12] to determine the appropriate communication and interference range. One such approach is discussed in [2].

In our solution, it is possible for the initiator of a diffusion to handoff this responsibility to other sensors as the diffusion can be initiated by any sensor as long as only one sensor initiates it. Thus, the current initiator can designate another sensor as subsequent initiator if the current initiator has low battery or if the initiating responsibility is to be shared by multiple sensors.

There are several questions raised by this work: For one, an interesting question is how to determine the initial sensor that is responsible for initiating the diffusion. In some heterogeneous networks where some sensors are more powerful and more reliable, these powerful/reliable sensors can be chosen to be the initiators. Alternatively, during deployment of sensors (e.g., by dropping them from a plane), we can keep several potential initiators that communicate with each other directly and use the approach in [8, 9] so that one of them is chosen to be the initiator. Another important concern is how to deal with errors in the location of the sensors. Specifically, we need to analyze the effects of these errors on the collision-free property of our algorithms.

References

[1] E. W. Dijkstra. Self-stabilizing systems in spite of distributed control. *Communications of the ACM*, 17(11), 1974. 18, 30

[2] Sandeep S. Kulkarni and Umamaheswaran Arumugam. Collision-free communication in sensor networks. Technical Report MSU-CSE-03-3, Department of Computer Science, Michigan State University, February 2003. 28, 30

[3] J. D. Ullman. *Computational Aspects of VLSI*. Computer Science Press, Rockville, MD, 1984. 28

[4] Evangelos Kranakis, Danny Krizanc, and Andrzej Pelc. Fault-tolerant broadcasting in radio networks. *Journal of Algorithms*, 39(1):47–67, April 2001. 28, 29

[5] Ted Herman. NestArch: Prototype time synchronization service. NEST Challenge Architecture. Available at: http://www.ai.mit.edu/people/sombrero/nestwiki/index/ComponentTimeSync, January 2003. 28, 29

[6] Jeremy Elson and Deborah Estrin. Time synchronization for wireless sensor networks. *In Proceedings of the International Parallel and Distributed Processing Symposium (IPDPS), Workshop on Parallel and Distributed Computing Issues in Wireless and Mobile Computing*, April 2001. 28, 29

[7] David E. Culler, Jason Hill, Philip Buonadonna, Robert Szewczyk, and Alec Woo. A network-centric approach to embedded software for tiny devices. In *EMSOFT*, volume 2211 of *Lecture Notes in Computer Science*, pages 97–113. Springer, 2001. 29

[8] Leszek Gasieniec, Andrzej Pelc, and David Peleg. The wakeup problem in synchronous broadcast systems. *SIAM Journal of Discrete Mathematics*, 14(2):207–222, 2001. 29, 30

[9] Bogdan S. Chlebus, Leszek Gasieniec, Alan Gibbons, Andrzej Pelc, and Wojciech Rytter. Deterministic broadcasting in ad hoc radio networks. *Distributed Computing*, 15(1):27–38, 2002. 29, 30

[10] Andrew J. Viterbi. *CDMA: Principles of Spread Spectrum Communication*. Addison Wesley Longman Publishing Co., Inc., Redwood City, CA, 1995. 29

[11] Vilgot Claesson, Henrik Lonn, and Neeraj Suri. Efficient TDMA synchronization for distributed embedded systems. In *Proceedings of the 20th IEEE Symposium on Reliable Distributed Systems (SRDS)*, pages 198–201, October 2001. 29

[12] Y. Choi, M. Gouda, M. C. Kim, and A. Arora. The mote connectivity protocol. Technical Report TR03-08, Department of Computer Sciences, The University of Texas at Austin, 2003. 30

Self-Stabilizing Pulse Synchronization Inspired by Biological Pacemaker Networks

Ariel Daliot[1], Danny Dolev[1]*, and Hanna Parnas[2]

[1] School of Engineering and Computer Science
The Hebrew University of Jerusalem, Israel
{adaliot,dolev}@cs.huji.ac.il
[2] Department of Neurobiology and the Otto Loewi Minerva Center for Cellular and
Molecular Neurobiology
Institute of Life Science, The Hebrew University of Jerusalem, Israel
hanna@vms.huji.ac.il

Abstract. We define the "Pulse Synchronization" problem that requires
nodes to achieve tight synchronization of regular pulse events, in the
settings of distributed computing systems. Pulse-coupled synchronization is a phenomenon displayed by a large variety of biological systems,
typically overcoming a high level of noise. Inspired by such biological
models, a robust and self-stabilizing pulse synchronization algorithm for
distributed computer systems is presented. The algorithm attains near
optimal synchronization tightness while tolerating up to a third of the
nodes exhibiting Byzantine behavior concurrently. We propose that pulse
synchronization algorithms can be suitable for a variety of distributed
tasks that require tight synchronization but which can tolerate a bound
variation in the regularity of the synchronized pulse invocations.

1 Introduction

The phenomenon of synchronization is displayed by many biological systems [27].
It presumably plays an important role in these systems. For example, the heart
of the lobster is regularly activated by the synchronized firing of four interneurons in the cardiac ganglion [13, 14]. It was concluded that the organism cannot
survive if all four interneurons fire out of synchrony for prolonged times [26].
This system inspired the present work. Other examples of biological synchronization include the *malaccae* fireflies in Southeast Asia where thousands of
male fireflies congregate in mangrove trees; flashing in synchrony [4]; oscillations
of the neurons in the circadian pacemaker; determining the day-night rhythm;
crickets that chirp in unison; coordinated mass spawning in corals and even au-
dience clapping together after a "good" performance [24]. Synchronization in
these systems is typically attained despite the inherent variations among the
participating elements, or the presence of noise from external sources or from
participating elements. A generic mathematical model for synchronous firing of

* This research was supported in part by Intel COMM Grant - Internet Net-
work/Transport Layer & QoS Environment (IXA).

S.-T. Huang and T. Herman (Eds.): SSS 2003, LNCS 2704, pp. 32–48, 2003.
© Springer-Verlag Berlin Heidelberg 2003

biological oscillators based on a model of the human cardiac pacemaker is given in [22]. This model does not account for either noise or the inherent differences among elements.

In computer science, synchronization is both a goal by itself and a building block for algorithms that solve other problems. In the "Clock Synchronization" problem, it is desired for computers to have their clocks set as close as possible to each other as well as to keep a notion of real time (see [7, 25, 12, 18, 23]).

It is desired for algorithms to guarantee correct behavior of the network in face of faults or failing elements, sometimes irrespective of any initial state of the system (self-stabilization). It has been suggested in [26] that similar fault considerations may have been involved in the evolution of distributed biological systems. In the example of the cardiac ganglion of the lobster, it was concluded that at least four neurons are needed in order to overcome the presence of one faulty neuron, though supposedly one neuron suffices to activate the heart. The cardiac ganglion must be able to adjust the pace of the synchronized firing according to the required heartbeat, up to a certain bound, without loosing the synchrony (e.g. while escaping a predator a higher heartbeat is required – though not too high). Due to the vitality of this network, it is presumably optimized for fault tolerance, self-stabilization, tight synchronization and for fast re-synchronization.

The apparent resemblance of the synchronization and fault tolerance requirements of biological networks and distributed computer networks makes it appealing to infer from models of biological systems onto the design of distributed algorithms in computer science. Especially when assuming that distributed biological networks have evolved over time to particularly tolerate inherent in-homogeneity of the cells, noise and cell death. In the current paper, we show that in spite of obvious differences, a biological fault tolerant synchronization model ([26]) can inspire a novel solution to an apparently similar problem in computer science.

We propose a relaxed version of the Clock Synchronization problem, which we call "Pulse Synchronization", in which all the elements are required to invoke some regular pulse (or perform a "task") in tight synchrony, but allow for some variation from complete regularity. Though nodes need to invoke the pulses synchronously, there is a limit on how frequent it is allowed to be invoked (similar to the linear envelope clock synchronization limitation). The "Pulse Synchronization" problem resembles physical/biological pulse-coupled synchronization models [22], though in a computer system setting it is required to give an algorithm for the nodes to reach the synchronization requirement.

We present a novel algorithm in the settings of self-stabilizing distributed algorithms, instructing the nodes how and when to fire in order to meet the synchronization requirements of "Pulse Synchronization". The core elements of the algorithm are analogous to the neurobiological principles of *endogenous* (self generated) *periodic spiking, summation* and *time dependent refractoriness*. The basic algorithm is quite simple: every node invokes a pulse regularly and sends a message upon invoking it (*endogenous periodic spiking*). The node sums messages received in some "window of time" (*summation*) and compares this to the continuously decreasing time dependent firing threshold for invoking the pulse (*time dependent refractory function*). The node fires when the counter of the summed messages crosses the current threshold level, and then resets its cycle.

The refractory function is the key element of our algorithm for achieving fault tolerant synchronization.

The algorithm performs correctly as long as less than a third of the nodes behave in a completely arbitrary ("Byzantine") manner concurrently. It ensures a tight synchronization of the pulses of all correct nodes, while not using any central clock or global pulse. We assume the physical network allows for a broadcast environment and has a bounded delay on message transmission. The algorithm may not reach its goal as long as these limitations are violated or the network graph is severely disconnected. The algorithm is Byzantine self-stabilizing and thus copes with a more severe fault model than the traditional Byzantine fault models. Traditional distributed algorithms assume the system is always within the predefined assumption boundaries. Moreover, many algorithms, particularly non-stabilizing clock synchronization algorithms, also make strong assumptions on the initial state of the nodes (such as assuming all clocks are initially synchronized, c.f. [7]). A self-stabilizing protocol converges to its goal within a finite time once the systems is back in an arbitrary state within the predefined assumption boundaries. For our protocol, once this happens, regardless of the state of the system, tight synchronization is achieved within finite time. It overcomes transient, permanent and intermittent faults, though for convergence we assume that there is a window of time during which no recovery of nodes takes place.

Our algorithm is uniform, all nodes execute an identical algorithm. It does not suffer from communication deadlock, as can happen in message-driven algorithms ([3]), since the nodes have a time-dependent state change, at the end of which they fire endogenously. It is fault-containing in the sense that the convergence time depends on the number of faulty nodes, f, and not on the network size (In Sect. 5 we discuss a relationship between the cycle length and the number of faults, imposed by our algorithm). The faulty nodes cannot ruin the synchronization; in the worst case, they can slow down the convergence and speed up the synchronized firing frequency up to a certain bound. The time complexity achieved is $O(f)$ cycles with a near optimal synchronization tightness of d (end to end network and processing delay). Comparatively, the time complexity of the digital clock synchronization problem in a similar model presented in [10] is exponential in the network size. The synchronization tightness achieved there depends on the network size. To the best of our knowledge that is the only paper describing an algorithm for Byzantine self-stabilizing clock synchronization algorithm. Note also that there are many papers that deal with self-stabilizing (digital) clock synchronization (see [17, 11, 1]), though not facing Byzantine faults. Nonetheless, the convergence time in those papers is not linear.

2   Assumptions, Definitions and Specifications of the Algorithm

The environment is a network of processors (nodes) that regularly invoke pulses, ideally every *cycle* time units. The invocation of the pulse is expressed by sending a message via a broadcast media; this is also referred to as **firing**.

In our environment, individual nodes have no access to a central clock or global pulse system. The hardware clocks of **correct nodes** have a bounded drift rate, ρ, from real time. The communication network does not guarantee any order on messages, though there is a bound on message delivery time once the network stabilizes.

The network and/or the nodes can behave arbitrarily, though eventually the network stabilizes to within the defined assumption boundaries in which at most f nodes may behave arbitrarily. The **network assumption boundaries** are:

1. Multicast message passing allowing for an authenticated identity of senders.
2. At most f of the nodes are faulty.
3. The subnetwork of correct nodes satisfies:
   (a) There is an upper bound δ on the physical end-to-end network delay.
   (b) Any message sent or received by any correct node will eventually reach every correct node within δ time units.

A node is **correct** at times that it complies with the following conditions:
1. Obeys a global constant $0 < \rho_{glob} << 1$, such that for every Newtonian time interval $[u, v]$, $(1 - \rho_{glob})(v - u) \leq$ 'physical clock' $\leq (1 + \rho_{glob})(v - u)$. Hereafter ρ_{glob} is denoted by ρ ($\rho \approx 10^{-6}$ in modern computers).
2. Operates according to an instructed protocol.
3. Accepts and sends only multicast messages.

Thus, a node is considered **faulty** when it violates one or more of the above. A faulty node can recover from its faulty behavior. The recovery is not necessarily immediate, but rather can take a certain amount of time until which the node is still considered faulty. We count the recovering nodes as part of the faulty nodes during a time window of length *cycle*. Thus, within the network assumption boundaries there can be at most f faulty and recovering nodes in every *cycle* time window. To overcome intermittent faults we need to assume some bound on how frequently the adversary can fail a recovered node, since, over time, all nodes may repeatedly fail and recover. We assume that eventually there is a window of at least $2(2f + 1)$ cycles within which there is no new recovery of nodes, which is proved in Theorem 3 to allow the system to converge.

Basic Notations:
   We use the following notations to define the quality of the solution, though nodes do not need to maintain them as variables.

- σ represents the target upper bound on the real time between the invocations of the pulses of different correct nodes (*tightness of synchronization*).

- $\Psi_p(t)$ is the number of endogenous (self generated) pulses node p would have invoked since its last recovery time to time t, had it been alone in the system.
- $\Phi_p(t)$ is the effective (actual) number of pulses a correct node p invoked since its last recovery time to time t.
- Let $a, b, g, h \in R^+$ be constants that define the linear envelope bound on the ratio between $\Psi_p(t)$ and $\Phi_p(t)$.
- $\phi_i \in R^+ \cup \{\infty\}$, $0 \le i \le n$, denotes the elapsed real time since the last time node p_i invoked a pulse. For a node, p_j, that has not fired since initialization of the system, $\phi_j \equiv \infty$.
- $d \equiv \delta + \pi$, where π is the upper bound on the message processing time.

Thus, d is an upper bound on the elapsed real time from the arrival of a message at a correct node and until a consequent message that is sent arrives at all other correct receiving nodes.

Basic Definitions:

- The **state** of the system at time t is given by: $State \equiv (t, \phi_0, \dots, \phi_{n-1})$.
- Let G be the set of all possible system states of a system S.
- A set of nodes, N, are called **synchronized** at time t if $\forall p_i, p_j \in N$, $\phi_i, \phi_j \le \frac{cycle}{1-\rho}$, then
  1. $|\phi_i - \phi_j| \le \sigma$,   or
  2. $\frac{cycle}{1-\rho} - \sigma \le |\phi_i - \phi_j| \le \frac{cycle}{1-\rho}$.
  Note that every correct node is always synchronized with itself. If $\forall p_i, p_j \in N$, it is Condition 1 that holds then we say that N is **strongly synchronized.**
- $s \in G$ is a **synchronized state** of the system at time t if the set of correct nodes are strongly synchronized at some time t_{syn} in the interval $[t, t + \sigma]$.
- $s \in G$ is a **sub-synchronized state** of the set of nodes N at time t, if a set of correct nodes in N are strongly synchronized at some time t_{syn} in the interval $[t, t + \sigma]$.

Note that when $||N|| = n$ for a set of nodes N, then the two definitions coincide. Observe that the definition of synchronized nodes is not transitive, and therefore the definition of a (sub-)synchronized state is not transitive.

The Self-Stabilizing "Pulse Synchronization" Problem

As long as the system is within its assumption boundaries:

Convergence: Starting from an arbitrary state, s, the system reaches a synchronized state after a finite number of steps.

Closure: If s is a synchronized state of the system at time t_0 then
1. all subsequent system states are synchronized states,
2. ≪Linear Envelope≫: for every correct node, p, and for every time $t \ge t_0$,
   $$a[\Psi_p(t) - \Psi_p(t_0)] + b \le \Phi_p(t) - \Phi_p(t_0) \le g[\Psi_p(t) - \Psi_p(t_0)] + h.$$

Note that the linear envelope resembles the linear envelope requirement of the clock synchronization problem.

3   The "Pulse Synchronization" Algorithm

We now present an algorithm that solves the "Pulse Synchronization" problem, inspired by and following a neurobiological analog. Each node sums the pulses that it learns about during a recent time window. If this sum (the Counter) crosses the current (time-dependent) threshold, then the node will fire. The refractory function describes the time dependency of the threshold. If reaching threshold level 0 then the node fires **endogenously,** irrespective of any inputs.

The Refractory Function

The cycle is the predefined time a correct node will count between two endogenous pulses. The refractory function R, is a step function. R_i is the time length of threshold level i. $R_i \in R^+$, $i = 1 \ldots n+1$, where, $\sum_{i=1}^{n+1} R_i \equiv cycle$. R_{n+1} is called the **absolute refractory period** of the cycle. Using the neurobiological analogy, this is the first period after a node fires; the node never fires within an absolute refractory period. We assume that $cycle \gg \sigma$ and require that $R_{n+1} > 2\sigma$ (satisfied by Restriction 5 presented later). We denote $R^p(t)$ the threshold level of node p at time t or $R(t)$ if it is clear what node is referred to. If a node fires at time t, then R is **reset** to $R(t) = n+1$.

The Messages

The content of a message M_p from a node p, is a Counter - the number of recent inputs received that caused the sending node to fire. A **k-sized input** is a set of k such messages that are received within a certain time window (defined in the appendix) that causes the value of the Counter of the receiver to be at least k.

The Summation Algorithm

A full description of the procedures used by the Summation Algorithm is provided in the Appendix. The Summation Algorithm is comprised of the following components:

The TIMELINESS procedure determines if the Counter contained in the message seems "reasonable" (timely). The bound on message transmission and processing time among correct nodes allows a node to estimate whether the content of a message it receives is plausible and therefore timely. If it is not then the node tables it for possible future use and after a certain time decays it. The MAKE-ACCOUNTABLE procedure determines by how much to increment the Counter following the arrival of a timely message. The node can take into account tabled messages, if necessary, for consistency reasons. The PRUNE procedure decays old messages and tables (currently) irrelevant messages.

SUMMATION(*at time t_{event} a new message M_p arrives or change in R*)

    if (*at time t_{event} a new message M_p arrives*) then

        if (TIMELINESS(M_p, t_{event})) then

            MAKE-ACCOUNTABLE(M_p)

                PRUNE(t);

    if (*change in R*) then

        PRUNE(t);

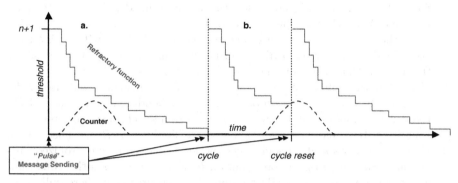

Fig. 1. Schematic example of the algorithm's mode of operation. (a.) A node fires endogenously if threshold=0 is reached. The counter of the summed messages does not cross the refractory function during the cycle, letting the threshold reach zero and consequently the node fires endogenously. (b.) The Counter of the summed messages increases sufficiently to cross the current refractory function, consequently the node fires and a new cycle of the node is initiated

The Event Driven Self-Stabilizing Algorithm (See Figure 1)

PULSE-SYNCHRONIZATION$(n, f, cycle)$

INIT:
  if $(n, f$ and $cycle$ are valid) then
      $R :=$ as determined by Eq. 2;
      reset R;
      set Counter $= 0$;
  else *exit;*
WAIT-FOREVER-LOOP:
  if (*at time t_{event} a new message M_p arrives* or *change in R*) then
      SUMMATION((M_p, t_{event}) or (*change in R*));
      if $(Counter \geq R(t))$ then
          Multicast Counter; /* Invocation of the Pulse */
          reset R;

4   Solving the "Pulse Synchronization" Problem

Due to the space constraints we only give an overview of the heuristics, in terms of the dynamics of the n-dimensional state space, that prove that the presented "Pulse Synchronization" algorithm solves the "Pulse Synchronization" problem. We assume the worst case of $n = 3f + 1$. In Sect. 5 we discuss various ratios between them and also about the relationship between the cycle length and f. A full account of the proofs of all the theorems in this paper can be found in [5].

1. Show that synchronized nodes identify a stable fixed point in state space (Lemma 1), which has a basin of attraction.
2. Show that we can associate every correct node exclusively with such a fixed point (called a "**synchronized cluster**") and prove that it is stable (Lemma 2), thus satisfying the closure requirement.
3. Show that the number of nodes associated with a synchronized cluster determines the span of its basin of attraction (depending on the shape of R). Explicitly formulate the basin of attraction of a synchronized cluster ("**absorbance distance**") as a function of its cardinality and R (see Theorem 1).
4. Show that every specific association of nodes with disjoint synchronized clusters has a matching linear constraint on R (Eq. 1). Satisfying this constraint under certain restrictions (Restrictions 1-5), ensures that there will be at least two synchronized clusters whose basins of attraction overlap in phase space ("within absorbance distance of each other") and thus synchronize (see Theorem 2).
5. Satisfying the set of all possible constraints (all possible associations of nodes with disjoint synchronized clusters) yields a refractory function that ensures Convergence of the system within finite time from an arbitrary state (see Corollary 2 and Theorem 3).
6. Present a solution to this set of linear equations on R (see Theorem 4).
7. Deduce from Corollary 2 and Theorem 4 that the algorithm thus solves the "Pulse Synchronization" problem (see Theorem 5).

We now cite the main lemmas, theorems, definitions and notations used:

- C_i – synchronized cluster number i.
- n_i – cardinality of C_i (i.e. number of correct nodes associated with synchronized cluster C_i).
- c current number of synchronized clusters in the current state; $c \geq 1$.
- $dist(p, q) \equiv |\phi_p - \phi_q|$ is the **phase difference** between nodes a and b.
- $dist(C_i, C_j) \equiv dist(\text{first node in cluster } C_i, \text{ first node in cluster } C_j)$.

Restriction 1: The Summation algorithm counts input messages such that: Following the arrival of a message from a correct node, every correct receiving node's Counter is incremented to hold a value greater than the Counter in the message.

Restriction 2: R_i is a monotonic decreasing function $R_i \geq R_{i+1}, i = 1 \ldots n-1$.

Restriction 3: $R_i > 3d, i = 1 \ldots n - f - 1$.

Restriction 4: $R_i > \sigma(1 + \rho) + \frac{\rho}{1+\rho} \sum_{j=1}^{n+1} R_j, i = 1 \ldots n$.

Restriction 5: $R_{n+1} \geq 2d(1 + \rho) \frac{(\frac{1+\rho}{1-\rho})^{n+3} - 1}{(\frac{1+\rho}{1-\rho}) - 1}$.

Lemma 1. *A set of correct nodes that are in a sub-synchronized state at some time t', remain in a sub-synchronized state as long as the network remains within its assumption boundaries.*

Lemma 2. *The set of nodes comprising a synchronized cluster at some time t remain in a sub-synchronized state as long as the network remains within its assumption boundaries.*

Corollary 1. *A synchronized cluster encompassing all the correct nodes implies the system is in a synchronized state, satisfying the objective of the Pulse synchronization problem.*

Theorem 1. *Given two synchronized clusters, C_i preceding C_j, Restriction 1 through Restriction 4 imply that if C_i fires due to a k-sized input $(0 \leq k \leq f)$[1] and **prior** to the firing of C_i,*

$$dist(C_i, C_j) \leq \frac{1}{1-\rho} \sum_{g=f+1}^{f+n_i} R_g - \frac{2\rho}{1-\rho^2} \sum_{g=f+1}^{n+1} R_g$$

then C_i absorbs C_j.

Theorem 2. *For n, f, cycle and a given clustering of $n - f$ correct nodes into $c > 1$ clusters at time t_0, for which Eq. 1 is satisfied, there will be at least one cluster that will absorb some other cluster by time $t_0 + (2\,cycle)$.*

Theorem 3. *Within at most $2(2f+1)$ cycle time units the pulse synchronization algorithm reaches a synchronized state of the system.*

Corollary 2. *For a given cycle, f and n, finding a solution to the problem of "Pulse Synchronization" employing the proposed algorithm, reduces to solving the set of linear constraints on R determined by Eq. 1.*

$$\sum_{j=1}^{c-1} \sum_{i=f+1}^{f+n_j} R_i + \sum_{i=1}^{n_c} R_i \geq (1 + \frac{2\rho}{1+\rho}(n-f))\,cycle, \text{ where } \sum_{j=1}^{c} n_j = n - f \ . \quad (1)$$

Theorem 4. *Given[2] $n > 3f + 1$ and cycle, the refractory function:*

$$R_i = \begin{cases} \frac{(1+\frac{2\rho}{1+\rho}(n-f))\,cycle}{n-f} & i = 1 \ldots n - f - 1 \\ \frac{R_1 - R_{n+1} - \frac{2\rho}{1+\rho}(n-f)\,cycle}{f+1} & i = n - f \ldots n \\ 2d(1+\rho)\frac{(\frac{1+\rho}{1-\rho})^{n+3}-1}{(\frac{1+\rho}{1-\rho})-1} & i = n+1, \end{cases} \quad (2)$$

constitutes a solution to the set of linear equations of R.

Theorem 5. *The algorithm of Sect. 3 solves the Pulse Synchronization Problem.*

---

[1] It is sufficient to limit the discussion to the case in which C_i receives a $k \leq f$-sized (faulty) input even though in the "real life" scenario C_i can by all accounts receive larger inputs. The justification for this assumption is that a greater than f sized input can actually be looked upon as though the f faulty nodes fired along with some cluster C_i, yielding an $f + n_i$-sized input. We therefore assume the discussed clusters are the clusters firing with or immediately following the k-sized (faulty) input, where $k \leq f$. The same reasoning is behind the consistency of the algorithm in case all/some of the faulty nodes actually behave correctly.

[2] An equivalent proof to Theorem 4 is given for the case $n = 3f + 1$ in [5].

5   Analysis of the Algorithm and Comparison to Related Algorithms

Our algorithm does not depend explicitly on the actual behavior of the nodes. The convergence of the clusters depends on having at most f nodes that may behave arbitrarily. Therefore, our algorithm can withstand any faulty behavior, including dynamic failure and recovery of nodes (intermittent faults). Nodes that have just recovered need time to synchronize, therefore, we assume that eventually we have a window of time within which there are no newly recovered nodes, and within which the system inevitably converges (Theorem 3).

Authentication and Fault Ratio: The algorithm does not require the full power of unforgeable signatures, and only the equivalence of an authenticated channel is required. Note that the shared memory model ([10]) has an implicit assumption that is equivalent to an authenticated channel, since a node "knows" the identity of the node that wrote to the memory it reads from. A similar assumption is also implicit in many message passing models by assuming a direct link among neighbors, and as a result, a node "knows" the identity of the sender of a message it receives.

Many fundamental problems in distributed networks have been proven to require $3f + 1$ nodes to overcome f concurrent faults in order to reach a deterministic solution without authentication [15, 20, 7, 6]. We did not prove that this ratio is a necessary requirement for solving the "Pulse Synchronization" problem but results of related problems lead to believe that a similar result may exist for this problem.

There are algorithms that have no lower bound on the number of nodes required to handle f faults, but unforgeable signatures are required as all the signatures in the message are validated by the receiver [7]. This is costly time-wise, it increases the message size, and it introduces other limitations, which our algorithm does not have.

Time Complexity: A randomized self-stabilizing Byzantine digital clock synchronization algorithm in [9, 10] designed for a fully connected communication graph synchronizes in $M2^{2(n-f)}$ pulses, where M is the upper bound on the clock values held by individual processors. The algorithm uses broadcast message passing, it allows transient and permanent faults during convergence, requires at least $3f+1$ processors, but utilizes a global pulse system. An additional algorithm in [10], does not use a global pulse system and is thus partially synchronous similar to our model. The convergence time of the latter algorithm is $O((n - f)n^{6(n-f)})$. This is drastically higher than our result even if one takes into consideration the relationship between *cycle* and f of our solution(Eq. 3), which yields an $O(f^3)$ time units convergence complexity.

Our use of broadcasts is essentially similar to the type of broadcast used in [10], since we assume nothing on the order of arrival of the messages and concomitant messages from the same source are ignored. Thus, a faulty node can send two consecutive messages with differing values. Correct nodes will accept the first arriving one.

Message and Space Complexity: Each correct node multicasts exactly one message per cycle. This yields a message complexity of at most n messages per cycle. The system's message complexity to reach synchronization from any arbitrary state is at most $2n(2f + 1)$ messages per synchronization from any arbitrary initial state. The faulty nodes cannot cause the correct nodes to fire more messages during a cycle. Comparatively, the self-stabilizing clock synchronization algorithm in [10] sends n messages during a pulse and thus has a message complexity of $O(n(n - f)n^{6(n-f)})$. This is significantly larger than our message complexity irrespective of the time interval between the pulses.

The space complexity is $O(n)$ since the variables maintained by the processors keep only a linear number of messages recently received and various other small range variables. The number of possible states of a node is linear in n, but the node does not need to keep a configuration table.

Tightness of Synchronization: Using the presented algorithm, the invocation of the pulses of the nodes will be synchronized to within d real time units. This asymptotically equals the lower bound on clock synchronization $d(1 - 1/n)$ in completely connected, fault-free networks [19]. Were our algorithm to be used as a logical clock synchronization algorithm then the clocks would show a maximum time difference of $d(1 + \rho)$ between each other due to the hardware clock skew. Comparatively, the non-stabilizing clock synchronization algorithm of [7] reaches a synchronization tightness of $d(1+\rho) + 2\rho(1+\rho)R$ where R is the time between synchronization rounds. The Byzantine digital clock synchronization algorithm in [10], which does not assume a global pulse, reaches a synchronization tightness which is in the magnitude of $(n - f)d(1 + \rho)$. This is significantly less tight than our result.

Firing Frequency Bound ("Linear Envelope"): The firing frequency bound is around twice that of the original firing frequency of the nodes (linear envelope). This bound is determined by the fault ratio (the sum of the first f threshold steps relative to the cycle length). For $n = 3f + 1$ it translates to $\approx \frac{1}{2}cycle$. Thus, if required, the firing frequency bound can be closer to the endogenous firing frequency of 1 *cycle* if the fraction of faulty nodes is assumed to be lower. For example, for a fraction of $n = 10f$, the lower bound on the cycle length is approximately 8/9 that of the endogenous cycle length.

The Allowed Parameter Range (of n, f and *cycle*): Restrictions 2-5 determine the lower bound on the allowed length of each threshold step, R_i. There are exactly $n + 1$ threshold steps whose sum needs to equal exactly *cycle* time units. Restrictions 2-5 therefore also determine a required relationship between the input parameters n, f and *cycle*. To uncover this relationship and show that the solution space is not empty we need to verify that given $n, f, cycle$ and the solution specified by Eq. 2 then:

1. R_i, $i = 1 \ldots n - f - 1$, comply with Restrictions 3 and 4:

$$\frac{(1 + \frac{2\rho}{1+\rho}(n - f)) \, cycle}{n - f} > \max(3d, d(1 + \rho) + \frac{\rho}{1 + \rho} \, cycle) \ .$$

2. R_i, $i = n - f \ldots n$, comply with Restriction 4:

$$\frac{R_1 - R_{n+1} - \frac{2\rho}{1+\rho}(n - f) \, cycle}{f + 1} > d(1 + \rho) + \frac{\rho}{1 + \rho} \sum_{j=n-f}^{n+1} R_j \ .$$

3. R_i, $i = 1 \ldots n - f - 1$ comply with: $R_i > \sum_{j=n-f}^{n+1} R_j$.

This yields the following approximate required relationship between f and $cycle$ (assuming $n = 3f + 1$), ensuring that the solution of (Eq. 2) complies with Restrictions 2-5:

$$4df^2 < cycle \ . \tag{3}$$

A disadvantage of the algorithm is thus its scalability with respect to the fault ratio and cycle length should the fault ratio be taken at its bound, $n = 3f + 1$. This relationship improves though, with a decrease in d, the network delay. If we fix the solution for a boundary network size of $3f + 1$ and designate it as m, then executing the algorithm with any input network size of $n \geq m$ is acceptable.

6   Discussion

We developed a self-stabilizing fault tolerant algorithm for *pulse synchronization* in distributed computer networks. The "Pulse Synchronization" problem is a relaxed version of the clock synchronization problem. The linear envelope requirement defines a restriction that defies a straight forward simple solution. Moreover, the fact that there isn't a specific value that describes the pulse difference among nodes, eliminates the ability to use some sort of approximation approach ([8]) or consensus. Clock synchronization can be viewed as approximate agreement on a value representing real time.

The algorithm developed is inspired by and shares properties with the lobster cardiac pace-maker network; the network elements fire in tight synchrony within each other, whereas the synchronized firing pace can vary, up to a certain extent, within a linear envelope of a completely regular firing pattern. This behavior can be compared to the requirement of keeping the clocks of the network computers synchronized with each other ("precision") as well as being close to real time ("accuracy"). Pulse synchronization and clock synchronization have similar precision requirements but differ in the accuracy requirement.

Possible Applications: We offer the pulse synchronization scheme in general, and our Byzantine self-stabilizing pulse synchronization algorithm in particular. The algorithm has an improved fault tolerance (self-stabilization) in comparison to traditional clock synchronization algorithms and improved convergence time and synchronization tightness in comparison to Byzantine self-stabilizing digital clock synchronization. It is useful particularly when there is no real need to agree on the pulse counters or keeping a constant pulse frequency, but only obtain and maintain highly fault tolerant and tight synchronization.

A self-stabilizing pulse synchronization algorithm can be beneficial to solve TDMA based slot synchronization (in multi access channels such as cellular phones; slotted ALOHA) [28]. A similar suggestion appears in [21], though without supplying any fault tolerance. In this problem, if the participants are not tightly synchronized with respect to the frame starting point then collisions will occur. The exact starting time of the frame is of minor importance relative to the synchronization requirement. Should a central synchronizer be present then the network would be extremely sensitive to faults in the central station. Where no central station is available and connectivity changes rapidly a self-stabilizing distributed synchronization protocol would make the participants resynchronize without any exterior intervention, should the participant be out of synchronization. Other cases that could benefit from a self-stabilizing pulse synchronization scheme include global snapshots; load balancing; distributed inventory count; distributed scheduling; backup of distributed systems; debugging of distributed programs; and deadlock detection.

References

[1] A. Arora, S. Dolev, and M. G. Gouda, *"Maintaining digital clocks in step"*, Parallel Processing Letters, 1:11-18, 1991. 34

[2] G. E. Andrews, *"The Theory of Partitions"*, Encyclopedia of Mathematics and Its Applications, Vol. 2, Addison-Wesley, Reading, MA, 1976.

[3] J. Brzeziński, and M. Szychowiak, *"Self-Stabilization in Distributed Systems - a Short Survey,* Foundations of Computing and Decision Sciences, 25(1), 2000. 34

[4] J. Buck, and E. Buck, *"Synchronous fireflies"*, Scientific American, Vol. 234, pp. 74-85, May 1976. 32

[5] A. Daliot, D. Dolev, H. Parnas, *"Self-Stabilizing Pulse Synchronization Inspired by Biological Pacemaker Networks* Technical Report TR2003-1, Schools of Engineering and Computer Science, The Hebrew University of Jerusalem, March 2003. url://leibnitz.cs.huji.ac.il/tr/acc/2003/HUJI-CE-LTR-2003-1_pulse-tr6.ps 38, 40

[6] D. Dolev, J. Halpern, and H. R. Strong, *"On the Possibility and Impossibility of Achieving Clock Synchronization"*, J. of Computer and Systems Science, Vol. 32:2, pp. 230-250, 1986. 41

[7] D. Dolev, J. Y. Halpern, B. Simons, and R. Strong, *"Dynamic Fault-Tolerant Clock Synchronization"*, J. Assoc. Computing Machinery, Vol. 42, No.1, pp. 143-185, Jan. 1995. 33, 34, 41, 42

[8] D. Dolev, N. A. Lynch, E. Stark, W. E. Weihl and S. Pinter, *"Reaching Approximate Agreement in the Presence of Faults,* Journal of the ACM, 33 (1986). 43

[9] S. Dolev, *"Self-Stabilization,"* The MIT Press, 2000. 41

[10] S. Dolev, and J. L. Welch, *"Self-Stabilizing Clock Synchronization in the presence of Byzantine faults"*, Proc. Of the Second Workshop on Self-Stabilizing Systems, pp. 9.1-9.12, 1995. 34, 41, 42

[11] S Dolev and JL Welch, *"Wait-free clock synchronization"*, Algorithmica, 18(4):486-511, 1997. 34

[12] C. Fetzer and F. Cristian, *"An Optimal Internal Clock Synchronization Algorithm"*, Proceedings of the 10th Conference on Computer Assurance, 1995, pp. 187-196, Gaithersburg, MD, USA. 33

[13] W. O. Friesen, *"Physiological anatomy and burst pattern in the cardiac ganglion of the spiny lobster Panulirus interuptus"*, J. Comp. Physiol., Vol. 101, 1975. 32

[14] W. O. Friesen, *"Synaptic interaction in the cardiac ganglion of the spiny lobster Panulirus interuptus"*, J. Comp. Physiol., Vol. 101, pp. 191-205, 1975. 32

[15] M. J. Fischer, N. A. Lynch and M. Merritt, *"Easy impossibility proofs for distributed consensus problems"*, Distributed Computing, Vol. 1, pp. 26-39, 1986. 41

[16] T. Herman, *"Phase clocks for transient fault repair"*, IEEE Transactions on Parallel and Distributed Systems, 11(10):1048-1057, 2000.

[17] T. Herman and S. Ghosh, *"Stabilizing Phase-Clocks"*, Information Processing Letters, 5(6):585-598, 1994. 34

[18] B. Liskov, *"Practical Use of Synchronized Clocks in Distributed Systems"*, PODC 10, 1991, pp. 1-9. 33

[19] J. Lundelius, and N. Lynch, *"An Upper and Lower Bound for Clock Synchronization,"* Information and Control, Vol. 62, pp. 190-205, Aug/Sep. 1984. 42

[20] N. Lynch, *"Distributed Algorithms"*, Morgan Kaufmann, 1996. 41

[21] R. Mathar and J. Mattfeldt, *"Pulse-coupled decentral synchronization"*, SIAM J. Appl. Math, Vol. 56, No. 4, pp. 1094-1106, Aug. 1996. 44

[22] R. E. Mirollo and S. H. Strogatz, *"Synchronization of pulse-coupled biological oscillators"*, SIAM J. Appl. Math, Vol. 50, pp. 1645-1662, 1990. 33

[23] B. Patt-Shamir, *"A Theory of Clock Synchronization,* Doctoral thesis, MIT, Oct. 1994. 33

[24] Z. Nèda, E. Ravasz, Y. Brechet, T. Vicsek, and A.-L. Barabàsi, *"Self-organizing process: The sound of many hands clapping"*, Nature, 403, pp. 849-850, 2000. 32

[25] F. Schneider, *"Understanding Protocols for Byzantine Clock Synchronization"*, Technical Report 87-859, Dept. of Computer Science, Cornell University, 1987. 33

[26] E. Sivan, H. Parnas and D. Dolev, *"Fault tolerance in the cardiac ganglion of the lobster"*, Biol. Cybern., Vol. 81, pp. 11-23, 1999. 32, 33

[27] S. H. Strogatz and I. Stewart, *"Coupled Oscillators and Biological Synchronization"*, Scientific American, Vol. 269, pp. 102-109, Dec. 1993 32

[28] A. S. Tanenbaum, *"Computer Networks 3rd ed."*, Prentice Hall International. 44

7   Appendix: The Summation Algorithm

Heuristics:

1. When the input counter crosses the threshold level, either due to a sufficient counter increment or a threshold decrement, then the node sends a message (fires). The message sent holds the value of Counter at sending time.
2. The TIMELINESS procedure is employed at the receiving node to assess the credibility (timeliness) of the value of the Counter contained in this message. This procedure ensures that messages sent by correct nodes with Counter less than n will always be assessed as timely by other correct receiving nodes.
3. When a received message is declared timely and therefore accounted for it is stored in a "counted" message buffer ("Counted State"). The receiving node's Counter is then updated to hold a value greater than the Counter in the message by the MAKE-ACCOUNTABLE procedure.
4. If a message received is declared untimely then it is temporarily stored in an "uncounted" message buffer ("Uncounted State") and will not be accounted for at this stage. Over time, the timeliness test of previously stored timely messages may not hold any more. In this case, such messages will be moved from the Counted State to the Uncounted State by the PRUNE procedure.
5. All messages are deleted after a certain time-period by the PRUNE procedure.

Definitions and State Variables

Counter: an integer representing the node's estimation of the number of timely firing events received from distinct nodes within a certain time window. Counter is updated upon receiving a timely message. The node's Counter is checked against the refractory function whenever one of them changes. The value of Counter is bounded and non-monotonous; the arrival of timely events may increase it and the decay/untimeliness of old events may decrease it.

Signature Entry: a basic data structure represented as (S_p, t_{arr}) and created upon arrival of a message M_p. S_p is the id (or signature) of the sending node p and t_{arr} is the arrival time of the message. We say that two signature entries, (S_p, t_1) and (S_q, t_2), are **distinct** if $p \neq q$.

Counted State (CS): a set of distinct signature entries that determine the current value of Counter. The Counter reflects the number of signature entries in the Counted State. A signature entry is **accounted for** in Counter, if it was in CS when the current value of Counter was determined. We require exclusive write access to CS.

Uncounted State (UCS): a set of signature entries, not necessarily distinct, that have not been accounted for in the current value of Counter and that are not yet due to decay. A signature entry is placed in the UCS when its message clearly reflects a faulty sending node or because it is not timely anymore.

Retired UCS (RUCS): a set of distinct signature entries not accounted for in the current value of Counter due to the elapsed time since their arrival. These signature entries are awaiting deletion (decaying).

The CS and UCS are mutually exclusive and together reflect the relevant messages received from other nodes in the preceding time window. Their union is the node's **message state**.

We use the notation $Counter_q$ to mark node q's Counter, $Counter_{M_p}$ to mark the Counter contained in a message M_p sent by p and —message state— to mark the number of distinct signature entries in the message state.

- $T(p, M_p)$: denotes the time at node p at which it sent the message M_p.
- $T(M_p, q)$: denotes the arrival time of the message M_p at node q.
- $MessageAge(t, p)$: the elapsed time on a node's clock since the most recent arrival of a message from node p. Thus, its value at a node q at time t, is given by $t - T(M_p, q)$.
- $StateAge(t, k)$: denotes $MessageAge(t, \ldots)$ of the k'th most recent signature entry in the node's message state.
- $CSAge(t)$: denotes, at t, the largest $MessageAge(t, \ldots)$ among the signature entries in CS.

Procedures Used by the Summation Algorithm

We say that message M_p is **assessed** by q, once the following procedure is completed by q. A message M_p, is **timely** at time t_{arr} at node q once it is declared timely by the procedure.

TIMELINESS (M_p, t_{arr}):
   Timeliness Condition 1:
        If $(0 > Counter_{M_p}$ or $Counter_{M_p} > n - 1)$
        then return "M_p is not timely";
   Timeliness Condition 2:
        Create a new signature entry (S_p, t_{arr}) and insert it into UCS;
        If $(\exists (S_p, t)$ s.t. $t \neq t_{arr})^3$ in message state $\cup RUCS)$
        then
             delete from message state all (S_p, t'), where $t' \neq \max(T(M_p, q))$;
             return "M_p is not timely";
   Timeliness Condition 3:
        Let k denote $Counter_{M_p}$, and let $\tau(k) \equiv 2d(1 + \rho) \frac{(\frac{1+\rho}{1-\rho})^{k+1} - 1}{(\frac{1+\rho}{1-\rho}) - 1}$.
        If $(k < |\text{message state}|)$ AND $(StateAge(t_{arr}, k + 1) \leq \tau(k))$
             at some time in the interval $[t_{arr}, t_{arr} + d(1 + \rho)]^4$
        then return "M_p is timely";
        else return "M_p is not timely";

The following procedure atomically moves and deletes obsolete signature entries. It prunes the CS to hold only signature entries such that a message sent holding the resultant Counter will be assessed as timely at any correct receiving node. Counter is then updated.

PRUNE(t):

---

[3] We assume no concomitant messages are stamped with the exact same arrival times at a correct node. We assume that one can uniquely identify messages.

[4] We assume the implementation detects that these conditions are satisfied within the time window.

- Delete (decay) from RUCS all entries (S_p, t) whose $MessageAge(t, p) > \tau(n + 2)$;
- Move to RUCS, from the message state, all signature entries (S_p, t) whose $MessageAge(t, p) > \tau(n + 1)$;
- Move to UCS, from CS, signature entries, beginning with the oldest, until: $CSAge(t) \leq \tau(k - 1)$, where $k = \max(1, |CS|)$;
- Set $Counter = |CS|$;

This procedure atomically moves signature entries from UCS into CS and updates the value of Counter following the arrival of a new timely message M_p.

MAKE-ACCOUNTABLE(M_p):

- Move the $\max(1, Counter_{M_p} - Counter_q + 1)$ most recent distinct signature entries from UCS to CS;
- Set $Counter = |CS|$;

This set of procedures comprise the event driven Summation Algorithm.

Self-Stabilizing Algorithms for {*k*}-Domination

Martin Gairing[1,*], Stephen T. Hedetniemi[2,**], Petter Kristiansen[3], and Alice A. McRae[4]

[1] Faculty of Computer Science, Electrical Engineering and Mathematics
University of Paderborn, 33102 Paderborn, Germany
`gairing@uni-paderborn.de`
[2] Department of Computer Science,
Clemson University, Clemson, SC 29634, USA
`hedet@cs.clemson.edu`
[3] Department of Informatics,
University of Bergen, N-5020 Bergen, Norway
`petterk@ii.uib.no`
[4] Department of Computer Science,
Appalachian State University, Boone, NC 28608, USA
`aam@cs.appstate.edu`

Abstract. In the self-stabilizing algorithmic paradigm for distributed computing each node has only a local view of the system, yet in a finite amount of time the system converges to a global state, satisfying some desired property. A function $f : V(G) \rightarrow \{0, 1, 2, \ldots, k\}$ is a $\{k\}$-dominating function if $\Sigma_{j \in N[i]} f(j) \geq k$ for all $i \in V(G)$. In this paper we present self-stabilizing algorithms for finding a minimal $\{k\}$-dominating function in an arbitrary graph. Our first algorithm covers the general case, where k is arbitrary. This algorithm requires an exponential number of moves, however we believe that its scheme is interesting on its own, because it can insure that when a node moves, its neighbors hold *correct* values in their variables. For the case that $k = 2$ we propose a linear time self-stabilizing algorithm.

1 Introduction

A distributed system can be modeled with a connected, undirected graph G with node set $V(G)$ and edge set $E(G)$. If i is a node in $V(G)$, then $N(i)$, its *open neighborhood*, denotes the set of nodes to which i is adjacent. Every node $j \in N(i)$ is called a *neighbor* of node i. The *closed neighborhood* of node i, is the set $N[i] = N(i) \cup \{i\}$. For a set $S \subseteq V(G)$ we define $N[S] = \bigcup_{i \in S} N[i]$. A *dominating set* is a set $S \subseteq V(G)$ for which $N[S] = V(G)$. Denote $n = |V(G)|$ the number of nodes in the graph and $m = |E(G)|$ the number of edges.

Self-stabilization is a paradigm for distributed systems that allows a system to achieve a desired, or legitimate, global state, even in the presence of faults.

---

[*] Supported by the IST Program of the EU under contract numbers IST-1999-14186 (ALCOM-FT) and IST-2001-33116 (FLAGS).

[**] Research supported in part by NSF Grant CCR-0222648.

S.-T. Huang and T. Herman (Eds.): SSS 2003, LNCS 2704, pp. 49–60, 2003.

The concept was introduced in 1974 by Dijkstra [2], but serious work on self-stabilizing algorithms did not start until the late 1980s. (See [14, ch. 15] for an introduction to self-stabilizing algorithms.) Dolev [3] published the first book, that focuses completely on self-stabilization.

In our algorithmic model, each node executes the same self-stabilizing algorithm, maintains its own set of local variables, and changes the values of its local variables based on the current values of its variables and those of its neighbors. The contents of a node's local variables determine its *local state*. The system's *global state* is the union of all local states.

When a node changes its local state, it is said to make a *move*. Our algorithms are given as a set of rules of the form $p(i) \Rightarrow M$, where $p(i)$ is a boolean predicate, and M is a move which describes the changes to be made to one or more of the node's local variables. A node i becomes *privileged* if $p(i)$ is true. When a node becomes privileged, it may execute the corresponding move. We assume there exists a daemon, an adversarial oracle, as introduced in [2], which selects one of the privileged nodes. The selected node then makes a move. Following the serial model, we assume that no two nodes move at the same time. For our algorithm it's sufficient that adjacent nodes never move at the same time. This can be achieved using a protocol for local mutual exclusion [1].

The goal of the daemon is to keep the algorithm running as long as possible. When no further moves are possible, we say that the system is *stable* or is in a stable state. We say that a self-stabilizing algorithm is *correct* if, when the system executes the algorithm,

1) every stable state it can reach is legitimate, that is, every stable state has the desired global property, and
2) it always reaches a stable state after a finite number of moves.

Notice that it is quite possible for a correct self-stabilizing algorithm to reach a legitimate state which is not stable.

Problems that can be solved by a straightforward greedy method in the conventional algorithmic model often require a far more clever approach in the self-stabilizing model. For example, finding a maximal matching (i.e. a set of disjoint edges that cover all remaining edges) in a graph is trivial: starting with an empty set of edges, keep adding another disjoint edge to the set as long as one exists. To describe and prove the correctness of a self-stabilizing algorithm for this same problem takes considerably more effort [10, 11, 13].

2   {k}-Domination

For a graph G, let $f : V(G) \rightarrow \{0, 1, \ldots, k\}$ be a function from the node set $V(G)$ into the set of integers $\{0, 1, \ldots, k\}$, and let $f(S) = \sum_{v \in S} f(v)$ for any subset $S \subseteq V(G)$. Such a function is a {k}-*dominating function* [8, 4, 5], if for every $i \in V(G)$ we have $f(N[i]) \geq k$. A {k}-dominating function f is *minimal* if there does not exist a {k}-dominating function f' with $f' \neq f$ and $f'(i) \leq f(i), \forall i \in$

$V(G)$. Or equivalently, for every node i, if $f(i) \neq 0$, then there is a neighbor $j \in N[i]$ with $f(N[j]) = k$.

The general idea of {k}-domination is that every node in the network needs a minimum amount of a given resource, for example k units of it. It then becomes a resource allocation problem to locate a minimum quantity of this needed resource among the nodes so that each node can gain access to at least k units of this resource within its closed neighborhood. The node must either supply itself with this resource, if it does not exist among its neighbors, or it can use the resources of its neighbors. Examples of this resource might include a minimum number of firefighters, ambulances, or emergency vehicles, or a minimum number of CPU cycles, memory or servers. Of course, in the most general setting, all nodes have different resource needs, say as a function of their size, population, etc. Thus, we can associate with each node i, a minimum resource requirement r_i. We then seek an allocation of resources, at minimum cost, such that the total amount of resources assigned to each closed neighborhood $N[i]$ is at least r_i. In the definition of {k}-domination it is assumed that all nodes have the same resource requirement, i.e. k.

The concept of a {k}-dominating function gives rise to the following decision problem:

{k}-DOMINATING FUNCTION

INSTANCE: A graph G and a positive integer l.
QUESTION: Does G have a {k}-dominating function f, with $f(V(G)) \leq l$?

In the reduction below we use the following problem, first shown to be $\mathcal{NP}$-complete by Karp in [12]:

MINIMUM COVER

INSTANCE: A set $X = \{x_1, x_2, \ldots, x_n\}$ of n elements, a collection $S = \{S_1, S_2, \ldots, S_m\}$ of m subsets of X, and a positive integer $q \leq |S|$.
QUESTION: Does S contain a cover for X of size q or less, i.e., a subset $S' \subseteq S$ with $|S'| \leq q$, such that every element of X belongs to at least one member of S'?

Theorem 1. {k}-DOMINATING FUNCTION *is $\mathcal{NP}$-complete for all $k \geq 1$.*

Proof. {k}-DOMINATING FUNCTION is clearly in $\mathcal{NP}$. We reduce from MINIMUM COVER.

Given an instance (X, S, q) of MINIMUM COVER, we create an instance (G, l) of {k}-DOMINATING FUNCTION in the following manner: for each $x_i \in X$, there is an element component G_i consisting of k paths on three nodes. We label the nodes of path j, for $1 \leq j \leq k$: $a_{i,j}$, $b_{i,j}$, $c_{i,j}$. In addition, one node d_i is connected to each of the c-nodes $c_{i,1}, \ldots, c_{i,k}$. For each subset $S_{i'} \in S$ there is a subset node $u_{i'}$ which is is connected to all of the $a_{i,j}$ nodes in the element components corresponding to the elements in $S_{i'}$. All subset nodes are in turn connected to a common K_2, with nodes labeled v and w, by adding edges from all subset nodes $u_{i'}$ to v. The transformation is completed by taking $l = |X| \cdot k^2 + q + k$.

Assume T is a set cover with $|T| \leq q$. We construct a $\{k\}$-dominating function as follows: for the element components G_i we let $f(a_{i,j}) = 0$, $f(b_{i,j}) = k - 1$, $f(c_{i,j}) = 1$, and $f(d_{i,j}) = 0$. For the subset nodes we let $f(u_{i'}) = 1$ if $S_{i'} \in T$, and $f(u_{i'}) = 0$ if $S_{i'} \notin T$. Finally we let $f(v) = k$ and $f(w) = 0$.

Under f, all b-, c-, and d-nodes will have neighborhood sums of k. The a-nodes will each be adjacent to a b-node with value $k - 1$, and at least one u-node with value 1. The remaining nodes all have node v in their neighborhood, and will therefore have neighborhood sums of k. Note that, for each element component G_i we have $f(G_i) = k^2$. The f-values for the subset nodes will sum to at most q, and $f(v) = k$. This implies that $f(V(G)) \leq |X| \cdot k^2 + q + k$, and, therefore f is a $\{k\}$-dominating function of weight less than or equal to l.

Given a $\{k\}$-dominating function f for G, with $f(V(G)) \leq l$, we modify f as follows: 1) If $f(v) \neq k$, change $f(v)$ and $f(w)$ so that $f(v) = k$ and $f(w) = 0$. It is easy to see that the modified function will still be a $\{k\}$-dominating function with $f(V(G)) \leq l$. 2) Examine each element component G_i, one at a time. Note that the f-values of every abc-path within the component must sum up to at least k, otherwise the b-node of the path will not be $\{k\}$-dominated. Therefore, $f(G_i) \geq k^2$, for every element component G_i. There are two cases to consider: i) $f(G_i) = k^2$, and ii) $f(G_i) > k^2$. In case i) node d_i, which is not part of any abc-path must have $f(d_i) = 0$. Therefore the sum of the f-values for the b-, and c-nodes of every abc-path must be k, otherwise the c-nodes will not be $\{k\}$-dominated. It therefore follows that $f(a_{i,j}) = 0$, for all j. In case ii) we reassign the f-values of all the nodes in G_i, so that $f(a_{i,j}) = 0$, $f(b_{i,j}) = k - 1$, and $f(c_{i,j}) = 1$, for every j, and $f(d_i) = 0$. We then choose any u-node connected to G_i, say $u_{i'}$, and set $f(u_{i'}) = 1$ if $f(u_{i'}) = 0$. The modified f is still a $\{k\}$-dominating function, and the weight of f has not increased. With the modified f-function we find a set cover T by taking $T = \{S'_i : f(u_{i'}) \geq 1\}$.

Since $f(V(G)) \leq l = |X| \cdot k^2 + k + q$, we know that the f-values of the u-nodes sum to at most q (remember $f(v) = k$ and $f(G_i) = k^2$), therefore there are at most q u-nodes with f-value greater than zero. Each element component G_i will have one c-node, say $c_{i,j}$, with $f(c_{i,j}) \geq 0$, otherwise d_i will not be $\{k\}$-dominated. Therefore $f(b_{i,j}) < k$. Consider node $a_{i,j}$. We know $f(a_{i,j}) + f(b_{i,j}) < 0 + k$, so $a_{i,j}$ must be adjacent to some u-node $u_{i'}$ with $f(u_{i'}) > 0$. Every element component must therefore be adjacent to a u-node, say $u_{i'}$, with $f(u_{i'}) > 0$, the subsets corresponding to those u-nodes will constitute a set cover.   □

3   Minimal $\{k\}$-Dominating Function

In this section we present a self-stabilizing algorithm for finding a minimal $\{k\}$-dominating function in an arbitrary graph. The algorithm is based on a self-stabilizing algorithm for maximal 2-packing [6]. We assume that every node has a distinct identifier, or *ID*, and that there exists a total ordering on the IDs. Each node i has a local variable f, storing the function value associated with node i, a local variable σ storing a local copy of the value $f(N[i])$ and a pointer. We use the notation $i \rightarrow j$ and $i \rightarrow NULL$ to denote that the pointer of i points to j and that the pointer of i points to $NULL$, respectively. A node i can also point to itself, indicated by $i \to i$. For a node i we say that $\sigma(i)$ is *correct*, if $\sigma(i) = f(N[i])$. The algorithm is identically stored and executed in each node i. For simplicity we define the following shorthands:

- $predf(i) = f(N[i]) < k \vee (f(i) > 0 \wedge f(N[i]) > k \wedge \forall j \in N(i) : \sigma(j) > k)$
- $minn(i) = min\{j|j \in N(i) \wedge j \to j\}$ and $min(\emptyset) = NULL$.

The predicate $predf(i)$ is used to indicate whether node i should change its f-value or not. For a node i, $predf(i)$ is true if either $f(N[i]) < k$ or from the view of i, $f(i)$ can still be decreased, preserving the property that $f(N[j]) \geq k$ for all $j \in N[i]$. We define $minn(i)$ to be the minimum ID of a node in the open neighborhood of i, that points to itself. If no such node exists, $minn(i) = NULL$.

Algorithm 3.1: MINIMAL $\{k\}$-DOMINATING FUNCTION

---

local $f(\_) \in \{0, 1, \ldots, k\}$;
$\quad \sigma(\_) \quad$ integer;
$\quad \_ \to \_ \quad$ pointer;

ADD: if $predf(i) \wedge i \to NULL \wedge \forall j \in N(i) : j \to NULL$
$\quad$ **then** $\begin{cases} i \to i; \\ \sigma(i) = f(N[i]); \end{cases}$

UPDATE: if $\sigma(i) \neq f(N[i]) \vee (i \nrightarrow i \wedge i \nrightarrow minn(i))$
$\quad$ **then** $\begin{cases} i \to minn(i); \\ \sigma(i) = f(N[i]); \end{cases}$

RETRACT: if $i \to i \wedge \exists j \in N(i) : (j \to l \wedge l < i)$
$\quad$ **then** $\begin{cases} i \to minn(i); \\ \sigma(i) = f(N[i]); \end{cases}$

INCREASE: if $i \to i \wedge \forall j \in N(i) : j \to i \wedge f(N[i]) \leq k$
$\quad$ **then** $\begin{cases} f(i) = k - f(N(i)); \\ \sigma(i) = f(N[i]); \\ i \to NULL; \end{cases}$

DECREASE: if $i \to i \wedge \forall j \in N(i) : j \to i \wedge f(N[i]) > k$
$\quad$ **then** $\begin{cases} \sigma(i) = f(N[i]); \\ f(i) = f(i) - min_{j \in N[i]}\{(\sigma(j) - k), 0\}; \\ \sigma(i) = f(N[i]); \\ i \to NULL; \end{cases}$

The rules ADD, UPDATE and RETRACT are used to achieve mutual exclusion for the INCREASE and DECREASE moves and to make sure that whenever a node INCREASEs or DECREASEs, this move is based upon correct

σ-variables in its neighborhood. We will use the term *p-move* for an ADD, UP-DATE or RETRACT and *f-move* for an INCREASE or DECREASE.

A node i that has to change its f-value ($predf(i)$ is true) tries to ADD. It can make this ADD move if all of its neighbors (including i) point to $NULL$. When making an ADD move, node i sets its pointer to itself, indicating that i wants to change its f-value. The next time that node i gets scheduled it either changes its f-value (by an f-move) or it RETRACTs. The f-move is made if all neighbors of i point to i. When executing this f-move, node i updates $f(i)$ and sets its pointer back to $NULL$. The RETRACT move is made, if i has a neighbor that points to a node with lower ID than the ID of i. A RETRACT move sets the pointer of i to $minn(i)$, that is, the neighbor with smallest ID that points to itself (if it exists) or to $NULL$. A node i where $\sigma(i)$ is not correct, or a node that does not point to itself or to $minn(i)$ can UPDATE by setting its pointer to $minn(i)$. In every move node i also recalculates $\sigma(i)$.

We prove convergence of Algorithm 3.1 in two steps. First, we give an upper bound on the total number of p-moves that the daemon can make without making an f-move. We then show that the number of f-moves for each node is bounded by a constant. For the first step we assume that $predf(i) = TRUE$ for every node i. It is easy to see that this gives the daemon the most power, since otherwise all nodes j with $predf(j) = FALSE$ are not privileged by ADD.

Lemma 1. *The following holds in between two consecutive INCREASE or DE-CREASE moves:*
(a) Between two successive UPDATEs by node i, there must be a RETRACT or ADD by a neighbor of i.
(b) Between two successive ADDs by node i, there must be a RETRACT by a lower numbered node.

Proof. (a) After the first UPDATE, i points to $minn(i)$ and $\sigma(i) = f(N[i])$. For another UPDATE to occur, i must not point to $minn(i)$. This means that $minn(i)$ has changed.

(b) When node i ADDs, all of its neighbors point to $NULL$. For i to RE-TRACT at least one of its neighbors, say j, must point to a lower-numbered node, say z. By the time i ADDs again, j must have changed its pointer back to $NULL$. If $j = z$, then that means that z has RETRACTed. On the other hand, if $j \neq z$, then since $j \rightarrow NULL$ previously, at the moment that j changes its pointer to z, the node z points to itself. At the moment that j changes its pointer back to $NULL$, the node z must not point to itself. That is z has RE-TRACTed.   □

Assume that the nodes are numbered from 1 to n. Let $a(i)$ denote the number of times that node v_i executes an ADD rule and let $r(i)$ be the number of RETRACTs of node v_i. Obviously, ADDing and RETRACTing are closely linked. Indeed, $a(i) - 1 \leq r(i) \leq a(i) + 1$.

Lemma 2. *In between two INCREASEs or DECREASEs in the graph the number of ADDs for a node j is bounded by $a(j) \leq 2^j - 1$.*

Proof. By induction on j. Base case: Node v_1 can ADD only once by the above lemma.

For the general case, Lemma 1 says that between consecutive ADDs for node v_j, there must be a RETRACT of one of $v_1, \ldots, v_{j-1}$. This means that:

$$a(j) \le 1 + \sum_{i<j} r(i) \le 1 + \sum_{i<j} (1 + a(i)) \le 2^j - 1,$$

where the last inequality follows from the inductive hypothesis.   □

Lemma 3. *At most* $(n+1) \cdot 2^{n+2}$ *ADDs, UPDATEs and RETRACTs can be made without executing DECREASE or INCREASE.*

Proof. By Lemma 2, the total numbers of ADDs and RETRACTs are both at most 2^{n+1}. By Lemma 1, the total number of UPDATEs is at most n times the total number of ADDs and RETRACTs combined.   □

We now show some properties that hold prior to, or just after an f-move.

Lemma 4. *If a node i makes an f-move for the second time, this move is based upon correct values of $\sigma(j)$ for all neighbors $j \in N[i]$.*

Proof. The first time a node i made an f-move all neighbors $j \in N[i]$ were pointing at i. After i INCREASEd or DECREASEd it sets its pointer back to $NULL$. In order for i to make an f-move again it first has to ADD. This only happens when all its neighbors $j \in N(i)$ are pointing to $NULL$. Then each neighbor j has to change its pointer back to i. At every pointer change j will set $\sigma(j) = f(N[j])$. Since $j \to i$ no other neighbor $z \in N(j) \setminus \{i\}$ can INCREASE or DECREASE. Therefore $f(N[j])$ will not change as long as $j \to i$ and i does not INCREASE or DECREASE. The lemma follows.   □

Lemma 5. *After the first INCREASE or DECREASE of node i, for the rest of the execution of the algorithm $f(N[i]) \ge k$.*

Proof. When node i INCREASEs it will set $f(i)$ such that $f(N[i]) = k$. It's easy to see, that after a DECREASE $f(N[i]) \ge k$. After an INCREASE or DECREASE move, $\sigma(i) = f(N[i])$. By the proof of Lemma 4 it follows that a later DECREASE of some neighbor $j \in N(i)$ will not push $f(N[i])$ below k.   □

To show that Algorithm 3.1 stabilizes we now prove that every node can make at most two f-moves.

Lemma 6. *The number of combined INCREASEs and DECREASEs for each node is at most 2.*

Proof. The first f-move that a node, say i, can make is either INCREASE or DECREASE. By Lemma 5 it follows that from there on $f(N[i]) \ge k$ and therefore the predicate for an INCREASE does not hold. Lemma 4 says, that from the second f-move on, when i DECREASEs again, for all neighbors $j \in N(i)$: $\sigma(j) = f(N[j])$. This implies, that after a DECREASE of node i either $f(i) = 0$ or $\exists j \in N[i] : f(N[j]) = k$ and $f(N[z]) \ge k, \forall z \in N[i] \setminus \{j\}$. In either case i will not DECREASE again.   □

Lemma 7. *When the algorithm stabilizes, the function f represents a minimal {k}-dominating function.*

Proof. In a stable configuration no node points to itself. Assume that there are nodes that point to themselves and let i be such a node with smallest ID. Either there is a node $j \in N(i)$ with $j \not\rightarrow i$, in this case j can UPDATE, or $\forall j \in N(i) : j \rightarrow i$, then i can INCREASE or DECREASE. Since in a stable state no node can ADD and by the previous statement $predf(i)$ has to be $FALSE$ for every node i. By the definition of $predf$, f is then a minimal {k}-dominating function.   □

Theorem 2. *Algorithm 3.1 stabilizes with a {k}-dominating function in at most $(2n + 1) \cdot (n + 1) \cdot 2^{n+2}$ moves.*

Proof. This follows directly from Lemma 3, 6 and 7.   □

4   Minimal {2}-Dominating Function

Since Algorithm 3.1 requires an exponential number of moves, we will now present a polynomial time algorithm that finds a minimal {2}-dominating function in a general graph. We don't consider a {1}-dominating function, because a minimal {1}-dominating function is equivalent to a *minimal dominating set* (see [9] for a self-stabilizing algorithm). For the case $k = 2$ we propose the following algorithm. Each node i has a variable f storing the function value associated with node i. The algorithm is identically stored and executed in each node i.

Algorithm 4.1: MINIMAL {2}-DOMINATING FUNCTION

---

local $f(\_) \in \{0, 1, 2\}$;

R1: if $f(N(i)) = 0 \wedge f(i) \neq 2$
  then $f(i) = 2$;

R2: if $f(i) = 0 \wedge f(N(i)) = 1$
  then $f(i) = 1$;

R3: if $f(i) = 1 \wedge |\{j \in N(i) : f(j) > 0\}| \geq 2$
  then $f(i) = 0$;

R4: if $f(i) = 2 \wedge f(N[i]) > 2$
  then $\begin{cases} \textbf{if } f(N(i)) = 1 \\ \quad \textbf{then } f(i) = 1; \\ \quad \textbf{else } f(i) = 0; \end{cases}$

The next two lemmas show that Algorithm 4.1 stabilizes with a $\{2\}$-dominating function.

Lemma 8. *If the system reaches a stable state, then the state is legitimate.*

Proof. If rules **R1** and **R2** do not apply, then f must be a $\{2\}$-dominating function; and if rules **R3** and **R4** do not apply, then f must be a minimal $\{2\}$-dominating function. □

Lemma 9. *If the system is in an illegitimate state, then there exists at least one node that can make a move.*

Proof. Assume the system is in an illegitimate state. There are two cases to consider: 1) the function f is not a $\{2\}$-dominating function, and 2) the function f is a $\{2\}$-dominating function, but not a minimal $\{2\}$-dominating function.

In case 1) there will exist a node i with $f(N[i]) < 2$. This node can execute rule **R1** if $f(N(i)) = 0$, rule **R2** if $f(i) = 0$ and $f(N(i)) = 1$.

In case 2) there will exist a node i with $f(N[i]) > 2$ and $\forall j \in N(i) : f(N[j]) > 2$. Either this node can execute rule **R3**, if $f(i) = 1$ and node i has at least two neighbors with positive f-value; or there will exist a node j adjacent to node i having $f(j) = 2$, and all other nodes adjacent to node i have f-value 0, in this case node j can execute rule **R4**. In either case, therefore, the non-minimal 2-dominating function does not constitute a stable state. □

We proceed by showing that any node executing rule **R1** can make no further moves, and that the remaining nodes can make only a finite number of moves.

Lemma 10. *If a node executes rule **R1** it will never make another move.*

Proof. A node i can only execute rules **R1** if $f(N(i)) = 0$. After i has executed rule **R1** no node in $N(i)$ can ever become privileged and make a move, therefore node i will also remain unprivileged. □

Lemma 11. *A node can only execute rule **R4** once.*

Proof. A node can only execute rule **R4** if $f(i) = 2$. If a node is to execute rule **R4** twice it must execute **R4**, **R1**, **R4**. But any node executing rules **R1** can never make another move. □

Let us represent the execution of Algorithm 4.1 as a sequence of moves $M_1, M_2, M_3, \ldots$, in which M_k denotes the k-th move. The system's initial state is denoted by S_0, and for $t > 0$ the state resulting from M_t is denoted by S_t. At time t we let

$$f_t = f(V(G)) \text{ , and}$$
$$p_t = |\{e = ij \in E(G) : f(i) > 0 \land f(j) > 0\}| \text{ ,}$$

where f_t is the total weight of the function f, and p_t is the number of edges, both of whose nodes have strictly positive function values.

Observation 1 *If rule **R2** is executed at time t, then $f_{t+1} = f_t + 1$ and $p_{t+1} = p_t + 1$.*

Observation 2 *If rule **R3** is executed at time t, then $f_{t+1} = f_t - 1$ and $p_{t+1} \leq p_t - 2$.*

Observation 3 *If rule **R4** is executed at time t, then $f_t - 2 \leq f_{t+1} \leq f_t - 1$ and $p_{t+1} \leq p_t$.*

Theorem 3. *Algorithm 4.1 finds a minimal $\{2\}$-dominating function in at most $3n + 2m$ moves.*

Proof. Assume that the algorithm runs forever. In an infinite execution sequence there must be two states S_n and S_m, such that $S_n = S_m$ and all moves M_l, $n \leq l \leq m$, are made by executing rules **R2** and **R3**. We cannot have $S_n = S_m$ if M_l is made by executing rule **R1**, and rule **R4** can never be executed more than n times. When $S_n = S_m$ we obviously have $f_n = f_m$ and $p_n = p_m$. Let x be the number of times rule **R2** is executed and y be the number of times rule **R3** is executed. We get the following pair of equations:

$$f_m = f_n + x - y = f_n \tag{1}$$
$$p_m = p_n + x - 2y = p_n \tag{2}$$

It follows from (1) that we must have $x = y$, and it follows from (2) that we must have $x = 2y$, a contradiction. Since this set of equations has no positive solutions we have that $S_n \neq S_m$ for all $n \neq m$, thus the algorithm terminates.

To prove the desired time bound we first observe that for all states S_t, we have $0 \leq f_t \leq 2n$, and $0 \leq p_t \leq m$.

We know from Lemma 10 that rule **R1** can be executed at most n times in total. Observations 1 and 3, and Lemma 11 imply that rules **R2** and **R4** can be executed at most $2n$ times in conjunction with each other, as rule **R4** can be executed at most n times. And it follows from Observations 1 and 2 that rules **R2** and **R3** can be executed at most $2m$ times in conjunction with each other; since for two states S_n and S_m with $f_n = f_m$, and all intermediate moves made by executing rules **R2** and **R3**, we must have $p_m \leq p_n - 1$. This implies that that the algorithm stabilizes in at most $3n + 2m$ moves.   □

Corollary 1. *If G is planar, then Algorithm 4.1 finds a minimal $\{2\}$-dominating function in $O(n)$ moves.*

5 Concluding Remarks

In this paper we have presented self-stabilizing algorithms for finding a minimal $\{k\}$-dominating function in general graphs. Algorithm 3.1 can be used for an arbitrary k, but requires an exponential number of moves. We believe that the scheme of Algorithm 3.1 is interesting on its own, since it can be used to ensure that certain moves are made based on neighbor variables that are correct. For instance this scheme can be used by a node to access variables of nodes that are at distance 2. With this property more complicated functions can be implemented.

Our second algorithm is dedicated to the case where $k = 2$. Here we have given a more efficient algorithm that stabilizes in at most $3n + 2m$ moves. It is interesting to consider whether a linear self-stabilizing algorithm exists for $\{3\}$-domination, and, indeed, for any fixed $\{k\}$-domination.

Subsequent to the development of Algorithm 3.1 for finding a minimal $\{k\}$-dominating function in an arbitrary graph, the authors of [7] designed a self-stabilizing algorithm for finding a minimal total dominating set in an arbitrary graph. At the end of this paper [7], the authors suggested that a self-stabilizing algorithm for $\{k\}$-domination can be constructed from the algorithm for finding a minimal total dominating set in [7]. However, this adaptation would involve the use of k pointers, and would be somewhat more complicated than Algorithm 3.1 presented in this paper.

Acknowledgment

The authors are grateful to the referees for making several suggestions for improving this paper. In particular, one referee suggested a simplified version of Algorithm 4.1, as follows:

$$\textbf{R1: if } f(i) \neq g(i) := \max\{2 - f(N(i)), 0\} \textbf{ then } f(i) = g(i);$$

Although this algorithm is different than Algorithm 4.1, it still produces a minimal $\{2\}$-dominating function and can be shown to stabilize in a linear number of moves.

References

[1] J. Beauquier, A. K. Datta, M. Gradinariu, and F. Magniette. Self-stabilizing local mutual exclusion and daemon refinement. In *DISC00 Distributed Computing 14th International Symposium, Springer LNCS:1914*, pages 223–237, 2000. 50

[2] E. W. Dijkstra. Self-stabilizing systems in spite of distributed control. *Communications of the ACM*, 17:643–644, 1974. 50

[3] S. Dolev. *Self-stabilization*. MIT Press, 2000. 50

[4] G. S. Domke. *Variations of Colorings, Coverings, and Packings of Graphs*. PhD thesis, Clemson University, 1988. 50

[5] G. S. Domke, S. T. Hedetniemi, R. C. Laskar, and G. Fricke. Relationships between integer and fractional parameters of graphs. In Y. Alavi, G. Chartrand, O. R. Ollermann, and A. J. Schwenk, editors, *Graph Theory, Combinatorics, and Applications, Proceedings of the Sixth Quadrennial Conference on the Theory and Applications of Graphs (Kalamazoo, MI, 1988)*, volume 2, pages 371–387. Wiley, 1991. 50

[6] M. Gairing, R. M. Geist, S. T. Hedetniemi, and P. Kristiansen. A self-stabilizing algorithm for maximal 2-packing. Technical Report 230, Department of Informatics, University of Bergen, 2002. 52

[7] W. Goddard, S. T. Hedetniemi, D. P. Jacobs, and P. K. Srimani. A self-stabilizing distributed algorithm for minimal total domination in an arbitrary system graph. In *Proceedings of the 8th International Workshop on Formal Methods for Parallel Programming: Theory and Applications (FMPPTA'03) in conjunction with IPDPS'03*, 2003. 59

[8] T. W. Haynes, S. T. Hedetniemi, and P. J. Slater. *Fundamentals of Domination in Graphs*. Marcel Dekker, 1998. 50

[9] S. M. Hedetniemi, S. T. Hedetniemi, D. P. Jacobs, and P. K. Srimani. Self-stabilizing algorithm for minimal dominating and maximal independent sets. *Comput. Math. Appl.*, to appear. 56

[10] S. T. Hedetniemi, D. P. Jacobs, and P. K. Srimani. Maximal matching stabilizes in time $O(m)$. *Information Processing Letters*, to appear. 50

[11] Su-Chu Hsu and Shing-Tsaan Huang. A self-stabilizing algorithm for maximal matching. *Information Processing Letters*, 43(2):77–81, 1992. 50

[12] R. M. Karp. Reducibility among combinatorial problems. In R. E. Miller and J. W. Thathcher, editors, *Complexity of Computer Computations*, pages 85–103. Plenum Press, New York, 1972. 51

[13] G. Tel. Maximal matching stabilizes in quadratic time. *Information Processing Letters*, 49(6):271–272, 1994. 50

[14] G. Tel. *Introduction to distributed algorithms*. Cambridge University Press, second edition, 2000. 50

Self-Stabilizing Group Communication
in Directed Networks*
(Extended Abstract)

Shlomi Dolev and Elad Schiller

Department of Computer Science
Ben-Gurion University of the Negev, Israel
{dolev,schiller}@cs.bgu.ac.il

Abstract. Self-stabilizing group membership service, multicast service, and resource allocation service in directed network are presented. The first group communication algorithm is based on a token circulation over a virtual ring. The second algorithm is based on construction of distributed spanning trees. In addition, a technique that emulates, in a self-stabilizing fashion, any undirected communication network over strongly connected directed network, is presented.

Keywords: Self-Stabilization, Group Communication, and Directed Networks.

1   Introduction

The group communication infrastructure is useful for numerous applications, starting in (video, audio, multimedia) virtual conferences, and including (safety) critical tasks that require exactly once transactions. On line on going systems are prone to unexpected state transition due to transient faults, thus, it is important to design such systems to recover automatically from any possible state.

Previous research towards self-stabilizing group communication services (including membership service, multicast service, and resource allocation services) considered undirected communication networks and ad hoc networks. It turned out that the techniques used for achieving self-stabilizing group communication are different for each such setting. The case of directed networks is important in heterogeneous communication systems that include base-stations, mobile hosts, sensors, servers, satellites, etc. Two-way communication is not always possible in such systems. The focus of this paper is self-stabilizing group communication services for directed networks.

Previous Work: Self-stabilizing group communication for fixed and dynamic undirected networks, and for ad hoc networks (in which servers may move) have

---

* Partially supported by NSF Award CCR-0098305, IBM faculty award, STRIMM consortium, and Israel ministry of defense. An extended version can be found in [12].

S.-T. Huang and T. Herman (Eds.): SSS 2003, LNCS 2704, pp. 61–76, 2003.

been studied in [11] and [13]. Self-stabilizing algorithms for directed networks have been addressed in [2, 1, 5, 4, 14].

Self-stabilizing mutual exclusion on directed graphs was considered in [2]. The communication graph is assumed to be a strongly connected directed graph that requires (non-distributed) preprocessing (see [16] for such an approach). The authors assume the existence of a distinguish node, a known number n of processors in the system, and of a central daemon [9, 8]. The first algorithm uses a token circulation on a virtual ring. Assuming that the degree of at least two nodes is in $\Theta(n)$, it is shown in [2], that the length of the virtual ring is in $\Omega(n^2)$. The second algorithm uses a spanning tree. The authors assume that the processors know the communication diameter d and that processors have distinct identifiers in the range of $\{0, \ldots, n-1\}$. Roughly speaking, the tree is repeatedly colored by colors in the range $\{0, \ldots, n-1\}$ in a round robin fashion granting the critical section to the processor with the current tree color. Thus, a processor must wait $O(nd)$ time (measured in asynchronous rounds) to reenter the critical section. A self-stabilizing algorithm for leader election and generic tree construction in a strongly connected directed network is presented in [1]. The algorithms of [1] stabilize in $O(n)$ time, where n is the number of processors. (The authors of [1] remark that by a slight change in the algorithm the stabilization time may be reduced, but this change leads to more complex proofs). A self-stabilizing algorithm for routing messages in a strongly connected directed network is presented in [5]. In [5] it is assumed that a distinguish processor exists and that every processor knows the exact number of processors in the system. A randomized self-stabilizing mutual exclusion algorithm in a uniform (directed) networks is presented in [4]. The algorithm uses a virtual ring that is constructed by keeping a pointer in each node and changing it in a round robin fashion. Delaet and Tixeuil presented in [14] a self-stabilizing census algorithm for strongly connected directed networks.

Our Contribution: We introduce the first self-stabilizing algorithms for group communication in directed networks using new building blocks such as membership and multicast services. We do not assume the existence of a distinguish processor, a central daemon, or that the actual number of processors (or the communication graph diameter) is known. Moreover, we do not require preprocessing. We prove that the length of a virtual ring is in $\Theta(n^2)$, even when the degree of every node is in at most three. Simple proofs show that our algorithms stabilize within the order of the system diameter. A transformer algorithm that emulates any undirected network over a strongly connected directed network is presented. In addition, we introduce a resource allocation algorithm for (asynchronous) strongly connected directed networks and (synchronous) weakly connected directed networks.

The rest of the paper is organized as follow. The system settings appear in Section 2. In Section 3, we specify our requirements from a group communication system, and design algorithms for achieving these requirements in Section 4. A general scheme for self-stabilizing emulation, of any undirected communication network over the directed network, is presented in Section 5. Resource allocation schemes appear in Section 6. Concluding remarks are in Section 7. Proofs are omitted from this extended abstract.

2   The System

The system consists of a set $\mathcal{P}$ of communicating entities, that we call *processors*. A processor is either a physical CPU or a process (a thread). There are $n < N$ processors in the system each processor has a distinct identifier. We represent the system by a communication graph $\mathcal{G}(\mathcal{V}, \mathcal{E})$, where every node in $\mathcal{V}$ represents a processor and every directed link in $(i, j) \in \mathcal{E}$ represents the possibility of p_i to communicate information to p_j. The device that conveys the information from p_i to p_j can be based on either wire or wireless technology. We model a communication link (i, j) by a *buffer* (or communication register) that stores the last message sent by p_i to p_j, and was not yet received. Thus, there is at most one message in every link and this message is stored in $buffer_{ij}$ with an indication of whether p_j has already received it (one may assume that send operations from p_i to p_j are spread enough to allow a message to arrive before the next message is sent).

The *in-neighbors$_i$* is a set that consists of all the nodes p_j such that the directed link (j, i) is in $\mathcal{E}$. The *out-neighbors$_i$* set is defined analogously. Processors may crash and recover during the execution. However, we concern ourselves with a period of time in which the communication graph is fixed for a long enough period that allows each processor to identify the correct *in-neighbors$_i$* and *out-neighbors$_i$* sets. The processors execute *atomic steps*. An atomic step consists of internal computations followed by a single *communication operation*. A *communication operation* of p_i through the out-going link (i, j) is a message send operation (a write to $buffer_{ij}$). A *communication operation* of p_i through the in-going link (j, i) is a message receive operation (a read from $buffer_{ji}$).

We define a system configuration as a vector of states of all the processors and the content of every buffer. A system *execution* (or *run*) $R = (c_1, a_1, c_2, a_2, \cdots)$ is an alternating sequence of configurations and steps. The system is asynchronous (though we remark that synchronous settings are considered in Section 6). The delay in message delivery (completeness of a write operation) is unbounded but finite. We measure the time complexity by the number of *asynchronous cycles* in an execution. Let R be an execution, and let $\mathcal{S}$ be a strongly connected component of the communication graph. We assume that no processor in $\mathcal{S}$ crashes during R. The first *asynchronous cycle* of $\mathcal{S}$ in R is a minimal prefix of R such that each processor p_i in $\mathcal{S}$ communicates with every neighbor: At least one message m_j is sent by p_i to every neighbor p_j in *out-neighbors$_i$*, such that p_j receives m_j during the first asynchronous cycle. The second asynchronous cycle of $\mathcal{S}$ in R is the first asynchronous cycle in the execution R', which starts in the configuration that immediately follows the first asynchronous cycle of $\mathcal{S}$ in R. In a similar manner, we define the rest of the asynchronous cycles. A *fair execution* is an execution with infinite number of asynchronous cycles.

The *task* τ of the system is defined by a set of legal executions *LE*. A configuration c is *safe* with relation to τ, and the system, if every execution that starts from c belongs to *LE*. We require that a self-stabilizing algorithm reaches a safe configuration within a certain number of asynchronous cycles in any execution that starts in an *arbitrary* initial configuration.

3   Group Communication Specifications

Group communication system typically provides various types of multicast services to a specific (dynamic) interest group. A member in the group may specify that a message should be delivered to the rest of the group members with certain reliability requirements and ordering guarantees. The multicast service is then responsible for delivering this message to the application layer of the group members under the defined requirements.

Several groups may coexist simultaneously in the system. However, we assume that no interaction among groups exists. Therefore, we choose a single group index g. A boolean variable $member_i$ is defined to (logically) represents the intention of p_i to be included in g. We use $v_i = \langle vid_i, members_i \rangle$ to represent the view maintained by processor p_i, where vid_i is a unique bounded integer *view identifier*, and $members_i$ is a list of processors indices. Roughly speaking, view identifier is used to distinguish two different incarnations of groups with the same set of members. Our requirements for message delivery are related to the view in which the message has been sent; requiring that every processor that belongs to the view in which the message has been sent and to every following view (if such views exist) will receive the message. For example, assume that message m has been sent by processor p_i when the view was $\langle 22, \{i, j, k\} \rangle$ and later only two more new views $\langle 23, \{i, j\} \rangle$ and $\langle 24, \{i, j, k\} \rangle$ were established, then p_k will not necessarily receive m. p_k can conclude that messages sent in view $\langle 22, \{i, j, k\} \rangle$ may not reach it. On the other hand, if the view identifier of the first (namely, 22) and the last (namely, 24) views were identical p_k could not conclude that some messages may never reach it. Another aspect of the above observation is that these definitions allow us to garbage collect old views (and messages) from the history.

Self-stabilizing algorithms use bounded variables, since a transient fault (or initial state) may corrupt the variable value and cause the variable to have the biggest value at once. Thus, we increment the view-identifier using a modulo operation over a bound V. We assume that all the processors participate periodically in establishing a view. This periodic establishment ensures conflict resolution among view identifiers (if exists) and allow the use of the modulo operation without losing the ordering among views. As we show in the sequel the participating process will rapidly have consistent histories.

Statements of requirements for self-stabilizing group communication appear in [11] and [13]. The first requirement is that in a legal execution every processor that wishes to join (or leave) the group eventually appears (respectively, does not appear) in the list of members $members_i$ of every configuration. In addition, if processors do not change their membership, then the *view identifier* of the group, vid_i, is eventually fixed.

The set of legal executions LE_{mem} for the group membership task, is associated with S, and includes executions R satisfying Requirements 1 and 2.

Requirement 1: *If the value of member$_i$ = true (member$_i$ = false) is fixed during R then there exists a suffix of R, in which p_i appears (respectively, does not appear) in all the views of group g in the connected component S.*

Requirement 2: *If the value of member$_i$ of every processor p_i of group g in the connected component S is fixed during R then there exists a suffix, in which all the views of group g in the connected component S are identical, the views have the same list of members and the* same view identifier.

The set of legal executions LE_{mcast} for the group multicast task, is a subset of LE_{mem}, and includes executions R satisfying Requirements 3, 4 and 5.

Requirement 3: *Suppose that two processors p_i and p_j are members of every view in R. If m is a message sent by p_j during R, then m is delivered to p_i.*

Requirement 4: *Suppose that the messages m_0 and m_1 are delivered to processors p_i and p_j during R. If m_0 is delivered to p_i before m_1 is delivered to p_i, then m_0 is delivered to p_j before m_1 is delivered to p_j.*

Requirement 5: *If a processor p_i is a member of two successive views of a group, v_j and v_{j+1}, then all messages sent in the group while v_j was the view of the group, have been delivered to p_i.*

Let m be a message sent by processor p_i, when $v_i = v$, then v is the *sending view* of m. If a message m is delivered to the application layer of every member in its sending view, then we say that m is *stable*. The system delivers a safety delivery indication (for m) to the application layer when m is stable. We view this indication as a best effort service; we do not require a delivery of a safety delivery indication, for every stable message.

In the sequel, we present self-stabilizing group communication algorithms in directed network that can achieve requirements 1, 2, 3, 4 and 5.

4   Group Communication Algorithms

In this section, we present two approaches for achieving self-stabilizing group communication in directed network. Token circulation (e.g., [6, 13]) is used in the first approach, while the second approach employs a distributed tree structure (e.g., [11]). Both approaches use the self-stabilizing update algorithm in directed network as a building block.

Update in Directed Networks: The update algorithm [7, 10] (for undirected networks) is useful for routing messages, collecting data, and distributing information. We present a version that is suitable for directed networks and can achieve topology update in directed networks. Then we use the resulting algorithm for achieving a variety of self-stabilizing algorithms: Ring construction, group membership, group multicast, β-synchronizer, general network topology emulation and resource allocation.

For the sake of completeness, we now present the basic ideas used by the (undirected) update algorithm of [7, 10]. Each processor p_i maintains a list $\mathcal{U}_i$ of no more than N tuples $\langle id, dis, parent \rangle$. In a legal execution, it holds that $\mathcal{U}_i$ lists the processors in $\mathcal{S}$. For every processor $p_j \in \mathcal{S}$, there is exactly one tuple $\langle j, dis, k \rangle \in \mathcal{U}_i$. The value of dis is the number of edges in a shortest path from p_i to p_j, and p_k is a neighbor of p_i that is in a shortest path to p_j.

Every processor repeatedly sends $\mathcal{U}$ to its neighbors, and accumulates the received lists of its neighbors in $\mathcal{TU}_i$. The content of $\mathcal{TU}_i$ is an input to a procedure that calculates $\mathcal{U}_i$. The value of the dis field of every tuple in $\mathcal{TU}_i$ is incremented by one. Then, the tuple $\langle i, 0, nil \rangle$ is included in $\mathcal{TU}_i$. For every specific id, we select the tuple with the minimal dis value, and remove the rest from $\mathcal{TU}_i$. We remove every tuple $\langle id, dis, parent \rangle$ such that there exists a positive $z < dis$ and there is no tuple with $dis = z$ in $\mathcal{TU}_i$. Finally we assign the value of $\mathcal{TU}_i$ to $\mathcal{U}_i$.

We now slightly change the update algorithm so that it fits directed networks. We extend the tuples of the update algorithm with a fourth field named *in-neighbors*. The field *in-neighbors* in the tuple $\langle i, 0, nil, in\text{-}neighbors \rangle \in \mathcal{U}_i$ consists of the *in-neighbors$_i$* list. Processor p_i repeatedly sends $\mathcal{U}_i$ to every $p_j \in$ *out-neighbors$_i$*. The procedure that calculates $\mathcal{U}_i$ from $\mathcal{TU}_i$, is the same for both directed and undirected versions of the update algorithm. The value of the list *in-neighbors$_i$* of every processor propagates to the entire connected component.

The correctness proof starts in the observation that following the first asynchronous cycle the tuples with distance field value 0 are correct, namely for every i there is a single tuple in $\mathcal{U}_i$ with distance 0, the tuple $\langle i, 0, null, in\text{-}neighbors_i \rangle$. Then, in the following cycle the tuples with distance field value 1 are computed using the tuples of the neighbors that have a distance value 0 and therefore are correct. The proof is completed by an induction over the value of the distance fields. The proof shows that within the order of the diameter of the graph, $\mathcal{U}_i$ contains the local topology of every processor p_i, and therefore, the connected component of p_i is known to p_i. The arguments are almost identical to the arguments presented in [8] for the undirected case, see also [14] for a similar proof for the census task (note that the census task, does not notify the processors with the system topology).

Next we describe how the directed version of the update algorithm is used as an underlying layer by several algorithms.

4.1   Token Algorithm:

The pioneering self-stabilizing algorithm of Dijkstra [9] uses a token ring. Token ring circulation was previously used by group communication algorithms (e.g., [6]). We describe how to construct a ring in a directed network, and the way to use it for a self-stabilizing membership and multicast services.

Token Ring Construction: A virtual ring construction (in a directed network) is defined by a function $next_i(p_j)$, a function from $in\text{-}neighbors_i$ to $out\text{-}neighbors_i$. We use the virtual ring definition to forward a token T (a short message) that arrives to p_i from p_j, to $next_i(p_j)$.

We call the forwarding process of T a *walk*. A walk defines a ring if, and only if, T arrives at every processor in the system at least once before returning to the processor in which the walk started in. Moreover, we require that a distinguish processor will be defined in the ring. Every processor p_i may access a predict $distinguish_i$, and there is exactly one processor in the system, such that $distinguish_i = true$.

We now present a straightforward approach for constructing a virtual directed ring (later we present more sophisticate schemes). List the processors according to their identifiers' value, and find a directed path from every two neighboring processors in the list (the graph is strongly connected and hence such a path must exist). Note that every processor can compute the virtual ring using the output of the self-stabilizing update algorithm. The number of nodes in the virtual ring is at most N^2. The distinguish (virtual) processor (represented by) the processor with the maximal identifier according to the update information, is defined to be the first processor in the virtual ring.

The algorithm in [9] is used on top of the virtual ring. Each processor p_i may act as several virtual processors $p_{i1}, p_{i2}, \cdots, p_{il}$, where l is the number of times p_i is visited during the walk. p_i maintains a variable x_{ij} for each p_{ij}. x_{ij} stores an integer value that is no smaller than zero and no larger than $2N^2 + 1$ (there are at most N^2 buffers in the virtual ring and N^2 local read values, we add one more possible value to ensure the existence of a missing value [8]). To define the configuration of the virtual ring we order the values of the x_{kj} variables according to their order of appearance in the (virtual) ring. p_i acts for every virtual node p_{ij}, repeatedly sending the value of every x_{ij} variables to the next node in the virtual ring. The message sent with x_{ij} carries additional values that may be interpreted as the values carried by a token. A token T *arrives* at the (virtual) distinguish node p_{ij}, if the value of x_{ij} is the same as the value in the arriving message sent by the (virtual) node p_{km} that precedes p_{ij} in the virtual ring. A token T *arrives* at a (virtual) non-distinguish node p_{ij}, if the value of x_{ij} differs from the value arriving to p_{ij} in the message sent by the (virtual) node p_{km} that precede p_{ij} in the (virtual) ring. In the sequel $T.y$ refers to the value of the y field in the token T.

Upon the arrival of the token at the distinguish node p_{ij}, p_{ij} increases x_{ij} by one modulo $2N^2 + 1$. Upon a token arrival at a non-distinguish node p_{ij}, p_{ij} assigns the value $T.x$ to x_{ij}. A node p_{ij} (distinguish or not), repeatedly sends the value of x_{ij} together with the rest of the fields (that may form a token) to the next node in the virtual ring.

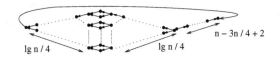

Fig. 1. A lower bound for the length of a ring

Tight Lower Bound for the Length of the Virtual Ring: We now turn to examine the problem of forming a virtual ring in a directed network. An Euler tour over a spanning tree of an undirected network forms a virtual ring of $\Theta(n)$ virtual nodes. We next show that the length of a virtual ring in a strongly connected *directed* network is $\Theta(n^2)$. Our lower bound proof uses only constant degree nodes in the system, as opposed to the assumption of degree in the order of n made in [2].

Assume that $n = 2^i$ for some integer $i > 1$. We construct two full binary trees of depth $d = \lg(n/4)$ one directed from the root to the leaves and the other from the leaves to the root. The number of leaves in each tree is $2^d = n/4$. Then we fuse the leaves of the trees one by one to form the directed *diamond* structure like the one presented in Figure 1. The diamond structure includes $2n/4 - 2 + n/4 = 3n/4 - 2$ processors. In addition, we connect the roots of the (fused) trees by a chain of $n - 3n/4 + 2$ processors.

Since any virtual ring must include all fused processors, and a path between any two fused processors is of length greater than $n/4 + 2$, then the length of the ring is in $\Omega(n^2)$. Since a virtual directed ring can be constructed with at most n^2 processors, we conclude that the length of the ring is in $\Theta(n^2)$.

Optimizing the Length of the Virtual Ring: We now present more sophisticated schemes for token ring configuration in which the length of the ring is optimized. Note that the virtual ring may include exactly n nodes (when the directed network is a directed ring). The problem of finding an optimal length virtual ring in a directed graph is known to be NP-hard [3]. Therefore, we may use an approximation algorithm to find an efficient virtual ring. Self-stabilizing update distributes the information on the communication graph to every processor in the system. Every processor may use a traveling salesman approximation algorithm (see [3]) as a heuristic method to find a near optimal Hamiltonian walk. The "salesman" should visit every city (a processor in $\mathcal{G}$) at least once. The cost of traveling among the cities u and v is ∞, if there is no directed edge from u to v in $\mathcal{G}$, and one otherwise.

We note that both deterministic and randomized approximation algorithms for the traveling salesman can be used. If a deterministic approximation algorithm is executed then the resulting virtual ring is identical in every processor. To use a randomized approximation algorithm we let the distinguish processor calculate the ring and then propagate it to the rest of the processors using the spanning tree rooted by itself (defined by the update algorithm). The distinguish processor will change the description of the ring that it propagates only when the current propagated ring has a length greater than the last computed ring.

Membership (Token Algorithm): We describe a membership algorithm that satisfies Requirements 1 and 2. Since there is no interaction between any two groups, we consider a specific group g and describe the membership service for g. We use the algorithm in [9] as an underlying algorithm. During the stabilization period of the underlying algorithms, there may be more than one token. When two tokens or more arrive at a single processor, a merge procedure is invoked. The tokens are merged to a single token where the merged token is either empty (see [13]), or is the result of resolving the minimum number of conflicts (see [11]).

We use time to live method (e.g., [15]) to remove stalled information from the token. The token carries a list, $members_g$, of processors that are members in the group g. The token also carries a list of corresponding time to live counters lvs; a counter value, lv_j, for each virtual processor in the virtual ring. The virtual processor p_i assigns the length of the virtual ring to lv_i, whenever a token arrives at p_i. Whenever a processor in the ring receives a token, it decrements the value of each $lv_i \in lvs$. While $lv_i > 0$, we consider p_i as an *active member* in g.

We note that we can order the virtual processors that each processor acts for according to the order of their appearance in the virtual ring. Thus, a processor p_m acting for $p_{m1}, p_{m2}, \cdots, p_{ml}$ will have only one counter in the lvs counters. lv_m (or lv_{m1}) will be set to n whenever the token arrives at p_{m1} and will be decremented by one only when arriving to the first representative of other processors, for example when arriving to p_{l1} that represents p_l. Here we present a version in which each virtual processor has its own counter, and an indication that one virtual processor is not active implies that the acting processor for this virtual processor is not active.

Processor p_i, chooses a new view identifier, whenever it holds a token, and discovers that the set of members in the group has changed. A change in the set of members can occur when a processor p_i voluntarily changes its membership status in group g, or there is an identification that processor p_k is *not* active.

The code of the membership algorithm is presented in Figure 2. Upon token T's arrival, we decrement every lv counter by one (line 1.1). Line 1.2 stores the current list of members (later used in line 1.6). Lines 1.3 to 1.3.2 remove a processor that has been flagged as not active. Lines 1.4 to 1.4.2 (1.5) adds (respectively, removes) i to (from) the members list upon a request. In the case, there were changes to the members of g, we establish a new view (lines 1.6). Line 1.11 forwards the token to the next neighbor in the virtual ring.

Multicast (Token Algorithm): The multicast algorithm that satisfies Requirements 3, 4 and 5. The *history* is a list of views and messages that should list the views of the system and the messages sent in each view according to the order of the view establishments and message send operations within the views. Whenever the token arrives at a processor p_j, the views and messages

---

Global constants:
V: upper bound on the number of view identifiers that can be concurrently active
$RingLength$: the number of nodes in the virtual ring
Token T data structure has fields:
$T.members_g$: the set of processors in group g
$T.lv_k$: (where p_k are the processors in $T.members_g$) counter
for the time to live of p_k
$T.vid$: identifier for the current view of the group
Local variables of processor p_i:
g_i: boolean indicating whether p_i is a member
   v_i: the value of the view for group g recorded at p_i
1. **Upon a token T arrival from p_k:**
1.1   for-every $T.lv_k \in T.lvs$ $T.lv_k \leftarrow T.lv_k - 1$
1.2 $members \leftarrow T.members_g$
1.3   for-every $T.lv_k \leq 0$
1.3.1   remove k from $T.members_g$
1.3.2   remove lv_k from $T.lvs$
1.4   if $g_i = true$ then
1.4.1   add i to $T.members_g$
1.4.2   add $lv_i = RingLength$ to $T.lvs$
1.5   else remove i from $T.members_g$
1.6   if $members \neq T.members_g$ then $T.vid \leftarrow T.vid + 1$ modulo V
($*$ For Multicast $*$)
1.11 send T to $next_i(p_j)$

Fig. 2. Self-stabilizing Membership in a Ring Algorithm, code for p_i

are delivered in a first-in first-out manner (with an appropriate view identifier) to p_j.

A view of a group becomes *old* when a new view has been established to the same group g. An old view $view_o$ is removed from the history, when every processor p_i, member in $view_o$ *and* in the current view, received all the multicast messages of $view_o$ (and also their delivery indications). A message is removed from the history also when the views are not changed following the send operation of the message, but there is an indication that every processor in the view received the message (and their delivery indication).

The code of the multicast algorithm is presented in Figure 3. Line 1.6.1 concatenates the current view with the history of views and messages. Line 1.7 adds the message m that p_i wishes to multicast to the list of messages of T that are related to the last established view (current view). Line 1.8 delivers new views to the application layer (and mark them as delivered to p_i, thus they are not new to p_i). Line 1.9 deliver new multicast messages (and mark them as delivered to p_i, thus they are not new to p_i). Lines 1.10 to 1.10.1 deliver safe indication for every view and multicast message that have been delivered to all the processors that they should be delivered to.

> 1.6.1 $T.history \leftarrow T.history + \langle T.vid, members \rangle$
> 1.7   if p_i wishes to send message m then add m to $T.messages$ of current view
> 1.8   for-every non-delivered view $v \in T.history$ deliver v to the application layer
> 1.9   for-every non-delivered $m \in T.messages$ deliver m to the application layer
> 1.10   for-every safe x that was not reported (x a safe view or message)
> 1.10.1   deliver report that x is safe

Fig. 3. Self-stabilizing Multicast in a Ring Algorithm, code for p_i

4.2 Tree Algorithm:

The second approach we present is based on a distributed tree structure defined by the update algorithm, and then the self-stabilizing β-synchronizer in directed network. The algorithm presented in this section executes the group communication tasks in the fastest time (in the order of the diameter) while the approach presented in Section 4.1 responds to a group membership request in time that is proportional to n the number of processors (or even to n^2). We note that the tree solution allows several messages that carry the group communication activity to be presented in a configuration, while in the ring solution there is at most one such message (see [13]).

β-Synchronizer: We use the β-synchronizer to coordinate view-updates in the membership service. The undirected β-synchronizer algorithm [8], uses a rooted tree. The processor p_l with the maximal identifier in $\mathcal{U}_i$ is the root of the tree. The tree is repeated colored by a finite set of *colors*.

Here we use two trees to implement the directed version of the β-synchronizer. Namely, we use the distributed tree structures *out-tree$_l$*, and *in-tree$_l$*. *out-tree$_l$* is used for broadcasting and *in-tree$_l$* for receiving feedback. Roughly speaking, the β-synchronizer makes two alternating phases named "propagation phase" and "feedback phase". Every pair of consecutive (successful) propagation phase and (successful) feedback phase is associated with a color chosen by the root p_l.

The root p_l repeatedly colors *out-tree$_l$* and *in-tree$_l$*. Suppose p_f is a leaf processor in *out-tree$_l$*, then the color of p_l propagates downwards until it reaches p_f (*propagation phase*). Eventually, after the new color reaches p_f, all p_f's children in *in-tree$_l$*, have the same color as the color of p_f. This color is propagated on the path of *in-tree$_l$* that is directed from p_f to p_l (*feedback phase*). When p_l receives a feedback on the new color propagation via *in-tree$_l$*, it chooses another color (in a round robin fashion, from a set of $4N$ colors).

Note that (unlike the undirected version of the algorithm) a legal execution might include a configuration in which the children of a processor p_i in *in-tree$_l$* are colored with a new color d, where its parent in *out-tree$_l$* is not colored with color d. This is a consequence of the existence of two different trees; one for propagation, and another for feedback.

Membership (Tree Algorithm): In a legal execution, only the user is privileged to change his/her membership status in a group. Such a change occurs in response to the application request. Here we describe how processor p_i may join (leave) a group g by local setting (respectively, resetting) $member_i$. We use the β-synchronizer to synchronize the changes of views as done in [11].

In a legal execution, processor p_l is responsible for membership updates. During the propagation phase, p_l propagates the view it maintains, v_l, together with a new color. The feedback phase is intended to inform on the completion of the propagation phase, and to gather membership requests from the application.

The values of $member_i$ are accumulated from every processor in $in\text{-}tree_l$ during the feedback phase. Once the feedback phase is completed, the root sends (during the next coloring phase) the received membership information, together with a view identifier. The view identifier changes merely when the set of members changes. Processor p_i accumulates the membership requests in a variable named $request_i$. We define $request_i[i]$ to be an alias to $member_i$. The entry, $request_i[j]$, is reserved for the value of $request_j$, where p_j is a predecessor processor of p_i in $in\text{-}tree_l$. The variable $request_i$ is an array of bits that are associated with every node in the sub-tree of $in\text{-}tree_l$ that is rooted at p_i (the k-th bit in the array is the k-th processor in a pre-order traversal on this sub-tree). The $members$ data structure of a view v_i is an array of bits with a structure that is identical to $request_l$ (where p_l is the root of $in\text{-}tree_l$).

The code of the β-synchronizer and the membership algorithm is presented in Figure 4. In line 1.1, the root (of the trees) tests whether the feedback phase has just ended. Line 1.1.1 chooses a new color. Line 1.1.2 establish a new view if the membership group g changes. Lines 1.2 to 1.2.2 are executed by processors other than the root. A message sent by these lines includes colors (for propagation and feedback) and the current view. In lines 2 to 2.3, the propagation phase color and current view are stored. In lines 3 to 3.3, the feedback phase color and membership requests are accumulated. For the sake of simplicity, we assume that $member_i$ is updated just before p_i reports to its parent in $in\text{-}tree_l$ on the completion of the feedback phase.

Multicast (Tree Algorithm): Here we describe a multicast algorithm that delivers messages and feedbacks to the members of the group. For the sake of simplicity, we assume that there is a single message that a processor p_i wishes to send (maybe an aggregation of several data-messages that are stored between consecutive feedback phases) whenever a color is changed in dc_i.

When p_i, wishes to send a multicast message it sends it towards p_l using $in\text{-}tree_l$. Upon the arrival of such a message, p_l uses $out\text{-}tree_l$ to deliver the message to every processor. The change in colors indicates the safe delivery of messages.

We extend the messages of the algorithm presented in Figure 4 with two additional fields dm (down message), and um (up message). Processor p_i stores its multicast message in $um[i]$. The messages that are in um_j (of every child p_j of p_i in $in\text{-}tree_l$) are sent from p_j to p_i, and stored in $um[j]$.

Local variables of processor p_i:
in-parent: the successor processor of p_i (*in-tree$_l$*)
in-children: the predecessor processors of p_i (*in-tree$_l$*)
out-parent: the predecessor processor of p_i (*out-tree$_l$*)
out-children: the successor processors of p_i (*out-tree$_l$*)
$uc, dc, uc[]$: two color variables and an array of colors used for synchronization
$req[]$: array that accumulates membership requests ($req[i]$ is *member$_i$*)
1 Upon timeout:
1.1   if *out-parent* $= NULL$ and $\forall p_k \in$ *in-children* $dc = uc[k]$ then
1.1.1 $dc \leftarrow dc + 1$ mod $4N$
1.1.2   if *v.members* $\neq req$ then $v \leftarrow \langle Choose(ViewIDs - \{v.id\}), req \rangle$
1.2   if *out-parent* $\neq NULL$
1.2.1   if $\forall p_k \in$ *in-children* $dc = uc[k]$ then $uc \leftarrow dc$
1.2.2   send $\langle uc, req \rangle$ to $p_{in-parent}$
1.3 $\forall p_k \in$ *out-children* send $\langle dc, v \rangle$ to p_k
2 Upon receiving $\langle dc_j, v_j \rangle$ from $p_{out-parent}$:
2.2 $dc \leftarrow dc_j$
2.3 $v \leftarrow v_j$
3 Upon receiving $\langle uc_j, req_j \rangle$ from $p_j \in$ *in-children$_i$*:
3.2 $uc[j] \leftarrow uc_j$
3.3 $req[j] \leftarrow req_j$

Fig. 4.   The β-Synchronizer and Membership Algorithm on a Tree, code of p_i

Eventually, p_l receives the messages sent by the processors in the system. The value m of um_l arrives at a processor p_i in the system, along with the next new color nc propagating through *out-tree*. We note that the propagating phase that follows the arrival of um_l can indicate that m was safely delivered.

The code of the multicast algorithm is presented in Figure 5. In lines 1.1.3 the root (of the trees) orders the messages sent by the processors of the *in-tree$_l$* (line 1.2.2), before they are sent on the *out-tree$_l$* (line 1.3). Line 2.1 to 2.1.3 deliver the multicast messages and their safe delivery indication. Line 3.1 stores and accumulates the messages sent on the propagation phase.

5   Emulating a General Topology

In this section we present a self-stabilizing scheme to emulate any undirected network over a directed network. Thus we can compose a self-stabilizing algorithm that assumes undirected communication graph with our emulation scheme. In particular we may combine the self-stabilizing group communication algorithm presented in [11] with the emulation scheme. Note that the convergence time and the space complexity of such a composition is usually greater than the ones of a solution that is build for the specific settings.

Assume that the input for the emulation algorithm is a general topology graph $\mathcal{G} = (\mathcal{V}, \mathcal{E})$, known to all processors. Let $(i, j) \in \mathcal{E}$ be a link from p_i to p_j

---

Local variables of processor p_i:
$dm, um[]$: a variable and array of messages $(um[i] \equiv um)$
1.1.3 $dm \leftarrow \text{Order}(um)$
. . .

1.2.2   send $\langle uc, req, um \rangle$ to $p_{in-parent}$
1.3 $\forall p_k \in out\text{-}children$ send $\langle dc, v, dm \rangle$ to p_k
2 **Upon receiving** $\langle dc_j, v_j, dm_j \rangle$ **from** $p_{out-parent}$:
2.1   if $dc \neq dc_j$ then
2.1.1   indicate that dm is safe
2.1.2 $dm \leftarrow dm_j$
2.1.3   deliver dm
3 **Upon receiving** $\langle uc_j, req_j, um_j \rangle$ **from** $p_j \in$ ***in-children_i***:
3.1   if $uc[j] \neq uc_j$ $um[j] \leftarrow um_j$

Fig. 5. The Multicast Algorithm on a Tree, code of p_i

(such that $p_i \notin in\text{-}neighbors_j$). We present two different approaches to provide an emulation of the edge (j, i) using the directed network.

Communicating over $in\text{-}tree_l$ and $out\text{-}tree_l$: We use the two anti-directed paths between p_i and p_j over $in\text{-}tree_l$ and $out\text{-}tree_l$ (these paths may traverse p_l for) emulating an undirected edge (i, j). The delay cost of message delivery (measured by the maximal number of hops that a message traverses) is within the order of the communication graph diameter.

Communicating over the Shortest Path: The update algorithm gathers and distributes the information concerning the communication graph topology to every processor in the system. The two shortest paths that are used to emulate the undirected edge (i, j), can be found by performing BFS twice, once from p_i (until reaching p_j) and once from p_j (until reaching p_i).

In order to ensure eventual delivery of messages, we use a self-stabilizing data link algorithm [8] over the two shortest paths that implement a virtual undirected link. Thus, the time complexity for emulating a message send operation over a link may be proportional to the network diameter, and the space overhead is related to the space required to implement the update algorithm [8].

6   Resource Allocation

We describe the resource allocation for a particular resource, the extension to the case in which there are several independent resources, each accessed in a mutual exclusion fashion, is straightforward.

Strongly Connected Networks: The scheme uses the self-stabilizing β-synchronizer presented in Section 4.2 for collecting requests for the resource and propagating the winning processor, the processor that can use the resource. Several requests may arrive at p_l the root of $in\text{-}tree_l$ and $out\text{-}tree_l$. p_l will store and manage the requests using a local queue $queue_l$. The feedback phase collects in a $requests$ list (using $in\text{-}tree_l$) the current requests in the system. p_l removes from $queue_l$ processors that did not request the resource during the feedback phase. Then p_l grants the resource to the processor p_i at the head of $queue_l$. p_l sends the identifier of the processor (p_i) that is allowed to access the resource to all the processors during the next propagation phase.

Weakly Connected Networks: We propose a self-stabilizing scheme for the case of synchronous systems (see e.g., [8]) in which there exists *single* strongly connected component from which there is a directed path to every other processor. Note that it is possible that a processor p_i may be reached from the strongly connected component but there is no path from p_i to any processor in the strongly connected component.

The processors in the strongly connected component learn the topology of the strongly connected component using the self-stabilizing directed update. Each processor p_i, that has $k \geq 1$ outgoing links that are not part of the strongly connected component, requests the resource on behalf of itself and on the behalf of the processors reached through these k outgoing links. We use the term *mysterious out-going* link for each of these k outgoing links. Once p_i is granted the resource (in a procedure that is identical to the one described for the strongly connected case) p_i uses the resource in a fair fashion, say, use the resource once in every $k + 1$ successive times in which the resource is granted to it. In each of the rest of the $k + 1$ times, p_i grants the resource to (the subsystem connected through) a (distinct) processor (chosen in a round robin fashion) connected via one of its mysterious edges. p_i always release the resource following B time units knowing that any (processor in such) subsystem that received the grant (lease) for the resource must release it within B time units.

7   Concluding Remarks

This paper presents schemes for achieving self-stabilizing group communication services in directed networks. We view our study as an important building block in understanding the possible and impossible middleware services in a faulty environment. Our lower bounds and techniques can be used for achieving other tasks in a directed network, in fact we show that we can simulate *any* undirected network over a strongly connected directed network in a self-stabilizing fashion.

References

[1] Y. Afek and A. Bremler, "Self-Stabilizing Unidirectional Network Algorithms by Power-Supply," *Chicago Journal of Theoretical Computer Science*, Vol. 1998, No. 3, December 1998. 62

[2] D. Alstein, J. H. Hoepman, B. E. Olivier, P. I. A. van der Put, "Self-Stabilizing Mutual Exclusion on Directed Graphs," In *Computing Science in the Netherlands (Utrecht, 1994)*, Stichting Mathematisch Centrum, Amsterdam, 1994, pp. 42–53. 62, 68

[3] J. Bang-Jensen and G. Gutin, "Digraphs: Theory, Algorithms and Applications," Springer Monographs in Mathematics, Springer-Verlag, London, 2000. 68

[4] J. Beauquier, M. Gradinariu, C. Johnen, J. Durand-Lose, "Token Based Self-Stabilizing uniform Algorithms," *Journal of Parallel and Distributed Computing (JPDC)*, 62(5):899–921, May 2002. 62

[5] J. A. Cobb and M. G. Gouda, "Stabilization of Routing in Directed Networks," *Proc. 5th Workshop on Self-Stabilization Systems*, pp. 51–66. 62

[6] F. Cristian and F. Schmuck, "Agreeing on Processor Group Membership in Asynchronous Distributed Systems," Technical Report CSE95-428, Department of Computer Science, University of California San Diego, 1995. 65, 67

[7] S. Dolev, "Self-Stabilizing Routing and Related Protocols," *Journal of Parallel and Distributed Computing*, 42:122–127, May 1997. 66

[8] S. Dolev, *Self-Stabilization*, MIT Press, 2000. 62, 66, 67, 71, 74, 75

[9] E. W. Dijkstra, "Self-stabilizing systems in spite of distributed control," *Communication of the ACM*, 17:643–644, 1974. 62, 66, 67, 69

[10] S. Dolev and T. Herman, Superstabilizing protocols for dynamic distributed systems. *Chicago Journal of Theoretical Computer Science*, 1997. 66

[11] S. Dolev and E. Schiller, "Communication Adaptive Self-stabilizing Group Membership Service," *5th Workshop on Self-Stabilizing Systems*, October, 2001. Also, Technical Report #00-02 Department of Computer Science Ben-Gurion University, Beer-Sheva, Israel, 2000. 62, 64, 65, 69, 72, 73

[12] S. Dolev and E. Schiller, "Self-Stabilizing Group Communication in Directed Networks," Technical Report #10-03 Department of Computer Science Ben-Gurion University, Beer-Sheva, Israel, 2003. 61

[13] S. Dolev, E. Schiller, and J. L. Welch, "Random Walk for Self-Stabilizing Group Communication in Ad-Hoc Networks," *21st Symposium on Reliable Distributed Systems*, IEEE Computer Society Press, pp. 70–79, 2002. 62, 64, 65, 69, 71

[14] S. Delaet and S. Tixeuil, "Tolerating transient and intermittent failures," *Journal of Parallel and Distributed Computing*, 62(5):961–981, 2002. 62, 66

[15] A. S. Tanenbaum, *Computer Networks*, Prentice Hall, 1996. 69

[16] M. Tchunte, "Sur l'auto-stabilisation dans un reseau d'ordinateurs," *RAIRO Informatique Theoretique*, 15:47–66, 1981. 62

Lyapunov Analysis of Neural Network Stability in an Adaptive Flight Control System[*]

Sampath Yerramalla[1], Edgar Fuller[2], Martin Mladenovski[1], and Bojan Cukic[1]

[1] Lane Department of Computer Science and Electrical Engineering
West Virginia University, Morgantown WV 26506
{sampath,cukic,martinm}@csee.wvu.edu
[2] Department of Mathematics, West Virginia University
Morgantown WV 26506
ef@math.wvu.edu

Abstract. The paper presents the role of self-stabilization analysis in the design, verification and validation of the dynamics of an *Adaptive Flight Control System* (AFCS). Since the traditional self-stabilization approaches lack the flexibility to deal with the continuous adaptation of the neural network within the AFCS, the paper emphasizes an alternate self-stability analysis approach, namely *Lyapunov's Second Method*. A Lyapunov function for the neural network is constructed and used in presenting a formal mathematical proof that verifies the following claim: While learning from a *fixed* input manifold, the neural network is self-stabilizing in a *Globally Asymptotically Stable* manner. When dealing with *variable* data manifolds, we propose the need for a real-time stability monitor that can detect unstable state deviations. The test results based on the data collected from an F-15 flight simulator provide substantial heuristic evidence to support the idea of using a Lyapunov function to prove the self-stabilization properties of the neural network adaptation.

1 Introduction

1.1 Background

Adaptive control is the latest trend in the application of Neural Networks (NN) in realtime automation, one of the world's leading markets for computer control systems. The concept of Neural Adaptive Flight Control is perhaps the most challenging of them all as constructing it with guaranteed stability that ensures peak performance of the aircraft requires a thorough understanding of the objective functions [19]. Qualitatively speaking, an adaptive flight control system that has the ability to sense its environment, process information, reduce uncertainty, plan, generate and execute control actions is considered an Intelligent Flight Control System (IFCS) [17, 16]. The goal of IFCS is to develop and flight evaluate

---

[*] This work was supported in part by NASA through cooperative agreement NCC 2-979. The opinions, findings, conclusions and recommendations expressed herein are those of the authors and do not reflect the views of the sponsors.

S.-T. Huang and T. Herman (Eds.): SSS 2003, LNCS 2704, pp. 77–92, 2003.

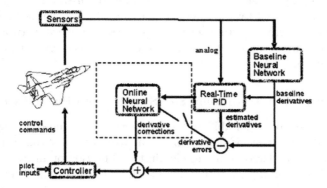

Fig. 1. An Intelligent Flight Control System Architecture

flight control concepts that incorporate emerging algorithms and techniques to provide an extremely robust system capable of handling multiple accident and off-nominal flight scenarios [12]. Figure 1 shows the architectural overview of an IFCS consisting of an Online Learning Neural Network (OLNN) that accounts for dramatic changes of the aircraft exceeding robustness limits [22].

A Baseline or Pre-trained Neural Net (PNN) is used for replacing linear maps from standard designs (like reference adaptive control) in order to produce a robust system that can handle nonlinearities. PNN is non-adaptive, meaning that once trained, it does not change during the flight. It is essentially a table-lookup scheme based on wind-tunnel experiments for the stable aircraft conditions. The adaptive nature of the IFCS is induced by the realtime Parameter Identification (PID), that uses an equation error technique employing Fourier Transform Regression algorithm. During off-nominal flight conditions (combat damage or major system failure), notable discrepancies between the outputs of the PNN and the real-time PID are generated that need to be accounted by the OLNN. This difference in output of the PNN and PID is termed as Stability and Control Derivative (SCD) error. The role of the OLNN is to store these SCD errors and provide a better estimate of the stored values for new flight conditions. The SCD outputs from the BLNN along with the estimated SCD errors form the OLNN ensure that the controller is able to compute control gains needed to make the aircraft stable and, consequently, safe.

Adaptive systems are hard to model as they are often accompanied with difficulties: many degrees of freedom, distributed sensors, high noise levels, and uncertainty. Nevertheless, greater the ability of the system to deal with these difficulties, the more intelligent is the system [17]. The central control goal of the IFCS is to calculate the present state of the system and determine a strategy to drive the system to a desired final state. If the system contains a provably self-stabilizing on-line learning neural network, it ensures that while IFCS achieves its central goal, states of the system do not deviate towards instability, thereby avoiding a potential disaster. However, verification of self-stabilization properties is usually a complicated task [13]. Our research goal is all the more challenging since we need to verify self-stabilization properties of a neural network which is able to adapt during the flight, potentially having direct consequences for the overall system safety.

1.2   Limitations of Traditional Self-Stabilization Proof Techniques

The original idea of self-stabilizing systems was introduced by Dijkstra in 1974 [8]. Traditional methodologies for the analysis of self-stabilization require a detailed system understanding, needed in the definition of an *invariance* condition. The role of an invariant function in self-stabilization has been described by Arora in [1]: *if the system is initiated appropriately, the invariant is always satisfied. If the system is placed in an arbitrary state to continue execution, it eventually reaches a state from where the invariant is always satisfied.*

The self-stabilization proof methodology applicable to distributed algorithms exhibits interesting analogies with feedback system stabilization in control engineering [23]. These analogies are based on the existence of invariants, but the proof mechanisms differ significantly. Therefore, very early in our research we had to ask ourselves whether it would be possible to apply any of the existing methodologies to prove the self-stabilization properties of a continuously evolving, topologically complex neural network embedded in an adaptive flight control environment.

A major practical limitation of application of traditional methodologies for proving self-stabilization properties of neural networks appears to be the *scalability* [2]. Standard approaches are based on the definition of the invariance. But in order to define the invariance, a detailed system description must be available. However, the goal of using an adaptive component in a flight control system is to cope with unanticipated and/or failure conditions. If these conditions were to be systematically described, the excessive size of the data (and the ensuing system designs) would make computing an invariance a complicated task. The second limitation of traditional approaches is their inability to handle *uncertainties*, regularly encountered in adaptive systems. But, even if we assume that uncertainty and scalability are of no concern, the challenge still remains: *Do traditional stabilization proof techniques work for adaptive systems?*

It should not come as a surprise that we discovered the need to define a different notion of self-stabilization and embarked on developing alternative verification techniques to reason about the self-stabilization properties of the specific type of neural network used in the intelligent flight control system.

1.3   Overview

The rest of the paper is organized as follows. Section 2 introduces the Lyapunov approach to self-stability analysis of dynamic systems. Section 3 describes the specific type of neural networks, so called Dynamic Cell Structures (DCS), used in the context of the adaptive flight control system. DCS neural networks are the object of our stability analysis. Section 4 presents our main result, formal stability proof for the DCS neural network. This proof deals with the flight conditions that exclude unexpected environmental conditions (failures). Therefore, Section 5 introduces the notion of on-line stability monitoring, which can provide early warnings by detecting the states leading to unstable system conditions. These concepts are further described in a case study involving the flight data collected in an F-15 flight simulator in Section 6. We conclude by a brief summary in Section 7.

2   Self-Stabilization Using Lyapunov Functions

Often, the mathematical theory of stability analysis is (mis)understood as the process of finding a solution for the differential equation(s) that govern the system dynamics. Stability analysis is the theory of validating the existence (or non-existence) of stable states. Theoretically, there is no guarantee for the existence of a solution to an arbitrary set of nonlinear differential equations, let alone the complicated task of solving them [7].

In the context of the analysis of the stability of adaptation in the IFCS, the problem is to find an effective tool applicable to the online learning neural network. It is often seen that adaptive systems that are stable under some definitions of stability tend to become unstable under other definitions [9]. This difficulty in imposing strong stability restrictions for nonlinear systems was realized as early as a century ago by a Russian mathematician A. M. Lyapunov. Details on Lyapunov's stability analysis technique for nonlinear discrete systems can be found in [4, 9, 27]. The fact that Lyapunov's *direct method* or Lyapunov's *second method* can be easily and systematically applied to validate the existence (or non-existence) of stable states in an adaptive system, intrigued us in using Lyapunov's concept of self-stabilization in our analysis as a means of answering the question posed earlier.

In the discrete sense, Lyapunov stability can be defined as follows:

Definition 1. *Lyapunov Stability*
If there exists a Lyapunov function, $V : \mathbb{R}^O \to \mathbb{R}$, defined in a region of state space near a solution of a dynamical system such that

1. *$V(0) = 0$*
2. *$V(x) > 0 : \forall x \in O, x \neq 0$*
3. *$V(x(t_{i+1})) - V(x(t_i)) = \Delta V(x) \leq 0 : \forall x \in O$*

then the solution of the system is said to stable in the sense of Lyapunov.

$x = 0$ represents a solution of the dynamical systems and $\mathbb{R}^O$, O represent the output space and a region surrounding this solution of the system respectively. Though this concept was intended for mathematics of control theory, Lyapunov stabilization in a general sense can be simplified as follows. A system is said to be stable near a given solution if one can construct a Lyapunov function (scalar function) that identifies the regions of the state space over which such functions decrease along some smooth trajectories near the solution.

Definition 2. *Asymptotic Stability (AS)*
If in addition to conditions 1 and 2 of Definition 1, the system has a negative-definite Lyapunov function

$$\Delta V(x) < 0 : \forall x \in O \tag{1}$$

then the system is Asymptotically Stable.

Asymptotic stability adds the property that in a region surrounding a solution of the dynamical system trajectories are approaching this given solution asymptotically.

Definition 3. *Global Asymptotic Stability (GAS)*
If in addition to conditions 1 and 2 of Definition 1, the Lyapunov function is constructed such that,

$$\lim_{t \to \infty} V(x) = 0 \tag{2}$$

*over the **entire** state space then the system is said to be Globally Asymptotically Stable.*

A notable difference between AS and GAS is the fact that GAS implies any trajectory beginning at *any* initial point will converge asymptotically to the given solution, as opposed to AS where only those trajectories begining in the neighborhood of the solution approach the solution asymptotically. The types of stability defined above have increasing property strength, i.e.

Global Asymptotic Stability $\implies$ Asymptotic Stability $\implies$ Lyapunov Stability.

Fig. 2. Relative strengths of Stability

The reverse implication does not necessarily hold as indicated by the Venn diagram of Figure 2. In simple terms, the system is stable if all solutions of the state that start *nearby* end up *nearby*. A good distance measure of *nearby* must be defined by a Lyapunov function (V) over the states of the system. By constructing V, we can guarantee that all trajectories of the system converge to a stable state. The function V should be constructed keeping in mind that it needs be scalar ($V \in \mathbb{R}$) and should be non-increasing over the trajectories of the state space. This is required in order to ensure that all *limit points* of any trajectory are stationary. Thus a strict Lyapunov function should force every trajectory to asymptotically approach an equilibrium state. Even for non-strict Lyapunov functions it is possible to guarantee convergence by LaSalle's invariance principle. In mechanical systems a Lyapunov function is considered as an energy minimization term, in economy and finance evaluations it is considered as a cost-minimization term, and for computational purposes it can be considered as an error-minimization term.

3   DCS Neural Network

In 1994 Jorg Bruske and Gerald Sommer of the University of Kiel, Germany, introduced the concept of DCS as a family of topology representing self-organizing NN [3, 5]. This Topology Preserving Feature Map (TPFM) generation scheme was motivated by Growing Neural GAS algorithm developed by Fritzke and the former work on Topology Representing Networks (TRN) by Martinetz [15].

DCS uses Kohonen-like adaptation to shift the weighted centers of the local neighborhood structure, closer to the feature manifold. When applied in conjunction with Competitive Hebb Rule (CHR) to update lateral connections of the neighbors, this produces a network representation that preserves the features of the input manifold. These two essential building blocks (rules) of the DCS algorithm, play a key role in the generation of a TPFM. Before we proceed for an in-depth analysis of the DCS algorithm we need to study and formulate these competitive rules that govern the DCS dynamical system.

3.1   Competitive Hebb Rule (CHR)

DCS NN rests upon a Radial Basis Function (RBF) and an additional layer of lateral connections between the neural units [3]. These lateral connection strengths are symmetric and bounded in nature, $c_{ij} = c_{ji} \in [0, 1]$. The goal of CHR is to update the lateral connections by mapping neighborhoods in the input manifold to neighborhoods of the network. Thereby, avoiding any restrictions of the topology of the network [5]. For each input element of the feature manifold, CHR operates by setting the connection strength between the two neural units that are closer to the input than any other neuron pair, to a highest possible connection strength of 1. These two neural units are referred to as the Best Matching Unit (*bmu*) and Second Best Unit (*sbu*). CHR then proceeds to decay the strength of all other existing lateral connections emanating from the *bmu* using a forgetting constant, α. If any of these existing connections drop below a predefined threshold θ, they are set to zero. The set of all neural units that are connected to the *bmu* is defined as the neighborhood of the *bmu*, and represented by *nbr*. All other connections of the network remain unaltered. In this way CHR induces a Delaunay triangulation into the network by preserving the neighborhood structure of the feature manifold.

$$c_{ij}(t+1) = \begin{cases} 1 & (i = bmu) \wedge (j = sbu) \\ 0 & (i = bmu) \wedge (j \in nbr - sbu) \wedge (c_{ij} < \theta) \\ \alpha c_{ij}(t) & (i = bmu) \wedge (j \in nbr - sbu) \wedge (c_{ij} \geq \theta) \\ c_{ij}(t) & i, j \neq bmu \end{cases} \tag{3}$$

It was shown in [15] that algorithms utilizing CHR to update lateral connections between neural units generate a TPFM.

3.2 Kohonen-Like Rule (KLR)

Unlike a typical feed-forward NN, the weight center $\boldsymbol{w_i}$ associated with a neural unit i of the DCS network represents the location of the neural unit in the output space. It is crucial to realize that these weighted centers be updated in a manner that preserves the geometry of the input manifold. This can be achieved by adjusting the weighted center of the *bmu* and its surrounding neighborhood structure *nbr* closer to the input element. For each element of the feature manifold, $\boldsymbol{u} \in I$, DCS adapts the corresponding *bmu* and its neighborhood set *nbr* in a Kohonen-like manner [18]. Over any training cycle, let $\boldsymbol{\Delta w_i} = \boldsymbol{w_i}(t+1) - \boldsymbol{w_i}(t)$ represent the adjustment of the weight center of the neural unit, then the Kohonen-like rule followed in DCS can be represented as follows

$$\Delta w_i = \begin{cases} \varepsilon_{bmu}(\boldsymbol{u} - \boldsymbol{w_i}(t)) & i = bmu \\ \varepsilon_{nbr}(\boldsymbol{u} - \boldsymbol{w_i}(t)) & i \in nbr \\ 0 & (i \neq bmu) \wedge (i \notin nbr) \end{cases} \tag{4}$$

where $\varepsilon_{bmu}, \varepsilon_{nbr} \in [0, 1]$ are predefined constants known as the learning rates that define the momentum of the update process. For every input element, applying CHR before any other adjustment ensures that *sbu* is a member of *nbr* set for all further adjustments within the inner loop of the DCS algorithm.

3.3 Growing the Network

Unlike traditional Self-Organizing Maps (SOM), DCS has the ability to grow or shrink the map by increasing or decreasing the number of neurons of the network. A local error measure associated with the network, namely *Resource*, is used to determine if the network experienced a large enough cumulative error, meaning there is a requirement for an additional neuron in the network. In most cases Euclidean distance between the best matching unit (*bmu*) and the training

```
while  stopping criteria is not satisfied
{
      for each training input stimulus
      {
                  find bmu, sbu
                  update connections using CHR
                  adapt weights using KLR
                  update resource error
      }
      compute cumulative network resource error
      if (cumulative network resource error) > (Predefined Error)
      {
                  grow the network
                  decrement all resource values
      }
}
```

Fig. 3. DCS Algorithm

input stimulus serves as a measure of the resource. After a cycle of adaptation (epoch), if needed an additional neuron is introduced into the network at the region between the highest and second highest resource neurons of the network.

3.4   DCS Algorithm

Knowing the operational aspects of the individual building blocks, we now analyze the DCS training algorithm. As shown in Figure 3, the DCS algorithm is allowed to train on the input stimulus until the network has reached a specific stopping criteria. For each training input stimulus, the network is searched for the two closest neurons, best matching unit (*bmu*) and second best unit (*sbu*). The lateral connection structure surrounding the *bmu* is updated using Hebb rule. Kohonen adaptation of the weights of the *bmu* and its neighbors (*nbr*) is performed.

The resource value of the *bmu* is updated correspondingly, marking the end of a training cycle (epoch). The cumulative resource error of the network is computed to determine the need for inserting an additional neuron into the network. Decreasing the resource values of all the neurons by a decay constant prevents the resource values from growing out of bounds.

We want to determine if the DCS algorithm will *reliably* learn a fixed input manifold $I \subset \mathbb{R}^I$, on successive applications. The question is then how much can the evolving state of the DCS algorithm, denoted by x_t, deviate from a previously learned stable state, denoted by x_0? Stability analysis in similar terms was performed by Kaynak et. al. for a backpropagation neural network that has a relatively simple topological structure in comparison with a DCS network [26].

A network basically consists of nodes (weights) and vertices (connections). Thereby, it can be completely represented using a weight center matrix, $W \subset \mathbb{R}^O$, and a connection strength matrix, $C \subset \mathbb{R}^O$. Considering the map generated by the DCS network as a graph, $G(W, C)$, we provide the following definition.

Definition 4. *DCS Network's Mapping*
DCS network's mapping $G(W, C)$ for a given feature manifold, $I \subset \mathbb{R}^I$, is an Nth order neural network representation of I in the output space, $O \subset \mathbb{R}^O$, generated by assigning N neural units in t_n steps of the DCS algorithm.

This definition characterizes the DCS process as a mapping which we can now proceed to analyze in the context of discrete dynamical systems.

4   Self-Stabilization of DCS Network

4.1   State Space of the DCS Network

Let the DCS network be learning from a set of training examples of the input space $\boldsymbol{u}(t) \in \mathbb{R}^I$. At some point of time during or after the learning, if a test input stimulus, $\boldsymbol{u}^\star(t) \in \mathbb{R}^I$ is presented, the network generates an estimated output, $\hat{\boldsymbol{y}} = G(W(t), C(t), \boldsymbol{u}^\star(t))$. The dynamics of such learning can be represented as:

$$\boldsymbol{x}(t) = f(\boldsymbol{x}(t), \boldsymbol{u}(t), t) : X \times \mathbb{R}^I \times \mathbb{R}$$
$$\hat{\boldsymbol{y}} = G(W(t), C(t), \boldsymbol{u}^\star(t)) : \mathbb{R}^O \times \mathbb{R}^O \times \mathbb{R}^I \qquad (5)$$

where $\boldsymbol{x}(t)$ represents the DCS networks learning state, X represents the learning profile. For the sake of simplicity we consider only discrete time variations. Specifically, whenever t is such that $t_i \leq t < t_{i+1}$ we will have $f(\boldsymbol{x}(t), \boldsymbol{u}(t), t) = f(\boldsymbol{x}(t), \boldsymbol{u}(t), t_i)$. This implies that the DCS network learning depends only on x and u. The dynamics from (5) can be re-written as:

$$\boldsymbol{\Delta x} = \boldsymbol{x}(t_{i+1}) - \boldsymbol{x}(t_i) = f(\boldsymbol{x}, \boldsymbol{u})$$
$$y(\boldsymbol{u}^\star) = G(W, C, \boldsymbol{u}^\star) \qquad (6)$$

4.2   Mathematical Verification of Self-Stabilization

Theorem 1. *During DCS network's representation of a fixed input manifold, the evolving state of the system due to neural unit's position adjustment, $x_W \in W$, is self-stabilizing in a globally asymptotically stable manner.*

Proof. Since the DCS network's learning is a time-varying process whose state changes according to the difference relations (6), we first need to construct a Lypaunov function that is non-increasing over the state trajectories.

To set up a Lyapunov function, we measure how accurately a current state of the algorithm models the input manifold in terms of the amount of geometry being preserved by the network. We formulate a function that measures the effectiveness of the placement of neural units by computing the amount by which a neural unit deviates from an element $u \in I$ of the input manifold for which it is the best matching unit. We then average this over the total number of neurons, N, in that phase of DCS approximation to get

$$V = \frac{1}{N} \sum_{u \in I} \| u - w_{bmu(u,t)} \| \tag{7}$$

Throughout this proof, V, commonly referred as the network's quantization error serves as the network's Lyapunov function.

First of all we need to show that the above presented Lyapunov function (V) is valid. It is obvious that $V \geq 0$ since $\| u - w_{bmu(u,t)} \| \geq 0$. Also $V(0) = 0$, since there are no neurons in the DCS network during zero state. To show that $\frac{\Delta V}{\Delta t} < 0$, first note that since the time step $\Delta t > 0$, the numerator ΔV will determine the sign in question. Over any learning cycle, DCS network adjusts the weights of the bmu and its neighbors, nbr, according to the Kohonen-like rule. Let $\| u - w_{bmu(u,t)} \|$ be represented by $d(u, t)$, then we see that over a single training cycle

$$\begin{aligned} \Delta V &= \frac{1}{N+1} \sum_{u \in I} d(u, t+1) - \frac{1}{N} \sum_{u \in I} d(u, t) \\ &= \frac{N \sum_{u \in I} d(u, t+1) - (N+1) \sum_{u \in I} d(u, t)}{N(N+1)} \\ &= \frac{N \sum_{u \in I} (d(u, t+1) - d(u, t)) - \sum_{u \in I} d(u, t)}{N(N+1)} \end{aligned}$$

$$\tag{8}$$

For any $u \in I$, we need to show that either the corresponding portion of the numerator is negative or that some other portion compensates when it is positive. There are three ways in which a neural unit's weighted center may get adjusted. It may get updated as

1. as the bmu for u,
2. as the bmu of some other $u' \in I$,
3. or as one of the neighbors of the bmu of some other $u' \in I$.

In the first case, to show that equation (8) evaluates to less than 0, it is sufficient to show that

$$d(u, t+1) - d(u, t) < 0 \tag{9}$$

Computation using the weight-adaptation rule followed in DCS network gives

$$
\begin{aligned}
d(\boldsymbol{u}, t+1) &= \|\boldsymbol{u} - w_{bmu(\boldsymbol{u},t+1)}\| \\
&= \|\boldsymbol{u} - (w_{bmu(\boldsymbol{u},t)} + \varepsilon_{bmu}(\boldsymbol{u} - w_{bmu(\boldsymbol{u},t)}))\| \\
&= \|(\boldsymbol{u} - w_{bmu(t)}) - \varepsilon_{bmu}(\boldsymbol{u} - w_{bmu(t)})\| \\
&= \|\boldsymbol{u} - w_{bmu(t)} - \varepsilon_{bmu}\boldsymbol{u} + \varepsilon_{bmu}w_{bmu(t)}\| \\
&= (1 - \varepsilon_{bmu})\|\boldsymbol{u} - w_{bmu(t)}\| \\
&= (1 - \varepsilon_{bmu})d(\boldsymbol{u}, t).
\end{aligned}
$$

Since $\varepsilon_{bmu} \in (0,1)$,

$$
d(\boldsymbol{u}, t+1) < d(\boldsymbol{u}, t),
$$

which implies (9).

In the second case, the best matching unit for $\boldsymbol{u} \in I$, $bmu(\boldsymbol{u})$, may get updated as the best matching unit for some other $\boldsymbol{u}' \in I$, $bmu(\boldsymbol{u}')$. The update as $bmu(\boldsymbol{u}')$ can either precede or follow the update as $bmu(\boldsymbol{u})$ and the effect on V depends primarily on which input stimulus is closest to $bmu(\boldsymbol{u}) = bmu(\boldsymbol{u}')$. When $\boldsymbol{u}$ is farthest from $bmu(\boldsymbol{u})$, the triangle inequality for the euclidean metric implies that $d(t) > d(t+1)$ regardless of the order of update. On the other hand, if $\boldsymbol{u}'$ is farther from $bmu(\boldsymbol{u})$, $d(t)$ may be smaller than $d(t+1)$ but any increase in the distance from $\boldsymbol{u}$ to its bmu is smaller than the decrease in the distance from u' to the same neuron since $\boldsymbol{u}$ is closer to $bmu(\boldsymbol{u})$. Again, this follows from the triangle inequality for the euclidean metric. The net effect in all cases is a decrease in V.

The third case will have $\Delta V < 0$ since $\varepsilon_{bmu} >> \varepsilon_{sbu}$ in general. In case the two values are comparable, the result follows from the same argument as in the second case above. As a result, the function V is a Lyapunov function for the state of position adjustments of the DCS network and furthermore since $\Delta V < 0$ and $V \to 0$ as $t \to \infty$, the network is asymptotically stable in the sense of Lyapunov. Finally, the decrease in V is independent of the initial placement of neurons in the DCS algorithm which implies that this stability is global.

The theorem verifies the fact that if we can construct a Lyapunov function as an error-minimizing term with initial boundary conditions ($V(0) = 0$), Lyapunov's stability theory can then guarantee the neural network's neighborhood structure, in terms of the best matching unit (bmu) to get closer to the training example in a globally asymptotically stable manner and thus preserving the features of the input manifold, which is the central goal of on-line learning neural network of the adaptive flight control system [24].

5   Online Stability Monitoring

It is of prime importance to understand if the neural network is convergent, meaning that trajectories converge to a stationary state even before we use them in real applications. Since we provided the required mathematical foundation to

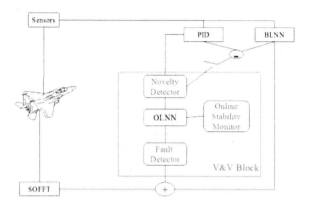

Fig. 4. V&V Mehtodology for OLNN

ensure the system to be stable, we now need to assure the robustness of system. In other words, if the online neural network encounters unusual data patterns that force the state of the system to deviate *away* from its current pattern, it always converges back to a stable equilibria within a *finite* amount of time. We may not always be able to assure robustness of the online network due to its implementation in an adaptive system, where the data patterns have no prior probability distribution. However, as the last resort of system assurance, we should at least be able to detect deviations of state that could lead to unstable behavior. This is is the objective of the Online Stability Monitor, shown in Figure 4.

An interesting question guiding the design of online monitoring feature is: *How much an evolving state of the system needs to deviate in order for the stability monitor to label it as unstable?*

Since, the objective functions for online adaptive systems evolve over time it is hard to establish a complete system description a priori. Hence, we cannot precisely specify what an unstable state (for adaptive neural network) is. The hope is that the on-line monitor will be able to *detect* it when it sees it. An inadequate Lyapunov function may, of course, cause the excess of false-positive warnings, but this risk cannot be avoided. Online Stability Monitor complements analytical stability analysis by being being able to detect system states that deviate *away* from stable equilibria in real-time.

6   Case Study

In order to better understand the role of Lyapunov functions in self-stabilization of the given system a case study has been performed. The learning data for the DCS neural network was collected in an *F-15* flight simulator. For the sake of simplicity, the simulation data depicts nominal conditions of approximately 4

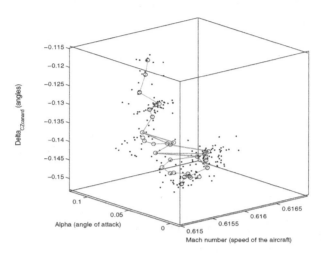

Fig. 5. Network Representation of Flight Control Variables

seconds of flight. During the simulation, the derivative outputs of the PID met the convergence criteria.

The plot in Figure 5 shows a portion of the DCS network learning behavior for the so called $DCS - C_z$ subnetwork, one of the five DCS neural networks used in the real implementation of the IFCS. The input to the $DCS - C_z$ network consisted of 186 data frames, each in a seven-dimensional space. Each input data frame consisted of 4 sensor readings and 3 stability and control derivative errors from PID and PNN.

In this figure, two *independent* input variables (from sensors) to the $DCS - C_z$ network are plotted against a third *dependent* input variable (from PID-PNN) 'fed' into the $DCS - C_z$ network. These independent variables represent Mach numbers, the speed of the aircraft as compared to the local speed of sound, and alpha, aircraft's angle of attack. The dependent variable is one of the aircrafts stability and control derivative errors, Cz_{canard}. Figure 5 depicts the DCS network approximation of the data configuration plotted in a three dimensional subspace of the total seven dimensional data space.

Since adaptive systems are associated with uncertainty, degrees of freedom and high noise-level in real flight conditions, we may not always be able to check to see if each dimension of the input data is effectively abstracted and represented by the network. The data sets being modelled here represent very short data sequences for one out of five neural networks in the intelligent flight control system. The use of the constructed Lyapunov function (V), as shown in Figure 6, reduces the need for checking effective learning by each dimension as $V \in \mathbb{R}$. Rather than looking onto several dozen graphs, the adequacy (stability) of learning can be assessed from the analysis of a single graph, the graph representing the Lyapunov function. Figure 6 depicts the convergence of V to a stable state within 10 epochs of neural network learning. Consequently, we can

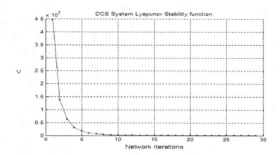

Fig. 6. Network's Lyapunov Function

pinpoint the precise time at which the network reaches a stable state using the rate of decay of the Lyapunov function.

7   Summary and Discussion

In this paper, we discussed practical limitations to the idea of applying traditional self-stabilization approaches to adaptive systems. As an alternate approach we emphasize the role of a Lyapunov function in detecting unstable state deviations. A Lyapunov function for a DCS neural network has been constructed and used in a formal proof that established the conditions under which on-line learning for this type of network is self-stabilizing.

Further, we propose the idea of online stability monitoring for adaptive flight control systems. The goal of on-line monitoring is to provide a real-time safety warning methodology. A simulation study was conducted and it provided further evidence of self-stabilizing properties of the DCS neural network learning.

References

[1] A. Arora, M. Demirbas and S. Kulkarni. *Graybox Stabilization*. International Conference on Dependable Systems and Networks (DSN'2001), Goteborg, Sweden, July 2001. 79

[2] A. Arora. *Stabilization*. Encyclopedia of Distributed Computing, edited by Partha Dasgupta and Joseph E. Urban, Kluwer Academic Publishers, 2000. 79

[3] Ingo Ahrns, Jorg Bruske, Gerald Sommer. *On-line Learning with Dynamic Cell Structures*. Proceedings of the International Conference on Artificial Neural Networks, Vol. 2, pp. 141-146, 1995. 82

[4] William L. Brogan. *Modern Control Theory*. II Edition, Prentice-Hall Inc., 1985. 80

[5] Jorg Bruske, and Gerald Sommer. *Dynamic Cell Structures*, NIPS, Vol. 7, Pages 497-504, 1995. 82

[6] Jorg Bruske, Gerald Sommer. *Dynamic Cell Structure Learns Perfectly Topology Preserving Map*. Neural Computations, Vol. 7, No. 4, pp. 845-865, 1995.

[7] Marc W. Mc. Conley, Brent D. Appleby, Munther A. Dahleh, Eric Feron. *Computational Complexity of Lyapunov Stability Analysis Problems for a Class of Nonlinear Systmes*. Society of industrial and applied mathematics journal of control and optimization, Vol. 36, No. 6, pp. 2176-2193, November 1998. 80

[8] Edsger W. Dijkstra. *Self-stabilizing systems in spite of Distributed Control*. Communications of the Assocoation for Computing Machinery, 17(11), 643-644, 1974. 79

[9] Bernard Friedland. *Advanced Control System*. Prentice-Hall Inc., 1996. 80

[10] Bernd Fritzke. *A Growing Neural Gas Network Learns Topologies*. Advances in Neural Information Processing Systems, Vol. 7, pp. 625-632, MIT press, 1995.

[11] Tom M. Heskes, Bert Kappen. *Online Learning Processes in Artificial Neural Networks*. Mathematical Foundations of Neural Networks, pp. 199-233, Amsterdam, 1993.

[12] Charles C. Jorgensen. *Feedback Linearized Aircraft Control Using Dynamic Cell Structures*. World Automation Congress, ISSCI 050.1-050.6, Alaska, 1991. 78

[13] J. L. W. Kessels. *An Exercise in Proving Self-satbilization with a variant function*. Information Processing Letters (IPL), Vol. 29, No.1, pp. 39-42, September 1998. 79

[14] Teuvo Kohonen. *The Self-Organizing Map*. Proceedings of the IEEE, Vol. 78, No. 9, pp. 1464-1480, September 1990.

[15] Thomas Martinetz, Klaus Schulten. *Topology Representing Networks*. Neural Networks, Vol. 7, No. 3, pp. 507-522, 1994. 82, 83

[16] Kumpati S. Narendra, Kannan Parthasarathy. *Identification and Control of Dynamic Systems Using Neural Networks*. IEEE Transactions on Neural Networks, Vol. 1, No. 1, pp. 4-27, March 1990. 77

[17] Kumpati S. Narendra. *Intelligent Control*. American Control Conference, San Diego, CA, May 1990. 77, 78

[18] Jurgen Rahmel. *On The Role of Topology for Neural Network Interpretation*, Proc. of European Conference on Artificial Intelligence, 1996. 83

[19] Orna Raz. *Validation of Online Artificial Neural Networks (ANNs)-An Informal Classification of Related Approaches*. Technical Report for NASA Ames Research Center, Moffet Field, CA, 2000. 77

[20] N. Rouche, P. Habets, M. Laloy. *Stability Theory by Liapunov's Direct Method*. Springer-Verlag, New York Inc. publishers, 1997.

[21] Marco Schneider. *Self-Stabilization*. Assocoation for Computing Machinery (ACM) sureveys, Vol. 25, No. 1, March 1993.

[22] The Boeing Company. *Intelligent Flight Control: Advanced Concept Program*. Project report, 1999. 78

[23] Oliver Theel. *An Exercise in Proving Self-Stabilization through Lyapunov Functions*. 21st International Conference on Distributed Computing Systems, ICDS'01, April 2001. 79

[24] Sampath Yerramalla, Bojan Cukic, Edgar Fuller. *Lyapunov Stability Analysis of Quantization Error for DCS Neural Networks*. Accepted for publication at International Joint Conference on Neural Networks (IJCNN'03), Oregon, July 2003. 87

[25] Wen Yu, Xiaoou Li. *Some Stability Properties of Dynamic Neural Networks*. IEEE Transactions on Circuits and Systems, Part-1, Vol. 48, No. 2, pp. 256-259, February 2001.

[26] Xinghuo Yu, M. Onder Efe, Okyay Kaynak. *A Backpropagation Learning Framework for Feedforward Neural Networks*, IEEE Transactions on Neural Networks, No. 0-7803-6685-9/01, 2001. 84

[27] V.I. Zubov. *Methods of A.M. Lyapunov and Their Applications.* U.S. Atomic Energy Commission, 1957. 80

Self-Stabilizing Token Circulation on Uniform Trees by Using Edge-Tokens*

Shing-Tsaan Huang[1] and Su-Shen Hung[2]

[1] Department of Computer Science and Information Engineering, National Central
University, Chung Li, Taiwan, 32054, R.O.C.
sthuang@csie.ncu.edu.tw
[2] Department of Computer Science, National Tsing Hua University,
Hsinchu, Taiwan 300, R.O.C.
sshung@itri.org.tw

Abstract. This paper presents a self-stabilizing token circulation algorithm for uniform tree networks by using edge tokens. An edge token with respect to an edge is a token maintained by the two nodes connected by the edge; one and only one of the two nodes has the edge token. This paper applies the concept of the edge token to solve the token circulation problem and works under the distributed scheduler with the read/write atomicity. The proposed algorithm only needs O(n) time to stabilize. The result is better than previous works either in stabilizing time or in its elegance.

Keywords: Edge token, mutual exclusion, token-circulation, self-stabilization.

1   Introduction

The term *self-stabilization* was introduced by Dijkstra in 1974 [7]. A self-stabilizing system guarantees to converge to a legitimate state in a finite time no matter what initial state it may start with. An attractive feature for a self-stabilizing system is that the system can recover from transient faults automatically without any outside intervention. This feature is highly desirable for distributed systems with fault-tolerance consideration.

The token circulation problem is to implement a token circulating among the nodes of the network and make each node get the token at least once in every circulation cycle. The solution to this problem can be used to achieve the mutual exclusion and synchronization goals. There are many self-stabilizing researches working on this problem. The earlier results can be found in [1,7,8] for ring networks and in [2] for linear array networks. The protocols proposed in [9,12,16,19,20] work for tree networks. In [9], the authors constructed a spanning tree firstly, then present a self-

---

* This research was supported in part by the National Science Council of the Republic of
China under the Contract NSC 90-2213-E-008-054.

S.-T. Huang and T. Herman (Eds.): SSS 2003, LNCS 2704, pp. 92–101, 2003.

stabilizing token circulation algorithm on the spanning tree in the depth-first order under the distributed scheduler with the read/write atomicity. A read/write atomicity requires that each process either reads the state of one of its neighbors or updates its local state but not both in an atomic step [9]. Petit and Villain also proposed several algorithms for rooted tree networks in [16,19] both for the oriented trees and unoriented trees. Besides those, Huang and Chen [13] firstly presented a self-stabilizing depth-first token circulation algorithm for arbitrary rooted networks without constructing a spanning tree. Subsequently, several protocols [5,10,11,15,17,18] were also proposed for general networks. But most of them need a distinguished node called root node, that is, they are not uniform systems. A system is *uniform* if all processes are identical and anonymous. The advantage of uniform systems is their fine scalability; that is, processes can be added onto or deleted from the system dynamically. The protocol proposed in [15] is a uniform algorithm, but the network must be prime size. Most of the above algorithms need O(n x *D*) stabilizing time except that the algorithm in [17] takes the fast stabilizing time O(n), where **n** is the network size and *D* is the degree of network.

Consider a connected graph with processes (or nodes) and edges. An *Edge Token* with respect to an edge is a token maintained by the two processes connected by the edge. The edge token is held by one of the two processes and is passed between them as needed. Basically, it is an algorithm to solve mutual exclusion problem for two processes. The problem is related to the dinning philosophers by Dijkstra[4] and the drinking philosophers by Chandy and Misra[6] although they are not self-stabilizing algorithms. The first self-stabilizing algorithm for edge tokens was presented in [14]. This paper adopts the algorithm in [14] to implement the edge token with slight modification. The major difference is that, in [14], the processes holding edge tokens have the privilege to pass edge tokens, but in the proposed algorithm, only the processes holding no edge token have the privilege to get edge tokens. However, in both algorithms, each process maintains only two three-state variables for each edge token; the two alogrithms also works under the distributed scheduler with the read/write atomicity.

In this paper, we propose a self-stabilizing token circulation algorithm for uniform tree based on the edge token algorithm. The proposed algorithm only needs O(n) rounds to stabilize. A round is the minimum time period that each process is scheduled to execute at least once [16]. This is better than previous results in stabilizing time. Besides, the proposed algorithm works under the distributed scheduler with the read/write atomicity; whereas, previous results are not designed for such consideration except [9]. Although the proposed algorithm in [9] also works under the distributed scheduler with the read/write atomicity, but it is not a uniform algorithm and needs O(nx*D*) stabilizing time, where *D* denotes the degree of network.

The rest of the paper is organized as follows. Section 2 describes the self-stabilizing edge token algorithm. The proposed token circulation algorithm is presented in Section 3; its correctness proof and analysis are given in Section 4. Section 5 gives concluding remarks.

2   The Self-Stabilizing Edge Token Algorithm

In this section, we propose a self-stabilizing algorithm to implement the edge token. An edge token is maintained with respected to an edge; the algorithm guarantees that after stabilizing, there is one and only one edge token held by one of the two neighboring processes connected by the edge. The algorithm also provides a mechanism to pass the edge token between the two processes as needed. In the following, to avoid confusing with the traditionally defined token, we use the word *Etoken* for the term *edge token*.

Assume P_i, P_j are two neighboring processes. First, let each process maintains two variables: one is a 3-state (ranging from 0 to 2) variable S and the other is the image of its neighbor's S. Let S maintained by P_i be denoted as S.i, and the image of S.j maintained by P_i be denoted as (S.j).i. The image variables are updated if they don't match their real values in the neighbors. The S values are ordered by $0<1<2<0$. We say that P_i holds the *Etoken* if S.i > (S.j).i. Meanwhile P_j can get the *Etoken* from P_i by setting S.j = (S.j-1) mod 3.

In our design, the action of updating image variables always has the highest priority, hence we assume (S.j).i = S.j and (S.i).j = S.i in the following discussion. There are two cases need to be considered:

(1) S.i ≠ S.j

The process with the larger S value (by the order $0<1<2<0$) holds the *Etoken*. And the process which without *Etoken* has the privilege to decide whether to get the *Etoken* from its neighbor or not. Assume S.i (=2) > S.j (=1), then P_i holds the *Etoken*; P_j may get the *Etoken* from P_i by setting S.j = (S.j-1) mod 3 = 0. Then, since S.i (=2) < S.j (=0), P_j gets the *Etoken*.

(2) S.i = S.j

We design a randomized rule to break the symmetry.

Once the symmetry is broken, there is one and only one *Etoken* held by P_i or P_j. A formal description of the algorithm is as follows:

Process P_i

Variables:
S.i: 0,1,2
   (S.j).i: image of S.j at P_i; P_j is a neighbor of P_i.

State predicate:
EToken(i,j) ≡ S.i > (S.j).i

Procedure:
GetEToken(i,j): if ¬EToken(i,j) then S.i := (S.i -1) mod 3 fi.

Rules:
R0: (S.j).i ≠ S.j → (S.j).i := S.j
R1: S.i = (S.j).i → S.i = Random(0,1,2)

There are only two rules in the algorithm: Rule (R0) is used to update the image variables of neighbors and Rule (R1) is used to break the symmetry. Rule (R0) has higher priority than Rule (R1).

Figure 1 shows a stabilizing example for the *Etoken* between P_i and P_j. Initially, both processes update the image variables, then P_i randomizes its S value to break the symmetry at state (2). The *Etoken* is stabilized after state (4). Meanwhile, states (4), (5) and (6) show the passing of the *Etoken* from P_i to P_j.

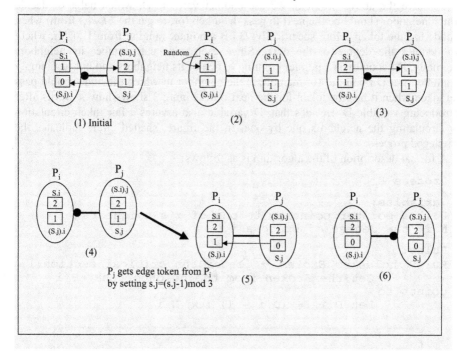

Fig. 1. An example for *Etoken* stabilizing. P_i randomizes its S value to break the symmetry at state (2). The *Etoken* is stabilized after state (4), and states (4), (5) and (6) show the passing of the *Etoken* from P_i to P_j

The algorithm can be generalized from two processes to multiple processes. Each process maintains two 3-states variables for each neighbor individually and takes actions independently.

3   The Token Circulation Algorithm

In this section, we propose a self-stabilizing token circulation algorithm for uniform trees. The algorithm is based on the *Etoken* algorithm presented in the previous section. For a tree of *n* processes, there are *n-1* edges; hence there are *n-1* *Etoken*s. It implies that there is at least one process holding no *Etoken*. The idea is to let the process holding no *Etoken* to own the privilege, which is called token traditionally.

Then the privileged process releases the token by getting an *Etoken* from one of its neighbors. The proposed algorithm guarantees there is one and only one token eventually and the token circulates among the processes of the tree fairly. The problem is that the token may be bounced back and forth between two nodes if the token passing does not follow a fair pattern. Figure 2 shows an example that the token bounces back and forth between P_s and P_t. In the figure, the shaded circle indicates the privileged process, which has the token.

To solve the above problem, we use another variable D, which helps to decide which neighbor should be the next to pass the token (or, to get the *Etoken* from) when a node has the token. More specifically, D.i is a pointer ranging from 1 to *N.i*, where *N.i* denotes the degree of the node. Since each node can number its neighbors internally, D.i actually is a pointer pointing to one of its neighbors and not just simply a number. Let D.i point to (or memorize) the neighbor to which the node should pass the token when it has the token for the next time. Figure 3 shows how it works after introducing variable D. Besides that, D variable also assures a fair token circulation by circulating the neighbors one by one. In the figure, shaded circle indicates the privileged process.

A formal description of the algorithm is as follows:

Process P_i

Variables:
D.i: a pointer pointing to one of i's neighbors.
N.i: the degree of process i.

Rules:
R0: P_i holds no *Etoken* → (enter the critical section;)
        Get the *Etoken* from the neighbor that D.i
points to;
            Let D.i := (D.i + 1) *mod* N.i.

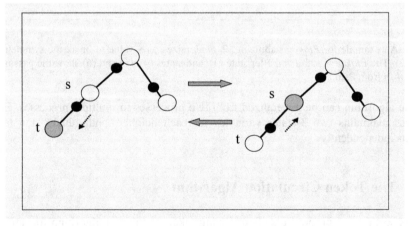

Fig. 2. *Etoken* bouncing back and forth. P_s and P_t may pass *Etoken* to each other infinitely

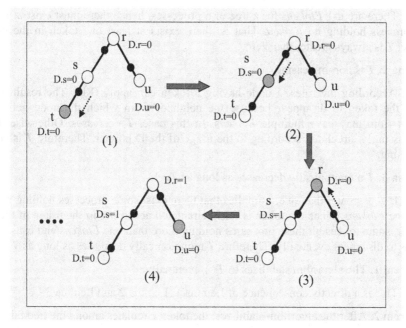

Fig. 3. Following the direction for *Etoken* passing, P_s gets *Etoken* from P_r at state (2) and then changes its D variable for next time

4   The Correctness Proof and Analysis for the Token Circulation Algorithm

In this section, we prove the correctness of the token circulation algorithm and analyze its complexity.

4.1   Correctness Proof

As the stabilizing property of the edge token algorithm is rather obvious, here we omit the proof for the correctness of the self-stabilizing algorithm for *Etoken*s. And assume this part is stabilized, that is, there is one and only one *Etoken* with respect to each edge. We just focus on the correctness of the token circulation algorithm.

According to our design, the process holding no *Etoken* owns token. In the following, we will prove that there exists one and only one token in the tree eventually, and the token is fairly circulated among the processes of the tree.

Definition Let T denote the number of tokens in the tree, that is, the number of processes holding no *Etoken* in the tree.

Lemma 1. T is always greater than zero.

Proof. There are n-1 *Etoken*s for a tree of n processes, hence there must exist at least one process holding no *Etoken*. That is, there exists at least one token in the tree. Hence, T is always greater than zero.

Lemma 2. T is non-increasing.

Proof. According the rules, a node having a token can apply (R0). The result may cause the token to disappear because the neighbor from which the node gets the *Etoken* from may have multiple *Etoken*s. In this case, T decreases. Otherwise, the token is fairly circulated according to the usage of the D pointer. Therefore T is non-increasing.

Lemma 3. T monotonically decreases as long as $T > 1$.

Proof. If T is greater than one, it implies that there exist some processes holding more than one *Etoken*s. Since the token is fairly circulated according to the usage of the D pointer, some tokens hit these processes holding more than one *Etoken*s and cause the tokens to disappear eventually. Therefore T monotonically decreases as long as $T > 1$.

Theorem 1. The algorithm stabilizes to $T = 1$ eventually.

Proof. This is a directly consequence of Lemma 1, Lemma 2 and Lemma 3.

Theorem 2. After the algorithm stabilizes; the token circulates among the tree fairly.

Proof. This is obvious according to the usage of the D pointer.

4.2   Complexity Analysis

In this subsection, we analyze the time complexity of the proposed algorithm. For time complexity, we adopt the measurement of round defined in [16].

Definition A *round* is the minimum time period that each process in the tree is scheduled to execute at least once.

Lemma 5. It takes at most 2 rounds to stabilize to exactly one *Etoken* for each edge.
Proof. Consider the edge that connected by P_i and P_j, we say that the *Etoken* is stabilized for the edge if $S.i \neq S.j$. Let us define two states:

State 0 $= \{(S.i, S.j) \mid S.i = S.j\}$
State 1 $= \{(S.i, S.j) \mid S.i \neq S.j\}$

And let p_{ij} denote the transition probability from state i to state j. According to the design, State 1 is a stabilized state and remains still; State 0 may enter State 1 or remains at State 0 by random. Hence the transition probabilities are $p_{00} = 1/3$, $p_{01} = 2/3$, $p_{10} = 0$ and $p_{11} = 1$. According to Markov chain theorems, the expected timeμ_{01} from State 0 to State 1 is:

$$\mu_{01} = 1 + p_{00}\mu_{01}$$

that is, $\mu_{01} = 1 + 1/3\mu_{01}$

$$\mu_{01} = 3/2$$

Hence, it takes at most 2 rounds to stabilize to exactly one *Etoken* for each edge.

Lemma 6. It takes at most 2(n-1) rounds for *T* to decrease to one.

Proof. According to Theorem 1, there is one and only one token eventually. Since the nodes which are visited by the surviving token don't make it disappear, so these nodes must hold one and only *Etoken* before visiting. It takes 2(n-1) rounds for a token to traverse all the nodes in the tree because the token passes each edge twice in a circulation cycle. Hence the surviving token takes 2(n-1) rounds to visit all the nodes and after that all the nodes hold one *Etoken* except one. Therefore, all the tokens must disappear except one in 2(n-1) rounds. Figure 4 shows an example. In the figure, P_s and P_t both own tokens at some time and the token owned by P_s is the final survived token. There exists another node P_k holding more than one *Etokens* on the path between P_s and P_t. Then before the surviving token is passed to P_k, the token owned by P_t must disappear.

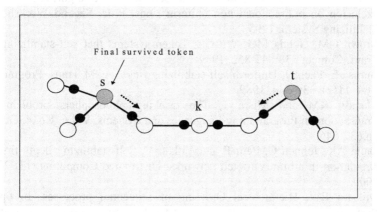

Fig. 4. P_s and P_t both own tokens and P_k holds more than one *Etoken*s. Then before the surviving token is passed to P_k, the token owned by P_t must disappear

Theorem 3. The maximum stabilizing time of the algorithm is O(**n**) rounds.
Proof. According to Lemmas 5 and Lemma 6, it takes at most 2*D rounds to stabilize all *Etoken*s, where D is the degree of network, and 2(n-1) rounds to one token. Therefore the maximum stabilizing time of the algorithm is 2*D + 2(n-1) ≤ 4(n-1) rounds. That is O(**n**) rounds.
Theorem 4. After the algorithm stabilizes, it spends 2(n-1) rounds to accomplish a token circulation cycle.
Proof. It is obviously that each edge is traversed twice for a token circulation; hence it spends 2(n-1) rounds to take a token circulation cycle after stabilizing.

5   Concluding Remarks

In this paper, we presented a uniform self-stabilization token circulation algorithm by using edge tokens, which works under the distributed scheduler with the read/write atomicity. The maximum stabilizing time of the algorithm is O(**n**) rounds. The result is better than previous works. Most of the previous works need O($\mathbf{n} \times \mathbf{D}$) rounds, where $\mathbf{D}$ is the degree of network. The protocol in [17] also needs O($\mathbf{n}$) time complexity, but it is not a uniform algorithm.

Due to the D pointer deign, the token circulates among the nodes of the tree fairly and follows the depth-first-search order. No matter how many tokens exist initially, one and only one token will survive. Before this surviving token completes one circulation cycle, all other initially existing tokens must disappear. Therefore, we may say that the proposed algorithm has the snap stabilizing property for this surviving token.

References

[1]   Beaquier J, Debas O, An optimal self-stabilizing algorithm for mutual exclusion on bidirectional non uniform rings, Proc. Second Workshop Self-Stabilizing System, 1995.

[2]   Brown GM, Gouda MG, Wu CL, Token systems that self-stabilizing. IEEE Trans. Comput , 38:845-852, 1989.

[3]   Burns JE, Pachl J, Uniform self-stabilizing rings. ACM Trans. Program Lang. Syst. 11(2): 330-344, 1989.

[4]   Chandy KM and Misra J, The drinking philosophers problem. ACM Transaction on Programming Languages and Systems, Vol.6, No. 4, Oct. 1984, pp.632-646.

[5]   Datta AK, Johnen C, Petit F and Villain V, Self-stabilizing depth-first token circulation in arbitrary rooted networks. Distributed Computing, 13: 207-218, 2000.

[6]   Dijkstra EW, Hierarchical Ordering of sequential processes. In operating Systems Techniques, C.A.R Hoare and R.H. Perrott, Eds., Academic Press, New York, 1972.

[7]   Dijkstra EW, Self stabilizing systems in spite of distributed control. *Communications of the Association of the Computing Machinery*, 17:643-644, 1974.

[8]   Dijkstra EW, A belated proof of self-stabilization. Distributed Computing, 1:5-6, 1986.

[9]   Dolev S, Israeli A, and Moran S Self-Stabilizing of dynamic systems assuming only read/write atomicity. Distributed Computing, 7:3-16, 1993.

[10]   Johnen C, Alari G, Beaquier J and Datta AK, Self-stabilizing depth-first token passing on rooted networks. In WDAG97 Distributed Algorithms 11th International Workshop Processings, Springer-Verlag LNCS:1320, page 260-274,1997.

[11]   Johnen C and Beaquier J, Debas O, Space-efficient distributed self-stabilizing depth-first token circulation. In proceedings of the second Workshop on Self-Stabilizing Systems, p.4.1-4.15, 1995.

[12]   Kruijer HSM, Self-stabilization (in spite of distributed control) in tree-structured systems. Information Process Letter, 8:91-95, 1979.

[13]   Huang ST and Chen NS, Self-stabilizing depth-first token circulation on networks. Distributed Computing, 7:61-66, 1993.

[14] Huang ST and Hung SS, Self-stabilizing Edge-Token and Its Applications. Journal of High Speed Networks Special Issue on SELF-STABILIZING SYSTEMS 2002, Submitting.

[15] Huang ST and Wuu LC, Self-stabilizing token circulation in uniform networks. Distributed Computing, 10:181-187, 1997.

[16] Petit F, Highly space-efficient self-stabilizing depth-first token circulation for trees. In OPOSDIS'97, International Conference On Principles Of Distributed System Proceedings, p221-235. 1997.

[17] Petit F, Fast Self-Stabilizing Depth-First Token Circulation. 5th International Workshop on Self-Stabilizing Systems (WSS '01), LNCS 2194, pages 200-215, 2001.

[18] Petit F, Villain V, Color optimal self-stabilizing depth-first token circulation. Third International Symposium on Parallel Architectures, Algorithms and Networks (I-SPAN'97), IEEE Computer Society Press, pages 317-323, 1997.

[19] Petit F, Villain V, Time and space optimality of distributed depth-first token circulation algorithms. DIMACS Workshop on Distributed Data and Structures, Carleton Univerty Press, pages 91-106, 1999. Also presented at Dagsthul Workshop on SS (October 2000).

[20] Petit F, Villain V, Optimality and self-stabilization in rooted tree networks. Parallel Processing Letters, 10(1):3-14, 2000.

Self-Stabilizing Atomicity Refinement Allowing Neighborhood Concurrency

Sébastien Cantarell[1], Ajoy K. Datta[2], and Franck Petit[3]

[1] LRI/CNRS, Université de Paris-Sud, France
[2] School of Computer Science, University of Nevada Las Vegas, USA
[3] LaRIA, Université de Picardie Jules Verne, France

Abstract. We propose a new resource sharing problem, called *Local Resource Allocation* (LRA) which deals with resource sharing problem among neighboring processes. LRA allows neighboring processes to access resources (i.e., their critical sections) concurrently provided the resources are not conflicting with each other. We first present a self-stabilizing solution to the LRA problem. We then use the proposed solution to design a self-stabilizing transformer to transform algorithms written using strong assumptions (e.g., central daemon or composite atomicity) to those using weaker assumptions (distributed read/write atomicity model). To our knowledge, this is the first self-stabilizing transformer which allows neighborhood concurrency. Moreover, the proposed solution preserves the silent property of the original algorithms.

1 Introduction

Many different resource sharing problems based on various assumptions have been studied. Mutual exclusion problem [7, 18] deals with accessing a resource by at most one process at one time. Group mutual exclusion problem [15] allows concurrent access by processes as long as all the processes use the same resource. The readers-writers problem [6] also allows concurrency among processes with some restriction on the type of access (read vs. write). There is another class of problems, called local mutual exclusion problems, which deal with restricting access to resources among neighboring processes. The dining philosophers problem [9] and drinking philosophers problem [5] belong to this category. In [17], Kean and Moir proposed a general structure for the resource sharing problems, called general resource allocation synchronization problem. Their solution is based on a new solution to the dining philosophers problem. This general framework provides solutions to many problems, including mutual exclusion, group mutual exclusion, reader-writers, and drinking philosophers. None of those solutions is self-stabilizing.

Many self-stabilizing algorithms have been written assuming that the neighboring processes communicate using communication registers. The strongest of such models is known as the *state* model in which processes can access the state of all its neighbors and update its own state in one atomic step [8]. The weakest communication model with registers is known as the *read/write atomicity*

S.-T. Huang and T. Herman (Eds.): SSS 2003, LNCS 2704, pp. 102–112, 2003.
© Springer-Verlag Berlin Heidelberg 2003

model [12], where a process can only atomically read the state of any one of its neighbors or atomically update its own state. In both models, concurrent execution of actions among processes is modeled by the interleaving model in which the actions are driven by a scheduler or daemon. The most common daemons are the *central* daemon (only one process can execute an atomic step at one time) and the *distributed* daemon (several processes can execute an atomic step at the same time). An orthogonal combination of of communication model and daemon constitutes the execution environment. The strongest model, sometime referred to as the *serial* model, assumes the state model and central daemon. The weaker model, referred to as the *distributed read/write atomicity* model, assumes the read/write atomicity model with the distributed daemon. The main goal of this paper is to design a transformation technique from stronger daemon based to weaker daemon based algorithms with an additional nice property of allowing the neighborhood concurrency.

Related Work. There has been a lot of research in the topic of daemon transformation in the recent years [1, 3, 13, 16, 20, 21, 22]. Nesterenko and Arora [22] used the phrase *Atomicity Refinement* to define a similar but a more general problem in the sense that atomicity refinement also includes daemon refinement. In [22], "high-atomicity" and "low-atomicity" models were used to refer to the strongest and the weakest model, respectively. As it is pointed out in [22], a straightforward solution to the daemon refinement problem is to execute every action of high-atomicity based algorithm mutually exclusively. This can be achieved by composing the original algorithm with a mutual exclusion algorithm written in the low-atomicity model. Although this is a simple solution to the daemon/atomicity refinement problem, this solution has a serious drawback — the neighboring processors must sequentially execute their actions. In other words, this approach does not allow concurrency among the neighboring processors. All the solutions use a local mutual exclusion mechanism which guarantees that no neighboring processes execute their critical sections simultaneously.

The transformation algorithm proposed in [20] uses unbounded timestamps [19]. Timestamps are also the basis of the solution proposed in [21] and [3]. The algorithm in [21] maintains the silent property [10]. Two algorithms are presented in [3]. One uses unbounded timestamps, and the other uses a bounded timestamp mechanism requiring only $O(\log n^2)$ bits. Both algorithms of [3] are not silent. The algorithms in [1, 13, 16, 22] are also solutions using bounded space. The algorithm in [22] achieves the best performance in terms of *step complexity* (the average number of low-atomicity actions a process executes to simulate a high-atomicity action) and *synchronization delay* (the average number of causally related low-atomicity actions executed between two high-atomicity actions). In a recent paper [16], two self-stabilizing algorithms assuming chromatic process identifiers (no two neighboring processes have the same identifier) were presented.

All existing (self-stabilizing) solutions to the daemon refinement problem (as discussed above) are based on a local mutual exclusion mechanism. So, they do not allow concurrent execution of neighboring processes. That is, in those solutions, even if two actions in two neighboring processes use disjoint sets of variables, they cannot be executed concurrently.

Contributions. The contribution of this paper is twofold. First, we define the *Local Resource Allocation* (LRA) problem. The LRA problem allows neighboring processes to enter their critical sections concurrently provided they do not use conflicting resources. We present a self-stabilizing solution to the LRA problem.

Second, we use the LRA algorithm to design a self-stabilizing atomicity refinement scheme. The proposed scheme transforms algorithms written in a high-atomicity model into the low-atomicity (distributed read/write atomicity) model. Unlike the previous solutions, the proposed solution allows neighborhood concurrency. Moreover, the presented scheme preserves the silent property.

Paper Organization. In the next section (Section 2), we describe the distributed systems and the model we consider in this paper. In Section 3, we present the specification of the LRA problem. Section 4 includes the LRA algorithm and its correctness proof. In section 5, the transformer is presented. Finally, concluding remarks are provided in Section 6.

2   Preliminaries

Distributed System. A *distributed system* $\mathcal{P}$ is an undirected connected graph whose nodes are processes and edges are *bidirectional communication links*. Each process p is assumed to have a unique identifier. A communication link (p, q) between processes p and q exists iff p and q are neighbors. Each process p maintains a set of distinct labels, denoted as N_p, such that each label identifies a (unique) neighbor. To simplify the presentation, we refer to a link (p, q) of process p simply by the *label* q.

Program. Each process consists of a (finite) set of *variables* and a (finite) set of *actions*. We refer to a variable v of process p as v_p. The communication among neighboring processes is carried out using *communication registers*, henceforth also referred to as *shared* variables. An atomic operation on shared variables is either a single read operation or a single write operation on one shared variable, i.e., we assume the read/write atomicity model [12]. Each action is uniquely identified by a label $\mathcal{A}$ and is of the following form:

$$\mathcal{A} :: \mathcal{G} \longrightarrow \mathcal{S}$$

Guard $\mathcal{G}$ of an action in the program of a process p ("an action of p", for short) is a boolean expression that depends on the values of variables of p and variables of its neighbor processes. When the guard $\mathcal{G}$ of an action labeled $\mathcal{A}$ of p is true, then the process p and the action $\mathcal{A}$ are said to be *enabled*. The statement $\mathcal{S}$ of an action $\mathcal{A}$ of p updates one or more variables of p and can be executed only if the guard $\mathcal{G}$ of $\mathcal{A}$ evaluates to true.

An assignment of values to variables of all processes in the system $\mathcal{P}$ is a *state* of $\mathcal{P}$. A *computation* of $\mathcal{P}$ is a *maximal fair* sequence of transitions $\alpha \mapsto \beta$ such that for each state α, β is obtained by executing the statement of some actions that are enabled in α. *Maximality* means that the sequence is either infinite, or it is finite and no action is enabled in the final state. *Fairness* means that if a processor p is continuously enabled, then p eventually executes an action.

Self-Stabilization. Let $\mathcal{X}$ be a set. $x \vdash P$ means that an element $x \in \mathcal{X}$ satisfies the predicate P defined on the set $\mathcal{X}$. We define a special predicate true as follows: *for any* $x \in \mathcal{X}$, $x \vdash$ true.

Let $\mathcal{P}$ be a distributed system and R and S predicates on the states of $\mathcal{P}$. R is *closed* if every state of the computation of $\mathcal{P}$ that starts in a state satisfying R also satisfies R. R *converges* to S in $\mathcal{P}$ if R is closed in $\mathcal{P}$, S is closed in $\mathcal{P}$, and any computation starting from a state satisfying R contains a state satisfying S. $\mathcal{P}$ *stabilizes* to R iff true converges to R in $\mathcal{P}$.

3   Local Resource Allocation

As in all mutual exclusion problems, we assume that a process follows a cycle, moving from its *remainder* (or *non-critical*) section to its *entry* section, then to its *critical* section, then to its *exit* section, and then back again to its remainder section. The LRA problem is to design a protocol, henceforth referred to as LRA protocol (or *layer*), for the entry and exit sections. The remainder and critical sections are assumed to contain the code of an application layer. A process can access a resource only inside its critical section. We assume that processes execute their critical section in finite but unknown time.

Definition 1 (Compatibility). *Two resources X and Y are said to be **compatible**, denoted by $X \rightleftharpoons Y$, if two neighboring processes can access X and Y concurrently. Otherwise, X and Y are said to be **conflicting**, denoted by $X \not\rightleftharpoons Y$.*

The LRA problem deals with sharing compatible resources among neighboring processes. More formally, the LRA problem is to design a protocol (for the entry and exit sections) so that the following two properties are true in every execution:

Resource Conflict Free (Safety):   If two neighboring processes p and q are executing their critical sections simultaneously using X and Y, respectively, then $X \rightleftharpoons Y$.

No Lockout (Liveness):   If a process p requests to enter its critical section, then p eventually executes its critical section.

To avoid unnecessary synchronization, we are looking for algorithms that allow higher degree of concurrency among the neighboring processors, i.e., a process p requesting to access a resource X must not lock a neighbor requesting to access a resource $Y \rightleftharpoons X$.

4   Self-Stabilizing LRA Protocol

A process p records the resource compatibilities in a *compatibility graph* $CG_p = (\mathcal{R}_p, \mathcal{C}_p)$ where $\mathcal{R}_p$ (the nodes of the graph) represents the set of resources that can be accessed by p, and $\mathcal{C}_p$ (the set of edges) denotes the pairs of compatible resources.

The application layer and LRA are synchronized using two variables $Request_p \in \mathcal{R} \cup \{\perp\}$ and a boolean variable $Grant_p$. When a process p does not request for any resource, $Request_p$ contains $\perp$. Every time p moves from its non-critical section to the entry section, p non-deterministically chooses a resource X from $\mathcal{R}$ which is stored in $Request_p$. Similarly, when p moves from its critical section to the exit section, p sets $Request_p$ to $\perp$. $Grant_p$ can only be written by the LRA layer. $Grant_p$ is used by the LRA layer to inform the application layer that p is granted entry to the critical section. So, $Request_p$ (respectively, $Grant_p$) is written only by the application layer (respectively, the LRA layer), and is a *read-only* variable for the LRA layer (respectively, the application layer). The application layer can be described as follows:

$$\vdots$$

Req :: $(Request_p = \perp) \wedge (\neg Grant_p) \wedge (\text{Resource } X \in \mathcal{R} \text{ is requested}) \longrightarrow$
$\qquad\qquad Request_p := X;$

CS :: $(Request_p \neq \perp) \wedge Grant_p \longrightarrow$
$\qquad\qquad << \text{Critical Section} >>; \; Request_p := \perp;$

$$\vdots$$

A process p maintains an integer variable c_p which is accessed only by the LRA layer. Each pair (c_p, p) constitutes the *timestamp* (or *logical clock*) [19]. For every pair of neighbors p and q, $(c_p, p) \prec (c_q, q)$ iff $(c_p < c_q) \vee ((c_p = c_q) \wedge (p < q))$. When a process p is not requesting to execute its critical section, c_p is set to 0. When $Request_p \neq \perp$ and $c_p > 0$, p is said to be a *competitor*, i.e., p is requesting a resource. It is well-known that $\prec$ defines a total ordering and defines a *precedence graph* [5] $\mathcal{H}$ (also called *wait-for graph*), which is a *dynamic directed* graph where the nodes are the processes. An edge (p, q) exists iff (*i*) p and q are neighbors and (*ii*) both p and q are competitors. Without loss of generality, the edge (p, q) is directed from p to q iff $(c_q, q) \prec (c_p, p)$.

Remark 1 ([5]). The graph $\mathcal{H}$ is acyclic.

Algorithm 1 consists of three actions.

1. Action A_1 is enabled when p wants to enter its critical section, i.e., p is ready to enter its entry section. p examines c_q of each of its neighbors q (in an arbitrary order) to find the maximum value of c_q (let us call it *max*), then sets c_p to $max + 1$.

Algorithm 1 Self-Stabilizing LRA Algorithm for Process p

Constants:
  N_p : The set of neighbors of p;
  $\mathcal{CG}_p = (\mathcal{R}_p, \mathcal{C}_p)$: The compatibility graph;

Uses:
  $Request_p \in \mathcal{R}_p \cup \{\bot\}$;

Variables:
  $Grant_p$: **boolean**;
  c_p: **positive integer**;

Macros:
  $p \prec q \equiv (c_p < c_q) \vee (c_p = c_q \wedge p < q)$
  $Ready_p \equiv (\forall q \in N_p : (c_q > 0) \Rightarrow$
    $((p \prec q) \vee ((Request_q \neq \bot) \Rightarrow (Request_p \rightleftharpoons Request_q))))$

Actions:

  $A_1 ::$ $(Request_p \neq \bot) \wedge (c_p = 0) \wedge \neg Grant_p \longrightarrow c_p := max(c_q|\ q \in N_p) + 1$;
  $A_2 ::$ $(Request_p \neq \bot) \wedge (c_p > 0) \wedge Ready_p \wedge \neg Grant_p \longrightarrow Grant_p := \mathbf{true}$;
  $A_3 ::$ $(Request_p = \bot) \wedge (Grant_p \vee (c_p > 0)) \longrightarrow Grant_p := \mathbf{false}; c_p := 0$;

---

2. In Action A_2, process p checks every contending neighbor q (in an arbitrary order). Process q is a contender if $c_q > 0$. p scans both c_q and $Request_q$. A neighbor q may prevent p to enter its critical section only when $q \prec p$ and $Request_q \neq Request_p$, i.e., when q requests for a resource which is in conflict with the resource requested by p and q made its request before p did. If none of the neighbors of p is in this state (all the neighbors of p which made their request before p requested for a compatible resource), then p is granted entry into its critical section ($Grant_p := \mathbf{true}$).

3. Action A_3 is enabled when p finishes using its resource. $Grant_p$ and c_p are reset to **false** and 0, respectively.

Note that as we consider the read/write atomicity model in this work, it the computations of the maximum c value and Macro $Ready_p$ (involving neighbors' registers) are not done in one atomic step.

4.1   Proof of Correctness

The proof follows the approach used in [21].
  We now define Predicate $\mathcal{T}$ on the system states.

Definition 2 (Predicate $\mathcal{T}$). *A state α satisfies Predicate $\mathcal{T}$ ($\alpha \vdash \mathcal{T}$) iff, for all possible transitions $\alpha \mapsto \beta$,*
if there exists a process p in α such that $c_p > 0$ and $Ready_p$ is true, then, if $c_p > 0$ in β and if a neighbor q of p sets c_q to x in the transition $\alpha \mapsto \beta$, then $((c_q, q) \prec (c_p, p)$ in $\beta) \Rightarrow x = 0$.

Even though the solution to the local mutual exclusion problem proposed in [21] does not set c_p to 0, the following result can be easily derived from their work:

Lemma 1 ([21]). *Algorithm 1 is self-stabilizing with respect to Predicate T.*

Theorem 1 (Resource Conflict Free). *If Predicate T holds, then if two neighboring processes p and q are executing their critical sections simultaneously using X and Y, respectively, then $X \rightleftharpoons Y$.*

Proof. Without loss of generality, let p be a competitor requesting Resource X. From Lemma 1 and Definition 2, if $Ready_p$ is true, then any neighbor q of p executing Action A_1 cannot set c_q to a value such that $(c_q, q) \prec (c_p, p)$. Assume by contradiction that while p does not execute Action A_3 (i.e., the time during which p is either executing or allowed to enter its critical section), a neighbor q of p exists such that q requests Resource Y, $X \neq Y$, and q enters its critical section. There are two cases:

1. $(c_q, q) \prec (c_p, p)$. To enter the critical section, $Ready_q$ must be true. So, $Resquest_q \rightleftharpoons Resquest_p$, which contradicts the assumption.
2. $(c_p, p) \prec (c_q, q)$. Then, $Ready_q$ is false, a contradiction.

$\square$

Next, we show (Lemma 2) that if process p is no longer enabled, then either p requests to enter its critical section a finite number of times, or p is never allowed by its neighbors to enter its critical section. This is used to prove the no lockout property (Theorem 2).

Lemma 2. *If Predicate T holds, a process p is infinitely often enabled iff none of the following two conditions is true forever:*

(1) $Request_p = \perp$,
(2) $\neg Ready_p$.

Proof. Case $\Rightarrow$. We prove this by contradiction. Assume that a process p is infinitely often enabled and $Request_p = \perp$ or $\neg Ready_p$ holds forever. We consider two cases:

1. $Request_p = \perp$ forever. Then, only Action $A3$ can be enabled infinitely often at p. (Actions $A1$ and $A2$ can be enabled infinitely often only if $Request_p \neq \perp$ infinitely often.) So, $(Grant_p \vee (c_p > 0))$ holds infinitely often. This contradicts the fact that Actions $A1$ and $A2$ are not infinitely often enabled.
2. $\neg Ready_p$ holds forever. Then, Action $A2$ is not enabled infinitely often on p. To execute either Action $A1$ or Action $A3$ infinitely often, c_p must be switched from 0 to $x \neq 0$, and again from $x \neq 0$ to 0. So, infinite execution of either Action $A1$ or Action $A3$ implies that $A1$ and $A3$ are alternatively executed infinitely often. Thus, $Request_p$ infinitely often switches from $\perp$ to $X \neq \perp$, and again from $X \neq \perp$ to $\perp$. To change $Request_p$ from $X \neq \perp$ to $\perp$, p must execute its critical section. This contradicts the assumption that $\neg Ready_p$ holds forever.

Case $\Leftarrow$. We prove this case also by contradiction. Assume that there exists a process p such that eventually, p is not enabled and none of the above two conditions ((1) and (2)) is true forever. Consider any state in which p is no longer enabled (forever). We need to consider the following two cases:

1. $Request_p = \perp$. If $Grant_p$ is true, then Action A_3 is enabled, which contradicts the assumption. If $Grant_p$ is false, then since $Request_p$ cannot be equal to $\perp$ forever, p eventually sets $Request_p$ to $X \neq \perp$ (by executing Req of the application layer). Then, Action A_1 is enabled, a contradiction.

2. $Request_p \neq \perp$. If $Grant_p$ is true, then p eventually sets $Request_p$ to $\perp$ (by executing Action CS of the application layer). That leads to Case 1. If $Grant_p$ is false, then $c_p > 0$ (otherwise, A_1 is enabled). Since by assumption, $Ready_p$ is eventually true, Action A_2 is eventually enabled, a contradiction.

$\square$

Theorem 2 (No Lockout). *If Predicate $\mathcal{T}$ holds, if a process p requests to enter its critical section, then p eventually executes its critical section.*

Proof. It is easy to verify that every process p which requests to access a resource is eventually in a state where $Request_p \neq \perp$, $Grant_p$ is false, and $c_p > 0$. Assume by contradiction that p never enters its critical section. So, $Ready_p$ is never true. Thus, there exists $q \in N_p$ such that $Request_p \neq Request_q$ and $(p \rightarrow q) \in \mathcal{H}$, where $(p \rightarrow q)$ is the directed edge from p to q in the precedence graph. Since Predicate $\mathcal{T}$ holds, eventually, no neighbor of p can be added to $\mathcal{H}'$, where $\mathcal{H}'$ is the subgraph of $\mathcal{H}$ reachable from p.

From Remark 1, at least one sink process exists in $\mathcal{H}'$. Let s be one of them. Since $s \in \mathcal{H}$, $Request_s \neq \perp$ and $c_s > 0$. From Lemma 2, no action among A_1, A_2, and A_3 is enabled at s iff either $Request_s = \perp$ forever, or $Ready_s$ is false forever. Process s not being waiting for another process (s is a sink), neither $Request_s = \perp$ forever nor $Ready_s$ is false forever. Thus, Process s eventually leaves $\mathcal{H}'$. Since there is a finite number of processes in $\mathcal{H}'$, by repeating the above argument on sink processes in $\mathcal{H}'$, p eventually becomes a sink process and $Ready_p$ becomes true. This contradicts the assumption. $\square$

From Lemma 1, Theorem 1, and Theorem 2, we can claim the following theorem:

Theorem 3. *Algorithm 1 is a self-stabilizing LRA algorithm.*

5   Atomicity Transformation

In this section, we describe how to use Algorithm LRA to transform any high-atomicity algorithm into the low-atomicity model considered in this paper, i.e., the read/write atomicity model.

Definition 3 (Action-Compatibility). *Let p, q be two neighboring processes. Two actions labeled A_p and A_q of a distributed program $\mathcal{P}$, respectively of p and q,* are said to be compatible w.r.t. $\mathcal{P}$, denoted by $A_p \rightleftharpoons_{\mathcal{P}} A_q$, iff none of the variables written in Action A_p (respectively, A_q) is read in Action A_q (respectively, A_p). When A_p and A_q are not compatible, they are said to be conflicting, denoted by $A_p \not\rightleftharpoons_{\mathcal{P}} A_q$.

Using Definition 3, for each process p, we build the *action-compatibility graph* of a high-atomicity program $\mathcal{P}$, $\mathcal{AG}_p = (\mathcal{A}_p, \mathcal{C}_p)$, as follows: The nodes $(\mathcal{A}_p)$ are the action labels of p and all its neighbors q, and an edge between two actions A_p and A_q indicates that these actions are action-compatible w.r.t. $\mathcal{P}$, i.e., $A_p \rightleftharpoons_{\mathcal{P}} A_q$.

We now build a new program, $\mathcal{P}^+$, as the result of the following composition:

1. $\mathcal{P}^+$ contains all the variables of both Program $\mathcal{P}$ and Algorithm LRA.
2. $\mathcal{P}^+$ contains Actions A_1, A_2, and A_3 of Algorithm LRA.
3. For each action $\mathcal{A}_X :: \mathcal{G}_X \longrightarrow \mathcal{S}_X$ of $\mathcal{P}$, we add the following two actions to $\mathcal{P}^+$:

$$
\begin{aligned}
\mathcal{A}_X^1 \quad &:: \quad (Request_p = \bot) \wedge (\neg Grant_p) \wedge \mathcal{G}_X \longrightarrow Request_p := X; \\
\mathcal{A}_X^2 \quad &:: \quad (Request_p = X) \wedge Grant_p \longrightarrow \mathcal{S}_X; \; Request_p := \bot;
\end{aligned}
$$

Note that if no guard of Program $\mathcal{P}$ is ever enabled, then no guard of Algorithm LRA is also ever enabled ($Request_p$ eventually becomes equal to $\bot$, and remains true forever). So, Algorithm $\mathcal{P}^+$ is a silent algorithm. Clearly, by construction, the resource conflict free property of the LRA algorithm guarantees that, if two neighboring processes p and q concurrently execute Actions A_p and Action A_q, respectively, then A_p and A_q are compatible. Also, the no lockout property of Algorithm LRA ensures that if a process needs to execute an action A_p of the high-atomicity algorithm, then A_p is eventually executed. Moreover, Algorithm $\mathcal{P}^+$ preserves the stabilization property of both Program $\mathcal{P}$ and Algorithm LRA. This leads to the following final result:

Theorem 4. *Algorithm $\mathcal{P}^+$ provides a silent algorithm for the atomicity refinement problem.*

6   Conclusion

We presented the local resource allocation (LRA) problem and gave a self-stabilizing solution to that problem. We use the LRA algorithm to design a self-stabilizing transformer to transform any algorithm written in a high-atomicity model into the low-atomicity model which is the distributed read/write atomicity model. The solution allows two neighboring processes to execute an action of the high-atomicity algorithm concurrently, provided that the actions do not interfere with each other. Moreover, the proposed solution preserves the silent property of the high-atomicity algorithm.

The proposed solution is based on the self-stabilizing local mutual exclusion algorithm presented in [21], which uses an unbounded variable. As pointed out by Mizuno and Nesterenko, we can assume that any process can detect an overflow. By triggering a reset algorithm working in the read/write atomicity model (e.g., [2]), the timestamp counters can be reset in the whole network. None of the existing solutions using bounded variables [3, 13, 16, 22] are silent. The reason is that all of them require that neighboring processes must be strongly synchronized, which is not directly compatible with the LRA problem. That indicates the difficulty of designing a bounded solution to the LRA problem. However, that is the main goal of our future research.

Acknowledgments

We are thankful to Vincent Villain for his helpful comments.

References

[1] G. Antonoiu and P. K. Srimani. Mutual exclusion between neighboring nodes in an arbitrary system graph tree that stabilizes using read/write atomicity. In *Euro-par'99 Parallel Processing, Proceedings, Springer-Verlag LNCS:1685*, pages 824–830, 1999. 103

[2] A. Arora and M. G. Gouda. Distributed reset. *IEEE Transactions on Computers*, 43:1026–1038, 1994. 111

[3] J. Beauquier, A. K. Datta, M. Gradinariu, and F. Magniette. Self-stabilizing local mutual exclusion and daemon refinement. In *Proceedings of the 14th International Conference on Distributed Computing (DISC 2000), Springer-Verlag LNCS:1914*, pages 223–237, 2000. 103, 111

[4] J. Beauquier, M. Gradinariu, and C. Johnen. Cross-over composition - enforcement of fairness under unfair adversary. In *Proceedings of the Fifth Workshop on Self-Stabilizing Systems, Springer-Verlag LNCS:2194*, pages 19–34, 2001.

[5] K. M. Chandy and J. Misra. The drinking philosophers problem. *ACM Transactions on Programming Languages and Systems*, 6(4):632–646, 1984. 102, 106

[6] P. J. Courtois, F. Heymans, and D. L. Parnas. Concurrent control with readers and writers. *Communications of the Association of the Computing Machinery*, 14(10):667–668, 1971. 102

[7] E. W. Dijkstra. Solution to a problem in concurrent programming control. *Communications of the Association of the Computing Machinery*, 8(9):569, 1965. 102

[8] E. W. Dijkstra. Self stabilizing systems in spite of distributed control. *Communications of the Association of the Computing Machinery*, 17:643–644, 1974. 102

[9] E. W. Dijkstra. Two starvation-free solutions of a general exclusion problem. Technical Report EWD 625, Plataanstraat 5, 5671, AL Nuenen, The Netherlands, 1978. 102

[10] S. Dolev, M. Gouda, and M. Schneider. Memory requirements for silent stabilization. In *PODC96 Proceedings of the Fifteenth Annual ACM Symposium on Principles of Distributed Computing*, pages 27–34, 1996. 103

[11] S. Dolev and T. Herman. Parallel composition of stabilizing algorithms. In *Proceedings of the Fourth Workshop on Self-Stabilizing Systems, IEEE Computer Society*, pages 25–32. IEEE Computer Society Press, 1999.

[12] S. Dolev, A. Israeli, and S. Moran. Self-stabilizing of dynamic systems assuming only read/write atomicity. *Distributed Computing*, 7:3–16, 1993. 103, 104

[13] M. Gouda and F. Haddix. The alternator. In *Proceedings of the Fourth Workshop on Self-Stabilizing Systems, IEEE Computer Society*, pages 48–53, 1999. 103, 111

[14] M. G. Gouda and T. Herman. Adaptive programming. *IEEE Transactions on Software Engineering*, 17:911–921, 1991.

[15] Y.-J. Joung. Asynchronous group mutual exclusion (extended abstract). In *Proceedings of the 17th Annual ACM Symposium on Principles of Distributed Computing (PODC)*, pages 51–60, June 28-July 2 1998. 102

[16] H. Kakugawa and M. Yamashita. Self-stabilizing local mutual exclusion on networks in which process identifiers are not distinct. In *Proceedings of the 21st Symposium on Reliable Distributed Systems (SRDS2002)*, pages 202–211, 2002. 103, 111

[17] P. Keane and M. Moir. A general resource allocation synchronization problem. In *Proceedings of the 23th IEEE International Conference on Distributed Computing Systems (ICDCS)*, pages 557–566. ACM Press, 2001. 102

[18] L. Lamport. A new solution of Dijkstra's concurrent programming problem. *Communications of the ACM*, 17(8):453–455, 1974. 102

[19] L. Lamport. Time, clocks and the ordering of events in a distributed system. *Communications of the ACM*, 21(7):558–565, 1978. 103, 106

[20] M. Mizuno and H. Kakugawa. A timestamp based transformation of self-stabilizing programs for distributed computing environments. In *WDAG96 Distributed Algorithms 10th International Workshop Proceedings, Springer-Verlag LNCS:1151*, pages 304–321, 1996. 103

[21] M. Mizuno and Nesterenko. A transformation of self-stabilizing serial model programs for asynchronous parallel computing environments. *Information Processing Letters*, 66(6):285–290, 1998. 103, 107, 108, 111

[22] M. Nesterenko and A. Arora. Stabilization-preserving atomicity refinement. *Journal of Parallel and Distributed Computing*, 62(5):766–791, 2002. 103, 111

A New Self-Stabilizing k-out-of-ℓ Exclusion Algorithm on Rings

Ajoy K. Datta[1], Rachid Hadid[2], and Vincent Villain[2]

[1] School of Computer Science, University of Nevada Las Vegas
datta@cs.unlv.edu
[2] LaRIA, Université de Picardie Jules Verne
5, rue de Moulin Neuf, 80000 Amiens France
{hadid,villain}@laria.u-picardie.fr

Abstract. We present an efficient self-stabilizing solution to the k-out-of-ℓ exclusion problem on a ring. The k-out-of-ℓ exclusion problem is a generalization of the well-known mutual exclusion problem — there are ℓ units of a shared resource, any process can request at most k $(1 \leq k \leq \ell)$ units of the shared resource, and no resource unit can be allocated to more than one process at one time. This solution is based on the circulation of ℓ tokens around the ring. A processor requesting NEED (NEED $\leq k \leq \ell$) units of the resource can enter the critical section only upon receipt of NEED tokens. We propose a simple and pessimistic method to handle the deadlock problem. So, after stabilization, no mechanism is needed for the deadlock detection. Moreover, in this paper, we give a formal definition of a new efficiency property, called (k, ℓ)-*liveness*, which is a desirable property of any k-out-of-ℓ exclusion solution. This property allows as many processors as possible to execute their critical sections simultaneously without violating the safety property. We generalize the technique introduced in [6] to maintain the right number (ℓ) tokens in the system. The tokens are counted without using any counter variable for all processors except one, called the Root. This solution improves the waiting time of an earlier solution [4] by maintaining a reasonable stabilization time. The waiting time is reduced from $(\ell + 2)(n - 1)$ to $2(n - 1)$, where n is the size of the ring. The stabilization time is $8n$ instead of $4n$ in [4]. One nice characteristic of our algorithm is that its space requirement is independent of ℓ for all processors except the Root.

Keywords: Fault-tolerance, k-out-of-ℓ exclusion, mutual exclusion, ℓ-exclusion, self-stabilization.

1 Introduction

The ℓ-*exclusion problem* is a generalization of the mutual exclusion problem — ℓ processors are allowed to execute the critical section concurrently. This problem models the situation where there is a pool of ℓ units of a shared resource and each processor can request at most one unit. The k-out-of-ℓ *exclusion* problem allows every processor to request at most k $(1 \leq k \leq \ell)$ units of the shared

S.-T. Huang and T. Herman (Eds.): SSS 2003, LNCS 2704, pp. 113–128, 2003.
© Springer-Verlag Berlin Heidelberg 2003

resources, but no unit can be assigned to more than one processor at the same time [10] . One example of this type of resource sharing is the sharing of channel bandwidth. The bandwidth requirements vary among the requests multiplexing the channel. For example, the demand would be quite different for a video from an audio transmission request. Algorithms (not self-stabilizing) for k-out-of-ℓ exclusion were given in [3, 8, 7, 10, 11]. All these algorithms are permission-based — a processor can access the resource after receiving a permission from all the processors of the system [10, 11] or from the processors constituting the quorum it belongs to [8, 7]. The only self-stabilizing solution to the k-out-of-ℓ exclusion algorithm is presented in [4]. This solution is based on the circulation of ℓ tokens around the ring. A processor requesting k_i ($k_i \leq k \leq \ell$) units of the resource can enter the critical section only upon receipt of k_i tokens. It is shown in [4] that this simple circulation of ℓ tokens is prone to deadlocks. Intuitively, let α be the number of the (critical section entry) requesting processors in the system and β the total number of tokens requested by α processors. If $\beta \geq \ell + \alpha$, then ℓ tokens can be allocated in such a manner that every requesting processor is waiting for at least one token. So, the system has reached a deadlock configuration. The deadlock problem is solved in [4] by using additional control messages.

Contributions. In this paper, we present a self-stabilizing solution to the k-out-of-ℓ exclusion problem on rings. We propose a new solution to the deadlock problem raised in [4]. Contrary to [4], when the system is stabilized, we need no extra control messages for the deadlock detection. The main idea of our solution is that only one of the requesting processors is given the permission to collect enough tokens to enter the critical section. That is, the process of receiving the permission and getting ready to enter the critical section is implemented as a mutually exclusive task. We show that our solution satisfies the (k, ℓ)-liveness property. In addition to its simplicity, this algorithm improves the waiting time of algorithm in [4] from $(\ell + 2)(n - 1)$ to $2(n - 1)$. The system may start in an arbitrary, possibly a deadlocked configuration. Therefore, in the stabilizing solution, we use a deadlock detection and resolution scheme which is used only during the stabilization phase. This detection/resolution scheme is very simple and efficient, and has only a constant overhead both in terms of space and size of messages. We add only a two-bit field in the message. We use a very simple token controller scheme to count and maintain the right number (ℓ) of tokens in the ring. The controller does not generate any additional messages (as produced in [4]). The space requirement of our algorithm is independent of ℓ for all processors except the Root. The stabilization time of the protocol is $8n$.

Outline of the Paper. In Section 2, we describe the model used in this paper. We present the specification of the k-out-of-ℓ exclusion problem in Section 3. We first present a non-self-stabilizing k-out-of-ℓ exclusion protocol in Section 4. Then in Section 5, we extend that solution to design a self-stabilizing k-out-of-ℓ exclusion algorithm. We only present the proof outline of this self-stabilizing solution due to lack of space. Finally, we make some concluding remarks in

Section 6. We use a composition scheme, called parametric composition in our protocol. The composition technique is described in [6] [4].

2   Preliminaries

The Model. The distributed system we consider in this paper is a uni-directional ring. It consists of a set of processors denoted by $0,1,..,n\text{-}1$ communicating asynchronously by exchanging messages. The subscripts $0,1,...,n\text{-}1$ for the processors are used for the presentation only. We assume the existence of a distinguished processor (Processor 0), called Root. Each processor can distinguish its two neighbors: the left neighbor from which it can receive messages and the right neighbor it can send messages to. The left and right neighbors of Processor i are denoted by $i-1$ and $i+1$, respectively, where indices are taken modulo n. We assume that the message delivery time is finite but unbounded. We also consider a message to be in transit until it is processed by the receiving processor. Moreover, each link is assumed to be of bounded capacity, FIFO, and reliable (the messages are neither lost nor corrupted) during and after the stabilization phase. Our protocols are *semi-uniform* as defined in [5] — every processor with the same degree executes the same program, except one processor (which we call Root). The messages are of the following form: $<message\text{-}type, message\text{-}value>$. The *message-value* field is omitted if the message does not carry any value. Some messages contain more than one *message-values*. The program consists of a collection of actions. An action is of the form: $<guard>$ $\longrightarrow <statement>$. A *guard* is a boolean expression over the variables of the processor and/or an *input* message. A *statement* is a sequence of assignments and/or message sending. An action can be executed only if its guard evaluates to true. We assume that the actions are atomically executed, meaning that the evaluation of a guard and the execution of the corresponding statement of an action, if executed, are done in one atomic step. The atomic execution of an action of p is called a *step* of p. When several actions of a processor are simultaneously enabled, then only the first enabled action (as per the text of the protocol) is executed. The *state* of a processor is defined by the values of its variables. The *state* of a system is a vector of $n+1$ components where the first n components represent the state of n processors, and the last one refers to the multi-set of messages in transit in the links. We refer to the state of a processor and the system as a (*local*) *state* and *configuration*, respectively.

Self-Stabilization. A protocol $\mathcal{P}$ is self-stabilizing for a specification $\mathcal{SP}$ (a predicate defined over the computations) if and only if every execution starting from an arbitrary configuration eventually reaches (*convergence*) a configuration from which it satisfies $\mathcal{SP}$ forever (*closure*).

3   The k-out-of-ℓ Exclusion Specification.

In this section, we first present the specification of the k-out-of-ℓ exclusion problem as defined in [10].

- **Safety:** Any resource unit can be used by at most one process at one time and at most ℓ resources can be used simultaneously.
- **Fairness:** If a processor requests at most k units, then its request is eventually satisfied and it enters the critical section.

Another performance metric, called *efficiency* has been introduced in [10]. Intuitively, an algorithm satisfying this property attempts to allow several processors to execute their critical section simultaneously. This property is defined as follows:

- **Efficiency:** As many concurrent requests as possible should be satisfied at the same time provided the safety and fairness are not compromised. This definition addresses the problem that maintaining efficiency may violate safety or fairness. However, our goal is to provide a more convenient parameter to simplify the proofs. In order to formally define this property, we assume that a processor can stay in the critical section forever. This assumption is necessary to formalize the concept of concurrency used in the definition of the efficiency property. Note that we make this assumption only to define this property. Our algorithm does assume that the critical sections are finite. We propose two definitions of the efficiency property. The first one is called *strict (k, ℓ)-liveness*. We then discuss the validity of this definition and show that it leads to a contradiction with fairness. The second derivation, called *(k, ℓ)-liveness*, defines a maximal concurrency property which can be maintained with no impact on the fairness issue.
- **Strict (k, ℓ)-liveness:** Let I be the set of processors executing their critical section forever, and every processor $i \in I$ using $u_i \leq k$ units of the shared resource such that $\sum_{i \in I} u_i = \ell - \beta$. If there exists a requesting processor j such that $u_j \leq \beta$ then, eventually at least one of these processors will enter the critical section.

As we claimed above, this definition may force the system to violate the fairness property. Let us consider an example of 3-out-of-4 exclusion on a network with three processors 0, 1, and 2. We assume that 0 executes the critical section forever with $u_0 = 2$, and 1 and 2 are requesting to enter the critical section with $u_1 = 2$ and $u_2 = 3$, respectively. $I = \{0\}$ and $\beta = 2$. Since our protocol satisfies the strict (k, ℓ)-liveness, Processor 1 must be able to enter the critical section. If we consider as similar situation where $I = \{1\}$, $\beta = 2$, $u_0 = u_1 = 2$, and $u_2 = 3$, then 0 must be able to enter the critical section. So, this protocol can generate the following execution: 0 requests for the CS[1] with $u_0 = 2$, then goes inside the CS. 1 and 2 request for the CS with $u_1 = 2$ and $u_2 = 3$. 1 enters the

---

[1] CS indicates "Critical Section".

CS. 0 exits the CS, but requests to enter again with $u_0 = 2$ while 1 is still in the CS. 0 enters the CS. 1 exits the CS and also requests to enter again with $u_1 = 2$. This execution creates starvation for Processor 2. This reasoning can be easily generalized for any type of k-out-of-ℓ exclusion and any type of network. We redefine the maximum property without violating the fairness:

– (k, ℓ)-**liveness:** Let I be the set of processors executing their critical section forever, and every processor $i \in I$ using $u_i \leq k$ units of the shared resource such that $\sum_{i \in I} u_i = \ell - \beta$. If all the requesting processors j satisfy $u_j \leq \beta$ then, eventually at least one of these processors will enter the critical section.

By using the definition of (k, ℓ)-**liveness**, in the above example, while 0 is in the CS, 1 and 2 do not satisfy $u_1 \leq 2$ and $u_2 \leq 2$. So, neither 1 nor 2 can get in the CS. This avoids the starvation of 2. The (k, ℓ)-**liveness** property characterizes the fact that if a protocol tries to increase the degree of concurrency too much, the protocol may violate fairness. Note that this definition is a well-founded generalization of the ℓ-liveness [1] since for $k = 1$ we match the ℓ-liveness property.

4   Non-self-stabilizing k-out-of-ℓ Exclusion Protocol

We briefly describe the interface between the k-out-of-ℓ exclusion protocol and any application program invoking the protocol. Then we discuss two component modules (*Permission* and ℓ-*Token-Circulation*) which are parametrically composed (denoted by $\triangleright_P$) to design the k-out-of-ℓ exclusion protocol.

The interface consists of three functions as described below:

1. Function STATE returns a value in {*Request, In, Out* }. The three values *Request, In,* and *Out* represent three modes of the application program "requesting to enter", "inside", and "outside" the critical section, respectively.
2. Function NEED returns the number of resource units (i.e., the tokens) requested by the application program.
3. Function ECS (Enter the Critical Section) does not return a value. This function is used by the ℓ-exclusion protocol to send a permission to the application program to enter the critical section.

The task of ℓ-Token-Circulation (in Algorithm 1) is to circulate ℓ tokens in rings such that a processor cannot keep more than k tokens while it is in the critical section. Every processor can request NEED($1 \leq$ NEED $\leq k \leq \ell$) tokens. Processors maintain a variable $T \in \{0, ..., k\}$ which contains the number of tokens held by a processor. A requesting processor can enter its critical section, i.e., access the requested (NEED) units of the shared resource only upon receipt of NEED tokens (Action A_{l2}). A processor needs to hold on to the tokens it already received until it gets all its requested (NEED) tokens (Action A_{l3}). Unfortunately, this "hold and wait" method may cause a deadlock situation which occurs as follows: Assume that ℓ tokens are distributed among the processors in the ring such that every requesting processor is waiting for at least one token. To correct

---

Algorithm 1 Permission $\rhd_P$ ℓ-Token-Circulation

ℓ-**Token-Circulation**(STATE(): {Request, In, Out},
                    NEED():0..k, ECS())

Permission (STATE(): {Request, In, Out }
/* Returns the status of the application
program : requesting to enter, inside,
outside the critical section */)

External Permission(STATE())
Parameters   Function STATE(): {Request, In,
                                    Out }

Public   Function Psend()
         $Ok := False$
         send $<PToken>$
         end Function

         Function Okay(): Boolean
             Return($Ok = True$)
         end Function

–

Variables Ok : Boolean Initially $False$

         /* Program of every processor. */
(A_{p1}) [] ((**receive** $<PToken>$)
         $\wedge$ (STATE() = $Request$)) $\longrightarrow$
             $Ok := True$

(A_{p2}) [] ((**receive** $<PToken>$)
         $\wedge$ (STATE() $\in \{In, Out\}$))) $\longrightarrow$
             Psend()

Variables T : 0..k Initially 0
             $t : 1..\ell$ /* Only for Root */
                          /* Only for Root */
(A_{l0}) [] **Upon Initialization** $\longrightarrow$
             Permission.Psend()
             for $t := 1$ **to** ℓ **do**
                 send $<Token>$

                 /* Program of every processor. */
(A_{l1}) [] ((STATE() = Out) $\wedge$ ($T > 0$)) $\longrightarrow$
             while $T > 0$ **do**
                 send $< Token >$
                 $T := T - 1$

(A_{l2}) [] ((STATE() = $Request$) $\wedge$ ($T \geq$ NEED())) $\longrightarrow$
             Permission.Psend()
             ECS()

(A_{l3}) [] (**receive** $<Token>$) $\longrightarrow$
             if Permission.Okay() **then**
                 $T := T + 1$
             else send $<Token>$

---

this problem, we move a special token, called *permission token* around the ring. (Henceforth, the ℓ token and permission token will be denoted as $Token$ and $PToken$, respectively.) The purpose of the $PToken$ is to ensure that only one processor can accumulate the $Token$s in the system at any time. The processor currently having the $PToken$ is the only processor which can hold on to the $Token$s (see Action A_{l3}). The implementation of the $PToken$ is as follows: Each processor i has a flag (Ok) which is set to true when the $PToken$ arrives at i (Action A_{p1}) and set to false when i sends it to $i + 1$ (Action A_{l2}). When a requesting processor receives the requested number (NEED) of tokens, it passes the permission (the $PToken$) to the next processor and enters the critical section (Action A_{l2}). Upon completion of the critical section execution, it releases all (NEED) tokens.

Let us now explain how the protocol achieves the deadlocks-freedom and the maximum degree of concurrency, i.e., the (k, ℓ)-liveness. We show that among all the requesting processors, eventually one processor enters the critical section. From the discussion in the previous paragraph, it is clear that a processor holds on to the tokens it receives only if it holds the permission token. From Action A_{l2}, before a processor i enters its critical section, it passes the $PToken$ to its right neighbor $i + 1$. From Algorithm 1, the $PToken$ can be stopped only by a requesting processor. So, there must exist a requesting processor i which will eventually receive the $PToken$ (Action A_{p1}). Then even if the rest of the $Token$s are being used by other processors which are in their critical section, since every critical sections is finite, eventually, those processors will exit the critical section and release the *Tokens*. As i is the only processor having the permission to hold the *Tokens*, the *Tokens* will eventually arrive and get accumulated at i. We assume that some processors are waiting to enter their critical section. By hypothesis of the (k, ℓ)-liveness, each processor needs at most $\ell - \beta$ tokens such that β is the number of tokens used by processors which are in their critical section. Then one requesting processor i will eventually receive the *PToken*. As i is the only processor having the permission to hold the *Token*, considering the fact that there are enough free tokens to satisfy the need ($NEED_i$) of i, i eventually receives $NEED_i$ tokens and enters the critical section.

Property 1. The parametric composition *Permission* $\rhd_P$ ℓ-*Tokens-Circulation* (Algorithm 1) guarantees the (k, ℓ)-liveness property.

After initialization, Algorithm 1 neither creates nor destroys any *Token*. The *PToken* implements a fair scheduling of ℓ tokens in the ring such that the next processor to enter the critical section is the first requesting processor reached by the permission token. By Property 1, we can claim the following result:

Theorem 1. *Algorithm 1 satisfies the k-out-of-ℓ exclusion specification.*

5   Self-Stabilizing k-out-of-ℓ Exclusion Protocol

In this section, we extend the non-self-stabilizing k-out-of-ℓ exclusion protocol of Section 4 to a self-stabilizing k-out-of-ℓ exclusion protocol. As in Algorithm 1, we design several modules separately and then compose them to get the final k-out-of-ℓ exclusion protocol.

5.1   Protocols

As in Section 4, we design an ℓ token circulation (Algorithm 2) and a single permission token circulation (Algorithm 4) protocols. However, that is not enough to design a self-stabilizing solution. We need to maintain the right number (ℓ) of tokens in the system. The token controller (Algorithm 3) serves that purpose. In Algorithm 1, we did not deal with the deadlock detection because we assumed a good initial configuration. But now, the system may start in an arbitrary initial configuration, possibly, in a deadlocked situation. So, we add a deadlock detection and resolution scheme (Algorithm 5).

Circulating and Maintaining ℓ Tokens. We use different types of tokens to exchange information among the processors. In addition to the ℓ tokens (*Tokens*) and the permission token (*PToken*), Algorithm 3 (called Token-Controller) circulates a token, called *CToken* to help Root count the number of tokens in the system.

The main function of Algorithm 2 is to circulate and allocate *Tokens*. It is very similar to Algorithm 1. Algorithm 2 uses some functions of Algorithms 3

Algorithm 2 ℓ-Token-Circulation

For Root	**For other processors**
(k, ℓ)-**Exclusion**(STATE(): {Request, In, Out}, NEED(): $0..k$, ECS())	(k, ℓ)-**Exclusion**(STATE(): {Request, In, Out}, NEED(): $0..k$, ECS())
External T-Controller(START, T) Permission(STATE())	**External T-Controller** (SENDTPASS, T, STOP) Permission(STATE())
Parameters Function START() for $t = 1$ to $\ell-$**T-Controller**.TCount do send $<Token>$ end Function	**Parameters** Function SENDTPASS() for $t = 1$ to **T-Controller**.TPass do send $<Token>$ end Function Function STOP(): Boolean Return($T > 0$) end Function
Variables T: $0..k$ $(k \le \ell)$ (used also as Parameter)	**Variables** T: $0..k$ $(k \le \ell)$ (used also as Parameter)

(A_{l1}) [] $((\text{STATE}() = Out)\vee$ $((\text{ STATE}() = Request)$ $\wedge \neg$ **Permission**.Okay())) $\wedge (T > 0) \longrightarrow$ **while** $T > 0$ **do** send $<Token>$ $T := T - 1$	(A_{l4}) [] $((\text{ STATE}() = Out)\vee$ $((\text{ STATE}() = Request)$ $\wedge \neg$ **Permission**.Okay())) $\wedge (T > 0) \longrightarrow$ **while** $(T-$ **T-Controller**.TPass$) > 0$ **do** send $<Token>$ $T := T - 1$ **T-Controller**.CGo()
(A_{l2}) [] $((\text{STATE}()= Request)\wedge$ $(T \ge \text{NEED}())) \longrightarrow$ **Permission**.Psend() ESC	(A_{l5}) [] $((\text{STATE}() = Request))\wedge$ $(T \ge \text{NEED}())) \longrightarrow$ **Permission**.Psend() ESC
(A_{l3}) [] (**receive** $<Token>$) $\wedge$ (**T-Controller**.TCount() $< \ell$) $\longrightarrow$ **T-Controller**.Count_t() **if Permission**.Okay() **then** $T := T + 1$ **else send** $<Token>$	(A_{l6}) [] (**receive** $<Token>$) $\longrightarrow$ **if Permission**.Okay() **then** $T := T + 1$ **else send** $<Token>$ **T-Controller**.CGo()

---

and 4 to circulate, count, and maintain the ℓ *Token*s (see Actions A_{l3}, A_{l4}, and A_{l6}). If the number of *Token*s is less than ℓ, Root replenishes the tokens (Function START in Action A_{c1}). If the number is more than ℓ, then the extra tokens are destroyed by Action A_{l3} and Function TCount. Any token arriving at Root in this situation (i.e., when TCount $= \ell$) is simply dropped.

In Algorithm 3, Root computes the number of *Token*s currently in the system and records it in a counter variable *Seen* (defined in Function TCount). Note that the variable *Seen* is maintained only at Root. Root initiates the circulation of *CToken* around the ring. When the *CToken* completes a full traversal of the ring and returns to Root, Root has counted the actual number of *Token*s in the system. The *CToken* circulation scheme is similar to the token passing scheme used in [2, 12]. Every time Root initiates a *CToken*, it uses a new sequence number ($CSentSeq$) in the $<CToken, Seq>$ message (Actions A_{c1} and A_{c2}). Other processors use two variables ($CSentSeq$ and $CRecSeq$) to store the old and new sequence numbers from the received *CToken* messages (Actions A_{c3} and A_{c4}). When Root receives a *CToken* message, it accepts and uses the information in the message provided the message carries the same sequence number as that placed by Root in the last *CToken* message it sent (Action A_{c1}). Otherwise, it considers the message as duplicate or corrupted, hence discards it. A processor i (not Root) accepts a $CToken$ message if the sequence number in the message is different from the one i used in the last message it sent (Actions A_{c3} and A_{c4}). The system may start with an arbitrary value of $CToken$ messages. However, the algorithm of the controller is self-stabilizing and eventually stabilizes for the predicate Single-CToken which is defined as follows: Single-CToken $\equiv$ " *there exists exactly one CToken in the system*". The $CToken$ is never held at the Root. The Root simply passes it to its right neighbor. However, other processors may hold the $CToken$ in some situations (to be discussed later).

Algorithm 3 Token-Controller

For Root	**For other processors**
T-Controller (	**T-Controller** (
START(), /* informs Root that the CToken	SENDTPASS(), /* informs that the CToken
has just passed */	has just passed */
T: Integer /* gives the number of tokens	T: Integer /* gives the number of tokens
held by Root when the CToken	held by the processor
leaves the Root */)	STOP(): Boolean /* indicates if the CToken
	must be stopped */)
Public **Function** TCount(): integer	**Public** **Function** CGo()
Return($Seen$)	**if** $T > 0$ **then**
end Function	$Passed := Passed + 1$
Function Count_t()	**if** $Passed =$ T **then** CSend
$Seen := Seen + 1$	$Passed := 0$
end Function	**else** Csend
	SENDTPASS()
Variables $CSentSeq : 0..\text{MaxSeq-1}$	$Passed := 0$
$Seen: 0..\ell$	**end Function**
	Function TPass(): Integer
(A_{c1}) [] ((**receive** $< CToken, Seq >$)	**Return** ($Passed$)
$\wedge(CSentSeq = Seq)) \longrightarrow$	**end Function**
$CSentSeq := (CSentSeq + 1)$	
$mod \, MaxSeq$	**Function** Csend()
START()	$CSentSeq := CRecSeq$
$Seen := T$	**send** $<CToken, CSentSeq>$
send $<CToken, CSentSeq>$	**end Function**
	Variables $CSentSeq, CRecSeq : 0..\text{MaxSeq-1}$
(A_{c2}) [] **timeout** $\longrightarrow$	$Passed: 0..k$
send $<CToken, CSentSeq>$	
	(A_{c3}) [] ((**receive** $<CToken, Seq>$)
	$\wedge((CSentSeq \neq Seq) \Rightarrow \neg \text{STOP}())) \longrightarrow$
	$CRecSeq := Seq$
	Csend
	(A_{c4}) [] ((**receive** $<CToken, Seq>$)
	$\wedge(CRecSeq \neq Seq)\wedge \text{STOP}()) \longrightarrow$
	$CRecSeq := Seq$

The *Permission* scheme (Algorithm 4) uses the same idea used in Algorithm 3 to circulate the $PToken$. The main difference here is that the $PToken$ can be held at any processor including Root because any processor can request for ℓ $Tokens$ to enter its critical section. Initially, the number of $PTokens$ in the system is arbitrary. However, since the algorithm is self-stabilizing, it will eventually stabilize for the predicate Single-PToken which is defined as follows:

Single-PToken ≡ *"there exists exactly one PToken in the system"*. Due to some wrong initial configurations, a processor i may be holding some tokens without the permission token ($STATE=$ *Request* $\wedge\neg$ *Permission*.Okay()). In this configuration, i must pass these tokens to its successor (see Actions A_{l1} and A_{l4}).

We now discuss the circulation of $CToken$ and $Tokens$. The $Token$ counting scheme must satisfy the following two conditions to get a correct count of the tokens:

- C_1: $CToken$ cannot pass any $Token$ because otherwise, the passed $Token$ will not be counted at Root (Actions A_{c3} and A_{c4}).
- C_2: A $Token$ cannot pass the $CToken$ to avoid repeated counting of the $Token$ at the Root (Actions A_{l4}, A_{l6}).

Algorithm 4 Permission

For Root	For other processors
Permission (STATE())	**Permission** (STATE())
External P-Controller(STATE())	**External P-Controller**(STATE(), OKAY(), PSEND())
Public Function Psend()	**Public Function** Psend()
$PSentSeq := (PRecSeq + 1)$	(*also used as Parameter*)
$mod\ Maxseq$	$PSentSeq := PRecSeq$
send $<PToken, PSentSeq>$	**send** $<PToken, PSentSeq>$
end Function	**end Function**
Function Okay(): Boolean	**Function** Okay(): Boolean
Return($PSentSeq = PRecSeq$)	(*also used as Parameter*)
end Function	**Return**($PSentSeq \neq PRecSeq$)
	end Function
Variables $PSentSeq, PRecSeq : 0..$MaxSeq-1	**Variables** $PSentSeq, PRecSeq : 0..$MaxSeq-1
(A_{p1}) [] (**receive** $<PToken, Seq>$)	(A_{p4}) [] (**receive** $<PToken, Seq>$)
$\wedge((PSentSeq = Seq) \Rightarrow$	$\wedge((PSentSeq \neq Seq) \Rightarrow$
$(STATE() \in \{In, Out\})$) $\longrightarrow$	$(STATE() \in \{In, Out\})$) $\longrightarrow$
$PRecSeq := Seq$	$PRecSeq := Seq$
Psend()	Psend()
(A_{p2}) [] (**receive** $<PToken, Seq>$)	(A_{p5}) [] (**receive** $<PToken, Seq>$)
$\wedge((PSentSeq = Seq)\wedge$	$\wedge((PSentSeq \neq Seq)\wedge$
$(STATE() = Request)) \longrightarrow$	$(STATE() = Request)) \longrightarrow$
$PRecSeq := Seq$	$PRecSeq := Seq$
(A_{p3}) [] **timeout** $\longrightarrow$	
send $<PToken, PSentSeq>$	

The above conditions ensure that during the $CToken$ traversal, all $Tokens$ visit the Root exactly once. To satisfy Conditions C_1 and C_2, processors hold on to $CToken$ and $Tokens$ in a queue. Hence, when i exits the critical section, tokens will be sent in the order they were received. Moreover, if a free token arrives at i when i is inside its critical section, i just enqueues this $Token$ and dequeues the $Token$ at the head of the queue. To implements the queue strategy, it is enough to use a counter variable ($Passed$) to know the number of tokens which follows $CToken$. This is shown in Figure. 1.(a) and (b) where $Passed$ is the number of tokens received by processor i after the $CToken$ and $\alpha =$NEED$_i$-$Passed$ tokens. When i receives another token (t) (Figure. 1.(a)), it increments

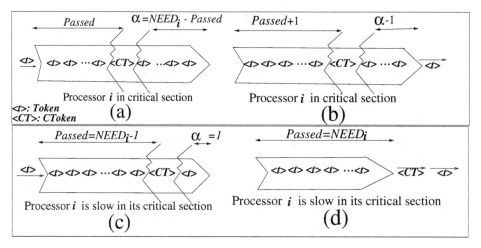

Fig. 1. An example to explain the counting of Tokens

Passed by one and it sends the token it receives (Figure 1.(b)) corresponding clearly to enqueue a token (incrementing *Passed*), hence α is decreased by one. We use a counter variable (*Passed*) to know the number of tokens which follow *CToken*.

So from C_1 and C_2, we can claim:

Property 2. Assuming *Token-Controller* is stabilized for the predicate Single-CToken, then Root is visited exactly once by every *Token* during a complete traversal of the *CToken*.

Handling Deadlocks. Deadlocks can occur due to wrong initial configurations. Deadlocks may also be formed during the stabilization phase. A typical deadlock configuration is shown in Figure 2. Assume that the number of *Tokens* in the system, ℓ' is less than ℓ, and all these tokens are held by a requesting processor $i \neq$ Root such that $\ell' < \text{NEED}_i \leq k \leq \ell$. Moreover, we assume that the *CToken* and *PToken* are stopped at $i \neq$ Root and no processor can execute any action (except the Root: A_{c2} and A_{p3}). It is obvious that the number of tokens *Tokens* in the system will remain ℓ' forever — a deadlock. We consider a 3-out-of-4 exclusion problem and Figure 2 to explain deadlocks. The deadlock configuration is shown in Part (b). Processor b needs three tokens and receives *PToken*, *Token*, and *CToken* in this order. To respect Condition C_1, *CToken* will remain at b until b receives enough tokens. So, *CToken* cannot complete its traversal, hence no *Token* will be added.

We use a very simple approach to handle deadlocks. We send a probe, called *DToken* (Algorithm 5) in the ring which carries a three state variable ({*Free*, *Deadlock*, *Remove*}). The Root records in variable *MyDetect* the value carried by the last *CToken* it sent. The circulation of *DToken* is also maintained

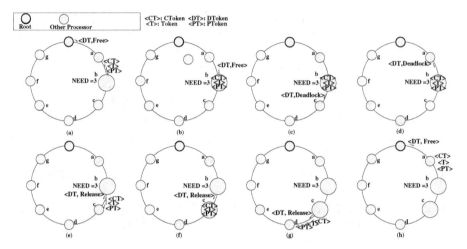

Fig. 2. An example to explain the handling of deadlocks

by a self-stabilizing token circulation scheme. So, it eventually stabilizes for the predicate Single-DToken which is defined as follows: Single-DToken ≡ *"there exists exactly one DToken in the system"*. When Algorithm 5 is stabilized, the Root initiates the $DToken$ with the value $Free$ meaning that the system is deadlock-free and it sets $MyDetect = Free$ as shown in Figure 2 (a) (see Action A_{d1}).

Upon receipt of the $DToken$ message carrying the $Free$ value, a processor i does the following (see Action A_{d5}): If the $PToken$ is stopped at i (i.e., Function OKAY returns true), then it sends the $DToken$ with the $Deadlock$ value to signal that a deadlock may have occurred in the system (see Action A_{d5} and Figure 2 (c)). Otherwise, it just forwards it to its successor. Then we consider two cases.

1. Assume that the $DToken$ did not meet any $PToken$ during its traversal. In this case, there is no deadlock in the system.

2. Assume that the $DToken$ met a $PToken$ in the system. Hence it carries a $Deadlock$ value. This situation is shown in Figure 2 (c). Processor b receives the $DToken$ with $Free$ value. Then it sends the $DToken$ with $Deadlock$ value to signal that a deadlock may have occurred in the system. Now, we consider two cases for the $DToken$ traversal.

   (a) Assume that a deadlock exists in the system (the $DToken$ did not find any other processor with any $Tokens$ during its last traversal in the ring). This situation is shown in Figure 2. Root eventually receives the message $DToken$ with $Deadlock$ value and it forwards it to its successor (see Action A_{d2} and Figure 2 (d)). This message eventually reaches Processor b (Figure 2 (d)). When b receives $DToken$ again with $Deadlock$ value, a deadlock exists in the system. Then b is forced to release the

Algorithm 5 Deadlock-Handler

For Root
P-Controller(STATE(): {Request, In, Out })

Variables $PCSentSeq : 0..MaxSeq-1$
$MyDetect :\in \{Free, Deadlock, Remove\}$

(A_{d1}) [] **receive** $<DToken, Seq, Free>$
               $\wedge\ (PCSentSeq = Seq) \longrightarrow$
               $PCSentSeq := (PCSentSeq + 1)$
                          $mod\ MaxSeq$
               send $<DToken, PCSentSeq, Free>$
               $MyDetect := Free$

(A_{d2}) [] **receive** $<DToken, Seq, Deadlock>$
               $\wedge\ (PCSentSeq = Seq) \longrightarrow$
               $PCSentSeq := (PCSentSeq + 1)$
                          $mod\ MaxSeq$
               if $MyDetect = Free$ **then**
                  send $<DToken, PCSentSeq,$
                            $Deadlock>$
                  $MyDetect := Deadlock$
               else send $<DToken, PCSentSeq,$
                            $Free>$
                  $MyDetect := Free$

(A_{d3}) [] **receive** $<DToken, Seq, Remove>$
               $\wedge\ (PCSentSeq = Seq) \longrightarrow$
               $PCSentSeq := (PCSentSeq + 1)$
                          $mod\ MaxSeq$
               send $<DToken, PCSentSeq, Free>$
               $MyDetect := Free$

(A_{d4}) [] **timeout** $\longrightarrow$
               send $<DToken, PCSentSeq,$
                        $MyDetect>$

For other processors
P-Controller(STATE(): {Request, In, Out },
    OKAY(): Boolean, /* indicates if the permission
                       token is stopped */
    PSEND() /* forces the processor to release its
                       permission token */)
Variables $PCSentSeq : 0..MaxSeq-1$

(A_{d5}) [] **receive** $<DToken, Seq, Free> \longrightarrow$
               if $(PCSentSeq \neq Seq)$ **then**
                  $PCSentSeq := Seq$
                  if OKAY **then**
                     send $<DToken, PCSentSeq,$
                               $Deadlock>$
                  else send $<DToken, PCSentSeq,$
                               $Free>$
               else send $<DToken, PCSentSeq,$
                               $Free>$

(A_{d6}) [] **receive** $<DToken, Seq, Deadlock> \longrightarrow$
               if $(PCSentSeq \neq Seq)$ **then**
                  $PCSentSeq := Seq$
                  if OKAY **then**
                     PSEND()
                     send $<DToken, PCSentSeq,$
                               $Remove>$
                  else if STATE() $= In$ **then**
                     send $<DToken, PCSentSeq,$
                               $Free>$
                  else send $<DToken, PCSentSeq,$
                               $Deadlock>$

(A_{d7}) [] **receive** $<DToken, Seq, Remove> \longrightarrow$
               if $(PCSentSeq \neq Seq)$ **then**
                  $PCSentSeq := Seq$
                  if OKAY **then** PSEND()
               send $<DToken, PCSentSeq, Remove>$

$PToken$ followed by the $Tokens$ (Action A_{d6} and A_{l4}) since a requesting processor cannot hold on to $Tokens$ without the $PToken$. Then b
changes the $DToken$ value to $Remove$ to force all processors to release
their tokens (see Action A_{d7}). Thus, the deadlock is resolved.

(b) Assume that there exists no deadlock in the system. If the $DToken$ met
at least a processor i in its critical section, then it passes the $DToken$
with the $Free$ value meaning that a deadlock did not occur (see Action A_{d6}). Otherwise, all $Tokens$ circulate in the ring, thereby eventually
reaching a processor holding the permission token.

5.2   Proof Outline

We first need to show that all types of tokens (*Token*, *CToken*, *PToken*, and *DToken*) circulate in the ring forever (deadlock-freedom). By Actions A_{d3} and A_{d4}, at least one *DToken* circulates in the ring infinitely.

The *DToken* is used to avoid the *CToken* from getting stuck at a processor i forever. Thus, a *CToken* eventually disappears or circulates in the ring forever. By using the fact that a *CToken* is never stuck at a processor i forever, it follows that a token is never held by a processor i forever. Otherwise, the system would reach a configuration where a *CToken* is also held by i forever. Thus, a *Token* eventually disappears or circulates in the ring infinitely. Similarly, we obtain that the *PToken* is never held by the processor forever. We can borrow some results of [2, 12] to claim that the predicate Single-CToken (respectively, Single-PToken and Single-DToken) holds if the two following conditions are satisfied:

– Constant $MaxSeq \geq nL_{Max} + n$, where n is the ring size and L_{Max} is the maximum capacity of the links.
– Any execution contains infinite steps of the *Token-controller* (respectively, *Deadlock-Handler* $\rhd_P$ *Token-Permission*).

Using $MaxSeq \geq nL_{Max} + n$, the fact that the *CToken* (respectively, *CToken* and *DToken*) is never stopped forever, we obtain the following result: If $MaxSeq \geq nL_{Max} + n$, then the *CToken* (respectively, *PToken* and *DToken*) stabilizes for the predicate Single-CToken (respectively, Single-PToken and *DToken*) regardless of the stability of ℓ-*Token-Circulation* in two *CToken* (respectively, *PToken DToken*) traversal time, i.e., $2n$.

By Action A_{l3} and Property 2, we can claim the following result (safety): Starting from any configuration which satisfies Single-CToken, the ℓ-Token-Circulation stabilizes for the predicate "there exist exactly ℓ tokens in the system after at most two *CToken* traversal time and will remain true forever."

Now, we show that starting from this configuration, the message *DToken* can force processors to release their tokens at least during one traversal. We assume that during its last traversal, the *DToken* has forced some processors to release their tokens (Actions A_{d6} and A_{d7}). By Algorithm 5, Root will eventually receive the *DToken* with the *Remove* value. Then it sends the *DToken* with the *Free* value in order to detect if a deadlock arises again in the system. Now, assume that the message *DToken* reach a processor i holding tokens and permission token (i is waiting for extra tokens to enter its critical section). So, i forwards the *DToken* with the *Deadlock* value. As the number of tokens in the system is ℓ, from this configuration onwards, the *DToken* with the *Deadlock* value never reach a processor holding the permission token, hence never forces a processor to release its tokens.

Thus, the system eventually reaches a configuration after which no *DToken* message can force a processor to release its tokens. Starting from this configuration, the system will behave exactly as Algorithm 1.

Stabilization Time. The *DToken* stabilizes after at most $2n$. Now, we calculate the number of traversals needed so that the *CToken* completes two traversals. After the *DToken* stabilization, the Root initiates the *DToken* to detect deadlock after at most one *CToken* traversal. Then we need four *DToken* traversals (two *DToken* traversals for each *CToken* traversal). After the *CToken* traversal, we need another extra *CToken* traversal to obtain ℓ tokens in the system. So, the stabilization time of our protocol is at most $8n$.

Waiting Time. The waiting time is the maximum number of times that all processors of the system can enter the critical section after a processor p requests to enter and before p enters the critical section [9].

The possibility for a processor i to enter the critical section depends on how quickly it receives the *PToken* in order to collect its necessary tokens. We consider the worst configuration γ such that the *PToken* is in the link connecting i to $i + 1$ and a maximal number of processors requesting only one token $(\min(\ell,\ n\text{-}1))$ have collected the token during the previous traversal of *PToken*, but they did not enter their critical sections yet. Now, starting from γ, these processors quickly enter their critical sections, execute, exit, and request to enter again before receiving the *PToken*. Thus, the waiting time of processor i is at most $2(n - 1)$.

6   Conclusion

In this paper, we present a solution to the k-out-of-ℓ exclusion. Our protocol satisfies the (k, ℓ)-liveness property. Moreover, it improves the waiting time of the solution proposed in [4] by maintaining a reasonable stabilization time. We also proposed a very simple token controller scheme which allows the Root to count and maintain the right number of tokens in the ring. The token counter is maintained only at the Root. A good feature of the controller is that it does not generate any additional messages. The method used to collect the required number of tokens before entering the critical section deserves some discussion. Only one processor is allowed to collect the tokens in our protocol. So, the obvious question would be how can this protocol achieve a high degree of concurrency? A study considering the probabilistic model or some benchmarks could clarify this question. We can make one observation here: If the average time of the critical section execution is higher than the message delivery time, then our protocol is very efficient on rings.

References

[1] U. Abraham, S. Dolev, T. Herman, and I. Koll. Self-stabilizing ℓ-exclusion. *Proceedings of the third Workshop on Self-Stabilizing Systems, International Informatics Series 7, Carleton University Press*, pages 48–63, 1997. 117

[2] Y. Afek and G. M. Brown. Self-stabilization over unreliable communication media. *Distributed Computing, Vol. 7*, pages 27–34, 1993. 120, 126

[3] R. Baldoni. An $o(n^{M/M+1})$ distributed algorithm for the k-out of-m resources allocation problem. *In Proceedings of the 14th conference on Distributed Computing and System.*, pages 81–85, 1994. 114

[4] A. K. Datta, R. Hadid, and V. Villain. A self-stabilizing token-based k-out-of-ℓ exclusion algorithm. *In Proceedings of the 8th International Europar Conference*, pages 553–562, 2002. 113, 114, 115, 127

[5] D. Dolev, E. Gafni, and N. Shavit. Toward a non-atomic era: ℓ-exclusion as test case. *Proceeding of the 20th Annual ACM Symposium on Theory of Computing, Chicago*, pages 78–92, 1988. 115

[6] R. Hadid and V. Villain. A new efficient tool for the design of self-stabilizing ℓ-exclusion algorithms: the controller. *In proceeding of the 5th International Workshop on Self-Stabilizing Systems, Lisbonne (Portugal), LNCS 2194, (WSS'01)*, pages 136–151, 2001. 113, 115

[7] Y. Manabe, R. Baldoni, M. Raynal, and S. Aoyagi. k-arbiter: A safe and general scheme for h-out of-k mutual exclusion. *Theoretical Computer Science, Vol 193*, pages 97–112, 1998. 114

[8] Y. Manabe and N. Tajima. (h, k)-arbiter for h-out of-k mutual exclusion problem. *In Proceedings of the 19th Conference on Distributed Computing System.*, pages 216–223, 1999. 114

[9] M. Raynal. Algorithm du parallélisme, le problème de l'exclusion mutuelle. *Dunod Informatique*, 1990. 127

[10] M. Raynal. A distributed algorithm for the k-out of-m resources allocations problem. *In Proceedings of the 1st conference on Computing and Informations, Lecture Notes in Computer Science, Vol. 497*, pages 599–609, 1991. 114, 116

[11] M. Raynal. Synchronisation et état global dans les systèmes répartis. *Eyrolles, collection EDF*, 1992. 114

[12] G. Varghese. Self-stabilizing by counter flushing. *Technical Report, Washington University (1993)*, 1993. 120, 126

A Framework of Safe Stabilization

Sukumar Ghosh* and Alina Bejan

University of Iowa, Iowa City IA 52242, USA
{ghosh,abejan}@cs.uiowa.edu

Abstract. Classical stabilizing systems do not take into consideration safety issues. This paper examines two different safety models for stabilizing distributed systems, and studies the cost of enforcing safety requirements in the context of various kinds of failures.

1 Introduction

Stabilization is an important mechanism for the design of fault-tolerant and adaptive distributed systems. Stabilization guarantees eventual recovery to a good configuration, but it does not specify anything about the intermediate configurations that the system has to go through. In the context of safety, this may not be adequate, since there are many applications in which certain intermediate states may violate one or more safety properties. Safety properties were formally introduced by Alpern and Schneider [1]. Safety invariants have important implications in application environments. For example, a load balancing system may never want to be in a state that reflects a "significant loss of balance," or a process control system may avoid a state that can cause two chemicals to mix with each other, leading to an explosion. This paper examines how to satisfy a given safety property when a system stabilizes to its legal configuration. It is more a declaration of the problem than an in-depth study of algorithmic techniques required to embed safety properties in stabilizing systems.

Yen [17] addressed the safety aspect of stabilization in the context of a token ring. She used signatures to safeguard against the inadvertent corruption of states that could falsely grant a token to a process. Another remedy to the same problem for trees has been proposed by Kiniwa [13]. Other refinements of stabilization are primarily performance guarantees: for example, fault-containment [9, 10] insures that recovery from all single failures takes place in $O(1)$ time, although there is an implicit safety requirement that non-faulty processes remain unaffected during recovery. Similar comments apply to other controlled recovery methods like superstabilization [8], or time-adaptive stabilization [14] or scalable stabilization[11].

In [5], Villain et al introduced *snap-stabilization* that addresses safety issues of stabilizing systems in a different way. Safety guarantees are produced on-demand, and user processes are required to send out a PIF wave, whose return

---
* This research was supported in part by the National Science Foundation under grant CCR-9901391.

S.-T. Huang and T. Herman (Eds.): SSS 2003, LNCS 2704, pp. 129–140, 2003.

echoes safety guarantee. However, any subsequent delay by the user in using the service can open the gate of additional failures. We will call such safety guarantees to be *dynamic*, which contrasts with the form of *static* safety being addressed in the present paper: at no time, the system should enter a configuration that violates the safety predicate. As an example, consider the absence of deadlock as a safety property. All correct stabilizing solutions trivially satisfy this property.

This paper provides a framework for the enforcement of safety in stabilizing systems, and studies the cost of such an enforcement. The contributions are three-fold: (1) formalizing the problem of safe stabilization, (2) accommodating different kinds of failures that may have implications on safety but not on stabilization, and (3) an impossibility result related to safe stabilization. The paper is organized as follows: Section 2 introduces some basic definitions and notations to be used in this paper. Section 3 describes a preliminary approach towards enforcing safety. Section 4 relates the problem of safe stabilization to various fault models. Section 5 outlines a few transformation rules for preserving safety in stabilizing distributed systems. Finally, Section 6 contains some concluding remarks.

2   Preliminaries

This section classifies safety into two different categories: *strong* and *weak*. The classification is relevant only in the context of stabilization.

2.1   Strong and Weak Safety

Define the global state (also called a configuration) of a distributed system as the set of the local states of all its component processes. Let the predicate L over the global state define legitimacy. When a failure occurs, the global state of the system may change to one in which L does not hold. At this time, the stabilization mechanism kicks in, and steers the system to a legitimate configuration. Define a set of configurations to be *safe*, when they satisfy a predicate Z. Ideally the system should always be in a safe configuration, otherwise the application might have catastrophic consequences. The following lemma is trivial:

Lemma 1. $L \Rightarrow Z$.

Our goal is to design a system that satisfies the following two conditions:

Stabilization. Starting from any initial configuration, the system stabilizes to a configuration that satisfies L.

Safety. Every configuration, including the starting configuration satisfies Z.

A stabilizing system that satisfies the above two criteria will be called *Z-safe L-stabilizing*.

Some safety predicates may trivially hold in every possible global state: for example, in a ring of n identical state machines $0..n-1$, if x_i (x_i is an element of the set of non-negative integers) denotes the state of process i, and $Z = \exists i, j (i \neq j) : x_i \geq x_j$, then Z is trivially true, regardless of failure. However, in general, the set of global configurations that violate Z is non-empty. When the extent of the failure is unknown, the first step towards guaranteeing safety is to ensure that Z holds in all starting configurations. The following lemma states a trivial impossibility result:

Lemma 2. *Given an arbitrary Z, it is impossible to design a Z-safe L-stabilizing system that tolerates an arbitrary number of faults.*

Proof. Any state can be transformed into a state that violates Z when an appropriate number of faults occur.   □

To design an L-stabilizing system that is Z-safe, we need to know the upper bound k of the number of faults. It is possible to fine tune this characterization: for example, in a system of ten processes p_0 through p_9, we can say that processes p_0 through p_3 are very reliable, so at most one of them can fail, but out of the remaining six processes p_4 through p_9, up to three can fail at any time. However to keep the discussions simple, we will stick to our simple characterization of failure by an overall non-negative integer k. The value of k plays a crucial role in the contract between the application and the system designer. If the number of faults exceeds k, then safety guarantee falls apart, since it is outside the contract. However, stabilization is guaranteed.

Safety violations can be handled in several different ways. One possible strategy for damage control is to reset the system to a special *failsafe* configuration $\perp$ that calls for external intervention. Accordingly we will define two versions of safe stabilization: *strongly safe* and *weakly safe*.

Definition 1. *A system is* strongly safe *and stabilizing when it satisfies the following three requirements:*

Stabilization. *Starting from a safe initial configuration, the system stabilizes to a configuration that satisfies L.*

Safety. *If the initial configuration is safe, and the number of failures does not exceed k, then every intermediate configuration is safe.*

Notification. *If and only if the configuration is unsafe, the system reaches a special failsafe configuration $\perp$ that requests for external intervention.*

The failsafe configuration $\perp \in \neg Z$. Once the system is in $\perp$, further recovery requires external intervention. Different systems can implement $\perp$ in different ways. It is application dependent, and is outside the scope of the current discussion.

The *weakly safe* version drops the notification requirement, but guarantees stabilization from *all* initial configurations.

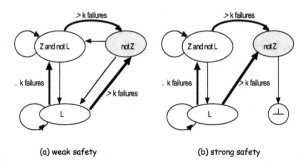

(a) weak safety   (b) strong safety

Fig. 1. Strong and weak safety in stabilizing systems

Definition 2. *A stabilizing system is* weakly safe, *when it satisfies the following two requirements:*

Stabilization. *Starting from any initial configuration, the system stabilizes to a configuration that satisfies L.*

Safety. *If the starting configuration satisfies Z, and the number of failures does not exceed k, then every intermediate configuration satisfies Z.*

Fig. 1 illustrates the behaviors of stabilizing systems that satisfy the weak or strong version of the safety criteria. In the rest of the paper, we primarily focus on the weakly safe version of stabilization. We will address strong safety in our concluding remarks.

2.2   Safety Margin

Let s designate the global state of a distributed system.

Definition 3. *The* distance *between two global states s_i and s_j, $D(s_i, s_j)$, is the smallest number of processes whose states need to be changed to transform one global state into the other.*

The state of a system can be transformed from safe to unsafe, when transient failures instantaneously change the states of more than k processes. To prevent this from happening, all safe configurations must be at a distance *greater than k* from any unsafe configuration *prior to the occurrence of the failure.* If the distance of the global state s from an unsafe configuration is $\leq k$, then technically the system would still be safe, but there will be no room for failures. Define Z_k as the *maximal set* of configurations for which the following holds:

$$\forall i, j : s_i \in Z_k \wedge s_j \notin Z :: D(s_i, s_j) > k$$

When $k > 0$, $Z_k \subset Z$.

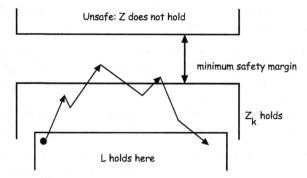

Fig. 2. The behavior of a process that is safe and stabilizing

Lemma 3. *A necessary condition for a stabilizing system to be weakly safe and tolerant to k or fewer faults is that the set of configurations prior to the occurrence of any failure is $\subseteq Z_k$.*

Proof. We do not know when and if processes will fail. It follows from the definition of Z_k that as long as the current configuration satisfies Z_k, no set of k instantaneous failures can lead the system to a configuration that violates Z. Fig. 2 illustrates the behavior of a process that is affected by failure(s), but is still safe and stabilizing.   □

Definition 4. *In a safe configuration, the maximum number of processes that are allowed to fail without violating the safety predicate is the safety margin.*

Some early comments about the fault model are in order here. Once failures bring the system to the edge of an unsafe configuration, we will hope that further failures do not occur, until the system state has been restored to one that belongs to Z_k. Otherwise, m ($m > 1$) quick successions of k failures is as damaging as one episode of $m.k$ failures, and safety can be compromised. Starting from any configuration in $\neg Z_k \wedge Z$ where there is no safety margin, the system must recover to a configuration in Z_k before the next failure occurs, otherwise the safety margin will be inadequate. These are relevant when the failure is bursty in nature.

3   A First Step

We will represent the program of a process by a set of rules. Each rule is a guarded action $g \rightarrow a$, where the guard g is a predicate involving the state of that process and those of its neighbors, and the action a modifies the local state of a process, causing the global state transition $s_i \rightarrow s_{i+1}$. We use a *serial scheduler* that allows only one process to apply a rule at any time. A computation is a sequence of states and actions $s_0 a_0 s_1 a_1 \cdots s_i a_i s_{i+1} \cdots$.

The following lemma shows how to transform a given L-stabilizing system into a Z-safe L-stabilizing system.

Lemma 4. *Let U be an L-stabilizing system. Derive a system S from U by replacing each guarded action $g \rightarrow a$ of U by $g' \rightarrow a$, where $g' = g \wedge (s_i \in Z_k) \wedge (s_{i+1} \in Z_k)$. Then S is Z-safe L-stabilizing, only if it does not deadlock.*

An implementation of the above strategy calls for the evaluation of the global state at every step. Two remarks are in order here.

Remark 1. If the starting state belongs to Z_k, and the next state is guaranteed to belong to Z_k before the step is taken, then there is apparently no need to verify the condition $s \in Z_k$ before every step. It is only justified in case more than k failures occur, and strong safety is the goal. However, the detection of an unsafe configuration requires an appropriate type of failure detector. If the detector is perfect, then strong safety can be guaranteed by adding the rule $s \notin Z \rightarrow s := \bot$. This step is not necessary, if the goal is weak safety.

Remark 2. If the global state is evaluated at every step, then there is no need to start from a stabilization algorithm that was designed with the assumption that processes only know about their neighbors' states. Perhaps, better algorithms can be designed to make use of the global state that is routinely collected before an action is taken. What fraction of the global state needs to be collected before a process takes a viable corrective step requires closer examination.

As an example, consider Dijkstra's stabilizing mutual exclusion algorithm [6] on a unidirectional ring with ten processes 0 through 9. Assume that Z corresponds to all configurations that have at most *five* privileges, and let $k = 1$. Then Z_k represents all configurations that have at most *three* privileges. This system is weakly safe by design [12]. Furthermore, the system guarantees safety when a burst of two failures occur in quick succession from a legal configuration before the progress of the recovery, since Z_k holds after the first failure.

Lemma 5. *Using the solution in Lemma 4, a system that is Z-safe L-stabilizing under a serial demon, is not necessarily Z-safe L-stabilizing under a distributed demon.*

Distributed demons parallelize actions and increase the risk. If T actions are executed simultaneously, then the scheduler has to look ahead T steps to enforce safety. If these actions interfere with one another [3], then there is no guarantee that the system will even stabilize under the distributed demon. Even when the actions are non-interfering, the combined effect is the same as that of T actions being sequentially executed, but without checking if the intermediate states are safe.

4   Relationship between Fault Models and Safe Stabilization

We now classify the various faulty behaviors, and refine the fault models in the context of safe stabilization. A transient failure alters the state of a process to an arbitrary value. Ordinarily we don't want to know either the duration or the frequency of occurrence of the faults. These have no impact on stabilization, as long as the faulty behavior eventually subsides, allowing sufficient time for recovery. Regardless of the extent of the state corruption, true recovery begins after the faulty behavior finally stops. No system can stabilize if the mean time between failures is smaller than the mean time to repair, or if the faulty processes continue their erratic behavior for ever.

When safety is an issue, not only is the frequency of the failures, but also the duration and the nature of the faulty behavior (which can be byzantine) are important factors. Assume that in any legal configuration, the safety margin is at least k. We consider several different cases here:

Case 1. k Instantaneous Failures.

Let faults instantaneously affect the states of k processes, and there is no interim period when the process exhibits byzantine behavior. Once the failure occurs, the system is allowed to stabilize before the next episode of failure. In this case, many published algorithms (but not all) that are designed to be fault-containing or time-adaptive trivially satisfy weak safety requirement since by definition $L \subseteq Z_k$, and L is closed under the actions of the algorithm.

Case 2. Burst Failures.

A *burst failure* consists of a sequence of m failures ($m > 1$) without allowing sufficient time for the system to recover from the effect of the previous failures. Each occurrence of a failure may instantaneously affect the states of up to k processes. The worst case is equivalent to Case 1 with $m.k$ failures. Note that the time interval between consecutive failures is an important parameter in the definition of burst failures.

Case 3. k Byzantine Failures.

A set of k processes exhibits byzantine failure for a finite non-zero period of time. In this case, we demonstrate that it is impossible to design a weakly safe stabilizing system that can tolerate k byzantine faults ($k > 0$), unless the topology is $(k + 1)$-connected. As a motivation, assume that $k = 1$, revisit the *fault-containment problem* [10] and examine its effectiveness in the context of safety.

Fault-containment provides the additional guarantee of stabilization from all cases of single failures in $O(1)$ time. All solutions expect only the faulty process to make a move to reverse the effect of the failure. However, the failure may also enable the guards of one or more non-faulty neighbors of the faulty process, making them eligible to execute their actions! Depending on which process executes a move, the failure is either contained, or it contaminates the non-faulty processes too. In many classical solutions to the fault-containment problem, a non-faulty process queries its faulty neighbor to obtain the states of its neighbor's neighbors and determines if it is the case of a single failure, so that appropriate corrective actions can be taken. However, if the single failure is byzantine for a finite duration, then the response from the faulty process cannot be trusted, and faulty answers could trigger unwanted moves that can aggravate the damage and violate safety. The following version of *Menger's theorem* [7] is relevant in this context:

Theorem 1. *The minimum number of nodes separating two non-adjacent nodes i and j is the minimum number of node-disjoint paths between them.*

Theorem 1 leads to the following result on weak safety and stabilization:

Theorem 2. *It is impossible to design a weakly safe stabilizing distributed system that tolerates k byzantine failures unless the connectivity is greater than k.*

Proof. The proof indirectly follows from [16], and hinges on how processes read the states of other processes. A process q reads the state of another process p as follows: it sends out a probe using *query-response* variables as in [11] via every edge incident on it. The responses contain copies of the state of process p. If there are k faulty processes in the system, and there are k node-disjoint paths, then no non-faulty process q can correctly read the state of another faulty process p, since each path can potentially contain one faulty process capable of tampering the response containing p's state. As a result, q can take an incorrect step that is equivalent to a faulty behavior. This increases the number of failures to $(k+1)$, and violates safety.   □

Corollary 1. *It is impossible to design a weakly safe and stabilizing system that tolerates even a single byzantine failure on an array of processes, or more than one failures on a ring of processes.*

Note. This is tangential to the impossibility results presented by Anagnostou and Hadzilacos [2] that studies *ftss* (fault tolerant and self-stabilizing) protocols for several well-known problems. The fault-tolerant part addresses permanent failures only. They do not address safety that is the focus of attention of the current paper. However, they present several results that illustrate the difficulty of tolerating crash failures and satisfying self-stabilization properties.

To obtain reliable information about the state of a remote process, the query-response has to be completed through *a path of non-faulty processes* only. However, no process has prior knowledge of which processes are faulty. The only assurance is that the duration of the failures is finite, and every process *eventually* receives the correct value of the state of every other non-faulty process after making a finite number of queries. We now modify the notion of a computation by increasing the *granularity of actions* as follows:

Definition 5. *Consider an* atomic read operation *consisting of reading the state of a remote process through* $(k+1)$ *node-disjoint paths using any viable query-response mechanism. The reading will be called* stable, *when all* $(k+1)$ *readings are identical.*

Lemma 6. *If a process q obtains a stable reading of the state of another non-faulty process p, then the reading must reflect the correct value of p's state.*

Proof. Since the maximum number of failures is k, and readings are being collected via $(k+1)$ node-disjoint paths, at least one of the $(k+1)$ readings is correct. Stable readings imply that all readings are equal, so all readings must be correct. No such guarantee can be given if the remote process is faulty, since it can exhibit byzantine behavior by sending out an incorrect value through each of the $(k+1)$ node-disjoint paths. □

This will slow down the system, but the waiting is guaranteed to be finite, and safety is not compromised.

5   Designing Algorithms for Safe Stabilization

This section addresses two different types of failures: instantaneous failures and byzantine failures, and outlines a transformation that preserves safety in the presence of byzantine failures.

Case 1. k Instantaneous Failures.

For safe stabilization, any algorithm that guarantees time-adaptive [15] or scalable stabilization [11] will suffice, *provided* it guarantees that contamination is impossible. It has been shown in [11] that as k increases beyond a threshold, scalable recovery may be possible, but only at the expense of some contamination that affects the states of non-faulty processes.

Case 2. k Byzantine Failures.

In the second case, given an algorithm A that guarantees safe stabilization with k *instantaneous failures*, one can derive an algorithm B for safe stabilization from k *byzantine failures* as follows: replace each guarded action $g \to a$ by $g_{stable} \to a$, where for any node i, $g_{stable}(x : x \in i \cup N(i)) = g(x : x \in i \cup N(i) \wedge stable(x))$. A node i computes the predicate g_{stable} as follows: for each target process, it sends out a probe (using query-response variables as shown in [11]) via all the edges incident on node i (Fig. 3), and the responses from the target node are compared with one another. When more than k responses are identical, the value can be used to compute g_{stable}, otherwise the computation is postponed. Since the byzantine failures have finite durations, eventually g_{stable} will be evaluated.

Theorem 3. *Algorithm B is weakly safe and stabilizing in the presence of k or fewer byzantine failures.*

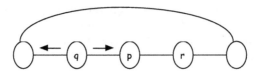

Fig. 3. Process p undergoes a byzantine failure. Process q queries about the state of r

Proof. Contamination, and consequently the violation of safety is possible when a non-faulty process takes an incorrect step during recovery, effectively increasing the number of failures. If the value of a remote variable is stable, then it means one of the following three things: (1) Either the remote process is now fault-free and responding consistently to all queries, or (2) the remote process is still faulty, but consistently sending wrong values and behaving like a non-faulty process, or (3) the remote process is responding inconsistently, but at least one process in the reading path is altering the readings and making it appear stable to the reader. In case 1, every computation of B is a computation of A and safe stabilization is guaranteed. In case 2, a faulty process may not behave as one, so safety is not compromised. In case 3, a non-faulty process may be forced to execute an action when it should not have done so, therefore safety may be violated. However, the duration of such failures is finite by assumption, so the suffix of every computation in B is a computation in A, and stabilization is guaranteed.   □

5.1   Performance

The space and time complexity of implementing weak safety will depend on how the K ($K > k$) copies of the states of the relevant remote processes are being read. The algorithm for state reading itself should be stabilizing. If d is the diameter of the network, then queries (and responses) have to travel a path of maximum length $2 \cdot d$ (Fig. 3). Thus, the stable value of even a neighboring process has to be collected at the expense of an d-fold increase in the state reading time. Depending on which self-stabilizing algorithm is used for reading the states of remote processes, the time needed for the query-response variables to stabilize can further increase this overhead. Two extreme scenarios are possible here. If all the queries are simultaneously sent out to expedite stabilization, then the time required to stabilize will go up by a factor of $\Omega(d)$. However, this will be possible at the expense of a K-fold increase in the space complexity per process, since all copies have to be locally stored prior to the evaluation of g_{stable}. On the other hand, by sending out the queries serially, g_{stable} can be evaluated using a space equivalent to that in the original stabilization protocol, but the time complexity will be determined by the overhead of serially collecting the K copies of the state of a remote process. Each query needs $\Omega(d)$ time to reach the target, so the time complexity will increase by a larger factor of $\Omega(K \cdot d)$.

6 Conclusion

The *contamination number*, which is the maximum number of processes that can change state before the system returns to a legal configuration [10], is an important safety criteria. Not all stabilization algorithms that help stabilize from k-faulty configurations in $O(k)$ time have a contamination number $\leq k$ [11], which is required for safety.

The implementation of strong safety requires that every unsafe configuration (i.e configurations with more than k failures) is eventually detected. This calls for appropriate types of failure detectors [4] – otherwise unsafe configurations may go undetected, or there may be *false alarms*. An interesting problem to explore here is the relationship between transient failure detectors and safe stabilization. A fail-safe configuration that is acceptable in many non-real time settings is the deadlock configuration. Algorithms that spontaneously deadlock, or return to designated fail-safe configuration when safety is violated, are currently under investigation.

The general framework does not address the handling of specific safety requirements that cannot be quantified using the number of faulty processes. Algorithms still need to be hand-crafted to meet such safety requirements.

References

[1] Alpern B. and Schneider F. B. "Recognizing Safety and Liveness," Distributed Computing 2(3), pp. 117-126, 1987. 129
[2] Anagnostou E. and Hadzilacos, V. "Tolerating Transient and Permanent Failures," Workshop on Distributed Algorithms (WDAG), pp. 174-188, 1993. 136
[3] Brown, G. M., Gouda, M. G. and Wu, C. L. "Token Systems that Self-stabilize," IEEE Transactions on Computers 38(6) 1989. 134
[4] Chandra, T., and Toueg, S. "Unreliable failure Detectors for Reliable Distributed Systems," Journal of the ACM, pp. 374-382, April 1996. 139
[5] Cournier A., Datta A. K., Petit F. and Villain V. "Snap-Stabilizing PIF Algorithm in Arbitrary Networks," ICDCS 2002: 199-208. 129
[6] Dijkstra, E. W. "Self-stabilizing Systems In Spite of Distributed Control," Communications of the ACM 17, pp. 643-644, Nov 1974. 134
[7] Diestel, R. "Graph Theory," Second Edition, Springer 2000. 136
[8] Dolev, S. and Herman, T. "Superstabilizing Protocols for Dynamic Distributed Systems," Chicago Journal of Theoretical Computer Science, 3(4), 1997. 129
[9] Ghosh, S. and Gupta, A., "An Exercise in Fault-containment: Leader Election on a Ring," Information Processing Letters 59, pp. 281-288, 1996. 129
[10] Ghosh, S., Gupta, A., Herman T., and Pemmaraju, S. V. "Fault-containing Self-stabilizing Algorithms," Proceedings of the 15th Annual ACM Symposium on Principles of Distributed Computing, pp. 45-54, 1996. 129, 135, 139
[11] Ghosh, S. and He, X. "Scalable Self-stabilization," J. Parallel and Distributed Computing 62(5), pp. 945-960, 2002. 129, 136, 137, 139
[12] Ghosh, S. and Pemmaraju, S. V. "Trade-offs in Fault-Containing Self-Stabilization," Proceedings of 3rd Workshop on Self-stabilizing Systems (Editors: Ghosh & Herman, Carleton University Press), pp. 157-169, Santa Barbara, August 1997. 134

[13] Kiniwa J. "Avoiding Faulty Privileges in Self-Stabilizing Depth-First Token Passing," ICPADS 2001: 390-397. 129

[14] Kutten, S. and Peleg, D. "Universal Fault-local Mending," Proceedings of the 14th ACM Symposium on Principles of Distributed Computing, pp. 20-29, 1995. 129

[15] Kutten, S. and Patt-Shamir, B. "Time-adaptive Self-stabilization," Proceedings of the 16th ACM Symposium on Principles of Distributed Computing, pp. 149-158, 1997. 137

[16] Lamport L. Shoshtak, R. and Pease, M. "Byzantine Generals Problem," ACM Transactions on Programming Languages and Systems 4(3) pp. 382-401, July 1982. 136

[17] Yen, I.-L. "A Highly Safe Self-stabilizing Mutual Exclusion Algorithm". Information Processing Letters (57), pp.301-305, 1996. 129

A Method for Evaluating Efficiency of Protocols on the Asynchronous Shared-State Model

Yoshihiro Nakaminami[1], Toshimitsu Masuzawa[1]*, and Ted Herman[2] **

[1] Osaka University, Japan,
{nakaminm,masuzawa}@ist.osaka-u.ac.jp
[2] University of Iowa,
herman@cs.uiowa.edu

Abstract. Distributed systems are commonly modeled by asynchronous models where no assumption is made about process execution speed. The asynchronous model is preferable to the synchronous one because the model reflects the fact that a distributed system consists of computers with different processing speeds. However, the asynchrony of the system makes it difficult to evaluate efficiency (performance) of distributed protocols. This paper defines a class of distributed protocols called linear state-transition protocols, in the state-communication model, and shows that efficiency of such protocols in the asynchronous distributed model can be derived from analysis of their synchronous execution, where all processes are synchronized in the lock-step fashion. This provides an effective method for evaluating efficiency of the linear state-transition protocols in the asynchronous distributed model. The paper also demonstrates the effectiveness of the method by applying it to the self-stabilizing alternator.

Keywords: Distributed system, distributed algorithm, asynchronous model, time complexity, synchronous execution, linear state-transition protocol

1   Introduction

Self-stabilization of systems and protocols is desirable, but can impose costs on performance. One challenging issue in the analysis of costs is the evaluation of time-efficiency: one would like to know the worst-case time of convergence and, for nonterminating protocols, some measure of the performance when the protocol executes legitimately. Typically, such evaluations are simpler for synchronous models than they are for asynchronous models, because the evaluation for synchronous executions is more deterministic (often the only nondetermistic

---

* Work supported in part by JSPS, Grants-in-Aid for Scientific Research ((c)(2)12680349) and by "Priority Assistance for the Formation of Worldwide Renowned Centers of Research - The 21st Century Center of Excellence Program" of the Ministry of Education, Culture, Sports, Science and Technology.
** Work supported in part by NSF grant CCR-9733541.

S.-T. Huang and T. Herman (Eds.): SSS 2003, LNCS 2704, pp. 141–153, 2003.

factor is the choice of the initial state). In this paper we are interested in the following question: what conditions should a protocol satisfy in order to simplify performance evaluation for asynchronous executions?

We start our investigation with the observation that there are some protocols in the literature of self-stabilization where the performance, measured in synchronous rounds, is the same as the performance measured in asynchronous rounds. This is true even though the asynchronous executions are nondeterministic, and include configurations that would not occur in a synchronous execution. We did not succeed to answer the general question in this paper, but we do present a sufficiency condition called "linear state-transition". Linear state-transition protocols have enough inherent determinism so that performance in an asynchronous execution is approximately the same as that in a synchronous execution. One of our contributions is thus to facilitate analysis in an asynchronous model essentially by reduction to analysis for the (simpler case of) synchronous model. We have identified several works in the literature that are linear state-transition protocols, demonstrating applicability of our results. We are able to derive new analysis of a synchronization protocol using these results.

The remainder of the paper is organized as follows. Section 2 defines the system model and its complexity measures. Section 3 introduces the linear state-transition criterion for protocols that we use in later sections. Section 4 presents theorems that relate synchronous and asynchronous executions of a linear state-transition protocol and the section also discusses how the theorems can be applied to evaluate efficiency of protocols. Then in Section 5 we use the results of Section 4 to analyze the alternator protocol [1].

2   Model

A **distributed system** $S = (P, L)$ consists of set $P = \{1, 2, \ldots, n\}$ of processes and set L of (communication) links. A link connects two distinct processes. When a link connects processes u and v, this link is denoted by (u, v). We say u is a **neighbor** of v if $(u, v) \in L$.

Each process v is a state machine and its state transition is defined by **guarded actions**:

$$< guard_v > \rightarrow < statement_v >$$

The guard $< guard_v >$ of process v is a boolean expression on its own state and its neighbors' states. When the guard is evaluated to be true, $< statement_v >$ is executed where only the state of v can be changed. In this paper, we assume that the guarded action can be atomically executed: evaluation of the guard and execution of the statement are executed in one atomic action. This model is the so-called shared-state model.

A **configuration** (i.e., a global state) of a distributed system is specified by an n-tuple $\sigma = (s_1, s_2, \ldots, s_n)$ where s_i stands for the state of process i. A process v is said to be **enabled** at a configuration σ when v has a guarded action whose guard is true at σ. A process v is said to be **disabled** at σ when it is not enabled at σ.

Let $\sigma = (s_1, s_2, \ldots, s_n)$ and $\sigma' = (s'_1, s'_2, \ldots, s'_n)$ be configurations and Q be any set of processes. We denote the transition from σ to σ' by $\sigma \overset{Q}{\mapsto} \sigma'$, when σ changes to σ' by actions of every enabled process in Q. (All enabled processes in Q make actions but no disabled processes in Q make actions.) Notice that $s_i = s'_i$ holds for process i if $i \notin Q$ or i is disabled at σ. We sometimes simply denote $\sigma \mapsto \sigma'$ without specifying the set of processes Q.

A **schedule** is an infinite sequence $\mathcal{Q} = Q_1, Q_2, \ldots$ of nonempty sets of processes. In this paper, we assume that any schedule is **weakly fair**, that is, all processes appear infinitely often in any schedule. If an infinite sequence of configurations $E = \sigma_0, \sigma_1, \sigma_2, \ldots$ satisfies $\sigma_i \overset{Q_{i+1}}{\mapsto} \sigma_{i+1}$ ($i \geq 0$), then E is called an **execution** starting from σ_0 by schedule $\mathcal{Q}$. For a process i, the **local history** of i in an execution E is the projection of E to process states of i with removal of the stuttering part.

A schedule specifies the order of processes that are activated to execute their guarded actions. In this paper, we consider an asynchronous distributed system where we make no assumption on the speed of processes. This implies that all weakly fair schedules are possible to occur. Among the schedules, we define the following two special schedules.

Synchronous Schedule: When a schedule $\mathcal{Q} = Q_1, Q_2, \ldots$ satisfies $Q_i = P$ for each i ($i \geq 1$), then we call $\mathcal{Q}$ a **synchronous schedule** and we call the corresponding execution a **synchronous execution**.

Sequential Schedule: When a schedule $\mathcal{Q} = Q_1, Q_2, \ldots$ satisfies $|Q_i| = 1$ for each i ($i \geq 1$), then we call $\mathcal{Q}$ a **sequential schedule** and we call the corresponding execution a **sequential execution**.

We consider schedules and executions to be infinite sequences. However sometimes, we consider finite parts of schedules and executions, and call them **partial schedules** and **partial executions**. Partial schedules and partial executions are defined as follows: A **partial schedule** is a finite sequence $\mathcal{Q} = Q_1, Q_2, \ldots, Q_m$ of nonempty sets of processes. If a finite sequence of configurations $E = \sigma_0, \sigma_1, \sigma_2, \ldots, \sigma_m$ satisfies $\sigma_i \overset{Q_{i+1}}{\mapsto} \sigma_{i+1}$ ($0 \leq i \leq m - 1$), then E is called a **partial execution** starting from σ_0 by schedule $\mathcal{Q}$.

To evaluate time complexity of protocols, we introduce **rounds** for an execution E. Let $E = \sigma_0, \sigma_1, \sigma_2, \ldots$ be an execution by a schedule $\mathcal{Q} = Q_1, Q_2, \ldots$. The first round of E is defined to be the minimal partial execution $\sigma_0, \sigma_1, \ldots, \sigma_i$ that satisfies $P = \cup_{1 \leq j \leq i} Q_j$. The second and later rounds of E are defined recursively for the execution $\sigma_i, \sigma_{i+1}, \sigma_{i+2}, \ldots$.

3   Linear State-Transition Protocol

A protocol is called a **linear state-transition protocol** (**LST protocol**) if it satisfies the following conditions **C1** and **C2**.

C1 (Linear State-Transition) For any configuration σ, each process has the same local history in all executions starting from σ. (This condition implies that the local history of each process is uniquely determined by the initial configuration σ.)

C2 (Non-interference) [8] Let σ be any configuration and v be any process. If v is enabled at σ, then v remains enabled until v executes an action. (This condition implies that an enabled process never becomes disabled by actions of other processes.)

The condition **C1** implies that the synchronous execution of a LST protocol is uniquely determined from the initial configuration. However, a LST protocol may have several executions even from the same initial configuration because of different asynchronous schedules.

Examples of LST protocols include the stabilizing alternator[1], the stabilizing agent traversal protocol[3], the stabilizing pipelined PIF protocol[4] and the synchronizers[5, 6, 7].

4 Efficiency Evaluation of the LST Protocols

This section presents key properties of LST protocols and proposes a method based on the properties for analyzing the efficiency of LST protocols.

4.1 Key Properties of the LST Protocols

First we define a special type of asynchronous execution, a *pseudo synchronous* execution. A pseudo synchronous execution simulates the synchronous execution in the sense that all configurations appearing in the synchronous execution also appear in the same order in an asynchronous execution (where both executions have the same initial configuration).

Definition 1. *Let σ_0 be any configuration. A **pseudo synchronous execution** starting from σ_0 is an execution by a sequential schedule $Q = Q^1 Q^2 \cdots$ with each term Q^i ($i \geq 1$) being a partial sequential schedule such that each process of P appears exactly once in Q^i, and such that the following holds:*

> *Let σ^j ($j \geq 0$) be the last configuration of the partial (pseudo synchronous) execution by the partial sequential schedule $Q = Q^1 Q^2 \cdots Q^j$. (For convenience, let $\sigma^0 = \sigma_0$.) Let $Enabled(\sigma)$ be the set of enabled processes at σ and $Disabled(\sigma)$ be the set of disabled processes at σ (i.e, $Disabled(\sigma) = P - Enabled(\sigma)$). Then all processes in $Disabled(\sigma^j)$ appear before any process in $Enabled(\sigma^j)$.*

> *The schedule $Q = Q^1 Q^2 \cdots$ is called a **pseudo synchronous schedule**.*   □

A pseudo synchronous execution is not uniquely determined from the initial configuration σ_0, but the configurations σ^j ($j \geq 1$) are uniquely determined for a LST protocol. Thus, the following lemma holds.

Lemma 1. *For a LST protocol, the subsequence of configurations $\sigma_0(= \sigma^0)$, σ^1, σ^2, ... appearing in a pseudo synchronous execution coincides with the synchronous execution.*

(Proof) Let $\sigma_0, \sigma_1, \sigma_2, \ldots$ be a synchronous execution. We can show by induction that $\sigma^i = \sigma_i$ holds for each i $(i \geq 0)$.
(Induction basis) It follows from the definition that $\sigma^0 = \sigma_0$ holds.
(Inductive step) With assumption of $\sigma^i = \sigma_i$, we prove $\sigma^{i+1} = \sigma_{i+1}$. The definition of the synchronous execution implies that every enabled process at σ^i executes a single action and no disabled process at σ^i executes an action between σ^i and σ^{i+1}.

Let $\mathcal{Q}^{i+1} = Q_1, Q_2, \ldots, Q_n$ be a partial pseudo synchronous schedule that leads from σ^i to σ^{i+1}. Recall from the definition of the pseudo synchronous schedule that $|Q_i| = 1$ holds for each i $(1 \leq i \leq n)$, and thus, let $Q_i = \{p^i\}$. In the partial pseudo synchronous schedule, there exists x $(0 \leq x \leq n)$ such that $Disabled(\sigma^i) = \{p^1, p^2, \ldots, p^x\}$ and $Enabled(\sigma^i) = \{p^{x+1}, p^{x+2}, \ldots, p^n\}$ hold. Let σ be a configuration reached from σ^i by applying the partial schedule $Q_1, Q_2, \ldots, Q_x$. It follows from $Disabled(\sigma^i) = \{p^1, p^2 \ldots p^x\}$ that no process executes its action between σ^i and σ. Thus, $\sigma = \sigma^i$ holds and all the processes in $Enabled(\sigma^i)$ remain enabled at σ. The condition **C2** guarantees that every process in $Enabled(\sigma^i)$ executes a single action by applying the schedule $Q_{x+1}, \ldots, Q_n$ to σ. For the resultant configuration σ^{i+1}, $\sigma^{i+1} = \sigma_{i+1}$ holds from the condition **C2**. □

Based on the condition **C1**, we introduce the precedence relation $<$ on the states of each process v.

Definition 2. *Let σ_0 be the initial configuration and s_0 be the initial state of process v. From the condition **C1**, the state transition of v is uniquely determined from σ_0 and let $s_0, s_1, s_2, \ldots$ be the local history of v (common to every execution starting from σ_0). For convenience, we assume without loss of generality that the states $s_0, s_1, s_2, \ldots$ are mutually distinct. Then, the precedence relation $<$ on the states of v is defined as: $s_i < s_j \iff i < j$. The precedence relation $\leq$ on the process states is defined as: $s_i \leq s_j \iff i \leq j$.* □

We define the precedence relation on the configurations from the precedence relation on the process states.

Definition 3. *For two configurations $\sigma = (s_1, s_2, \ldots, s_n)$ and $\sigma' = (s'_1, s'_2, \ldots, s'_n)$, the precedence relation $<$ on the configurations is defined as follows.*

$$\sigma < \sigma' \iff \forall i (1 \leq i \leq n) \, [s_i \leq s'_i] \wedge \exists j (1 \leq j \leq n) \, [s_j < s'_j]$$

The precedence relation $\leq$ on the configurations is defined as follows.

$$\sigma \leq \sigma' \iff \forall i (1 \leq i \leq n) \, [s_i \leq s'_i]$$

□

Lemma 2. *For a LST protocol, let E_{ps} be a pseudo synchronous execution starting from σ_0 and let σ be any configuration that appears in E_{ps}. Let E be any execution starting from σ_0 and let δ be any configuration that appears in E. If $\sigma < \delta$ holds, there exists a partial execution $E_{\sigma,\delta}$ that starts from σ and reaches δ.*

(Proof) We say that configuration α is β-reachable when there exists an execution that starts from α and reaches a configuration β. We say that configuration α is β-unreachable when α is not β-reachable. For contradiction, we assume σ is δ-unreachable.

From the definition, the initial configuration σ_0 is δ-reachable. It follows that a pseudo synchronous execution E_{ps} has a consecutive configurations γ and γ' ($\gamma < \gamma'$) such that γ is δ-reachable and γ' is δ-unreachable. Let v be the process that executes an action between γ and γ'. Since γ is δ-reachable, there exists a partial sequential execution, say $E_\gamma = \gamma, \omega_1, \omega_2, \ldots, \omega_{m-1}, \omega_m(=\delta)$ from γ to δ. Let $\mathcal{Q}_\gamma = v_1, v_2, \ldots, v_m$ ($v_i \in P$) be the partial sequential schedule for E_γ.

From the condition $C2$, process v is enabled at ω_1. Let ω_1' be the configuration that is reached when process v executes its action at ω_1. Similarly, process v_1 is enabled at γ'. Let ω_1'' be the configuration that is reached when process v_1 executes its action at γ'. From the condition **C1**, $\omega_1' = \omega_1''$ holds (Fig. 1).

Since ω_1' is reached from ω_1 and process v_2 is enabled at ω_1, v_2 is enabled at ω_1' from the condition **C2**. By repeating the similar discussion, we can construct a partial sequential execution $E_\gamma' = \gamma', \omega_1', \omega_2', \ldots, \omega_m'$ starting from γ' by $\mathcal{Q}_\gamma$. We can see that action of process v changes configuration from ω_i to ω_i' for each i ($1 \leq i \leq m$).

Since γ' is δ-unreachable, ω_i' is δ-unreachable. It follows for $\mathcal{Q}_\gamma = v_1, v_2, \ldots, v_m$ that $v_i \neq v$ ($1 \leq i \leq m$) holds. Then, for $\sigma = (s_1, s_2, \ldots, s_n)$, $\delta = (s_1', s_2', \ldots, s_n')$ and $\gamma = (s_1'', s_2'', \ldots, s_n'')$, $s_v > s_v'$ holds from $s_v = s_v''$. This contradicts $\sigma < \delta$.   □

Theorem 1. *Let σ_0 be any initial configuration. For a LST protocol, any action that is executed at round t in a pseudo synchronous execution starting from σ_0 is executed at round t or earlier in any execution starting from σ_0.*

(Proof) We prove the theorem by induction. For $t = 1$, the theorem obviously holds from the condition **C2**. Let $\sigma^t = (s_1, s_2, \ldots, s_n)$ and $\sigma^{t+1} = (s_1' s_2', \ldots, s_n')$ be the configurations at the ends of rounds t and $t+1$ in a pseudo synchronous execution respectively. For any execution E, let $\delta^t = (r_1, r_2, \ldots, r_n)$ and $\delta^{t+1} = (r_1', r_2', \ldots, r_n')$ be the configurations at the ends of rounds t and $t+1$ in any execution respectively.

For induction, we show $\sigma^{t+1} \leq \delta^{t+1}$ under the assumption that $\sigma^t \leq \delta^t$ (i.e., $s_i \leq r_i$ for each i ($1 \leq i \leq n$)). If process v is disabled at configuration σ^t (i.e., $s_v' = s_v$), $s_v' \leq r_v'$ obviously holds. If $s_v < r_v$ holds, $s_v' \leq r_v'$ obviously holds since v executes at most one action between σ and σ'. Thus, it is sufficient to show that process v is enabled at δ^t when v is enabled at σ^t and $s_v = r_v$ holds. From Lemma 2, σ^t is reachable to δ^t since we assume $\sigma^t \leq \delta^t$. Thus, from the condition **C2**, v is enabled at δ^t since v is enabled at σ^t and $s_v = r_v$. Consequently, $s_v' \leq r_v'$ holds.   □

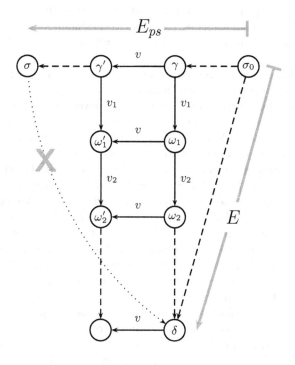

Fig. 1. Proof of Lemma 2

From Theorem 1, the following theorem immediately follows.

Theorem 2. *Let σ_0 be any initial configuration. For a LST protocol, any action that is executed at round t in the synchronous execution starting from σ_0 is executed at round t or earlier in any execution starting from σ_0.*   □

4.2   A Method for Evaluating Efficiency of the LST Protocols

Generally a distributed problem Π specifies the possible initial configurations and the expected executions starting from each of the initial configurations. A protocol for solving Π is required that all of its possible executions are the expected ones Π specifies.

In the following, we introduce two efficiency measures of a protocol, **performance** and **reach time**. In these efficiency measures, we focus on some set of specified actions or some set of specified configurations. These specified actions and configurations are determined according to the context of the problem. Typical examples of such specified actions include the token passing actions in a token circulation protocol and the *decide* actions in the repetition of a wave algorithm [9]. Typical examples of specified configurations include the configurations with solutions in non-reactive problems (e.g., leader election and tree construction problems) and the safe configurations [10] in self-stabilizing protocols.

Efficiency of a protocol is measured by the number of designated actions that are executed in some number of rounds. Theorem 2 implies for any LST protocol that each process executes no fewer actions by the end of round t in any asynchronous execution than it does in the synchronous execution. Thus the worst-case performance (i.e., the lowest performance) of a LST protocol in asynchronous executions can be directly derived from the performance of the synchronous execution starting from the same initial configuration.

The reach time measures efficiency of a protocol by the number of rounds until it reaches one of the specified configurations. We consider only specified configurations satisfying the *closure property*: once the protocol reaches one of these specified configurations, then all of the subsequent configurations are also among the specified configurations. For such specified configurations, Theorem 2 implies the following: if a LST protocol reaches a specified configuration at the end of round t in the synchronous execution, then it reaches a specified configuration at the end of round t or earlier in any execution from the same initial configuration. Thus the worst-case reach time of a protocol in asynchronous executions can be directly derived from the reach time of the synchronous execution from the same initial configuration.

It is valuable to mention what impact the above method makes especially on efficiency analysis of self-stabilizing protocols. For any self-stabilizing protocol the worst-case stabilizing time (i.e., the reach time concerning the safe configurations) in asynchronous executions can be directly derived from the stabilizing time of the synchronous execution, and the worst-case performance of asynchronous executions after recovery of a legal execution can be sometimes derived from the performance of the synchronous execution.

5   Application for Stabilizing Alternator

In this section, we evaluate the performance of **the stabilizing alternator** proposed by Gouda and Haddix [1, 2], which is an example of the LST protocols. Notice that Gouda and Haddix [1, 2] did not show the performance of the alternator and we first evaluate its performance using the properties of LST protocols.

5.1   Stabilizing Alternator

In this section, we briefly introduce the stabilizing alternator proposed by Gouda and Haddix [1].

The alternator is a transformation protocol: it transforms a protocol that works correctly under any sequential schedule to a protocol for the same task that works under any schedule. The transformation is important for the following

$$\forall w \in N_v[(q_v \neq q_w \lor v < w) \land (q_v \neq ((q_w - 1) \bmod 2d))]$$
$$\rightarrow q_v := (q_v + 1) \bmod 2d$$

Fig. 2. Actions for process v in the stabilizing alternator

reasons. Protocol design is much easier under the sequential schedules. In fact, many self-stabilizing protocols have been proposed under the sequential schedules. But the sequential schedule is not practical since real distributed systems allow several processes to execute actions simultaneously.

In the shared-state model, the action of each process is determined from the states of the process and its neighbors. This implies that protocols designed under the sequential schedules correctly work under any schedule if no neighboring processes execute actions simultaneously (i.e., local mutual exclusion). The alternator realizes the local mutual exclusion.

The alternator is a self-stabilizing protocol: starting from any initial configuration, the system reaches a configuration after which no neighboring processes execute actions simultaneously.

Figure 2 shows actions of process v. In the protocol, $q_v (0 \leq q_v \leq 2d - 1)$ is a variable of process v, N_v is a constant denoting the set of neibors of v, and d is a constant denoting the length of the longest simple cycle (if a distributed system has no cycle, then let $d = 2$).

The following lemma holds for the alternator.

Lemma 3. [1] *In any execution starting from an arbitrary initial configuration, the followings hold.*

1. *Each process v becomes enabled infinitely often (i.e., v updates q_v infinitely often).*
2. *There exists a suffix of the execution that satisfies $q_v \neq 2d - 1$ or $q_w \neq 2d - 1$ at every configuration for any neighboring processes v and w.*

The stabilizing alternator is utilized in protocol transformation. Let $\mathcal{A}$ be a self-stabilizing protocol that works correctly under any sequential execution. Transformation from $\mathcal{A}$ to a self-stabilizing protocol $\mathcal{A}'$ for the same task that works under any executions is realized as follows: Each process executes the actions of the self-stabilizing alternator and executes the actions of $\mathcal{A}$ concurrently only when variable q_v is updated from $2d - 1$ to 0.

Lemma 3 guarantees that any execution of protocol $\mathcal{A}'$ has an infinite suffix where no neighboring processes execute actions simultaneously. Since protocol $\mathcal{A}$ is a self-stabilizing protocol, $\mathcal{A}'$ converges to its intended behavior eventually.

5.2   Application of the Proposed Method

In this subsection, we first show that the alternator is a LST protocol and we evaluate its performance using the properties of a LST protocol. To show that the alternator is a LST protocol, we consider conditions $C1$ and $C2$. It is clear that $C1$ (linear state-transition) is satisfied because the only possible action of process v is $q_v := (q_v + 1) \mod 2d$. Thus, it is sufficient to show that the alternator satisfies $C2$ (non-interference).

Lemma 4. *In the alternator, once a process becomes enabled, then the process remains enabled until it executes an action.*

(Proof) Let v be a process and σ be a configuration such that v is enabled at σ. Without loss of generarility, we assume that $q_v = 0$ at σ. Since process v is enabled at σ, each neighbor w of v satisfies $2 \leq q_w \leq 2d - 1 \vee (q_w = 0 \wedge v < w)$. For contradiction, assume that v becomes disabled before it executes its action. Let w be the process whose execution of its action changes v to disabled. Two cases to consider are: (i) Case that $q_w = 0 \wedge v < w$ holds at σ: Since w cannot execute its action until v executes its action, w never changes v to disabled. (ii) Case that $2 \leq q_w \leq 2d - 1$ holds at σ: Process w can execute actions. But from the protocol, w satisfies $2 \leq q_w \leq 2d - 1$ after execution of its actions. Thus w never changes v to disabled. In each case, v remains enabled and it is contradiction. □

5.3   Performance Analysis

In this subsection, we consider synchronous execution of the alternator and show that the alternator reaches an **ideal** configuration (defined below) in $O(n)$ rounds from any configuration. We also show that all processes are enabled at every configuration after the ideal configuration.

We define an **ideal** configuration as follows: A configuration is ideal iff it satisfies the following condition:

$$\forall w \in N_v [\quad q_v \neq q_w$$
$$\wedge \; q_v \neq (q_w + 1) \mod 2d$$
$$\wedge \; (q_v + 1) \mod 2d \neq q_w \;]$$

From the protocol in Fig.2, we can see that all processes are enabled at any ideal configuration. In the synchronous execution, each process increments its variable at any ideal configuration. So the resultant configuration in the synchronous execution is also ideal.

Lemma 5. [1] *In the synchronous execution, the alternator eventually reaches an ideal configuration from any initial configuration.* □

To evaluate the number of rounds until the alternator reaches an ideal configuration, we define a directed graph $G.\sigma$ for a configuration σ as defined in [1].

Definition 4. *For a distributed system $S = (P, L)$ and a configuration σ, a directed graph $G.\sigma = (P, L')$ is defined as follows:*

$$L' = \{ (v, w) \in L \mid (q_v = q_w \; \wedge \; v > w)$$
$$\vee \quad (q_v = (q_w - 1) \mod 2d) \text{ holds at configuration } \sigma\}$$

(In $G.\sigma$, the vertex set of $G.\sigma$ is P. We do not distinguish the vertices from the processes. So we simply call a vertex in $G.\sigma$ a process.)   □

From the definition of $G.\sigma$ and the protocol of the alternator, process v is enabled iff v has no outgoing edge in $G.\sigma$.

Lemma 6. [1] *For any configuration σ, $G.\sigma$ has no directed cycle.*   □

Lemma 7. *In the synchronous execution from any initial configuration, the alternator reaches an ideal configuration within $2n$ rounds.*

(Proof) We consider graph $G.\sigma = (P, L')$ for any configuration σ of $S = (P, L)$. From Lemma 6, graph $G.\sigma = (P, L')$ has no directed cycle. Thus, if L' is not empty, $G.\sigma$ has a process that has no outgoing edge but has at least one incoming edge. We call this process a **head process**.

Let σ and σ' be consecutive configurations in the synchronous execution and v be a head process at σ'. There is two possible cases concerning the status of v at σ.

- Process v is a head process in $G.\sigma$: Since v is enabled at σ, v increments q_v between σ and σ'. It follows that any edge (u, v) in $G.\sigma'$ exists also in $G.\sigma$. This is possible only if $(q_u = q_v) \wedge (u > v)$ holds at σ.
- There exists an edge (v, w) where w is a head process in $G.\sigma$.

Let $\sigma_0, \sigma_1, \sigma_2, \ldots$ be the synchronous execution starting from σ_0. We define **an inheritance list** for each head process v in $G.\sigma_i$ as follows.

- The inheritance list of v at the initial configuration σ_0 is a list $\langle v \rangle$.
- If v is a head process in $G.\sigma_{i-1}(i > 1)$, the inheritance list of v at σ_i is that of v at σ_{i-1}.
- If v has an outgoing edge in $G.\sigma_{i-1}$, let w be any process such that edge (v, w) exists in $G.\sigma_{i-1}$. The inheritance list of v at σ is obtained by appending v to the list of w in $G.\sigma_{i-1}$.

We define the length of an inheritance list to be the number of processes contained in the list. Let ℓ_i be the minimum length of the inheritance lists existing at σ_i. From the definition of the inheritance list, it is obvious that the sequence $\ell_0, \ell_1, \ell_2, \ldots$ is monotonically non-decreasing. From the following observation, we can show that for any consecutive configurations σ_i, σ_{i+1} and σ_{i+2}, $\ell_i < \ell_{i+2}$ holds if there exists a head process at σ_{i+2}: if $\ell_i = \ell_{i+1}$ holds, then the head processes at σ_{i+1} with the inheritance list of length ℓ_{i+1} are the head process at σ_i. Such a process (say v) does not have any neighbor w such that $q_v = q_w$ at σ_{i+1}, and thus, it is not a head process at σ_{i+2}. This implies $\ell_{i+2} > \ell_i$

In what follows, we show that any process appears in any inheritance list at most once.

For contradiction, we assume that a process v appears twice in an inheritance list. Let $\langle v = v_0, v_1, v_2 \ldots, v_{m-1}, v_m = v \rangle$ $(m \leq d)$ be a part of the inheritance list, and without loss of generality, assume $v_i \neq v$ for each $i (1 \leq i \leq m-1)$. Notice that the partial list forms a simple cycle. This implies that the inheritance list is inherited along the cycle.

Let σ^{v_i} be the configuration where the process v_i becomes a head process inheriting the inheritance list from v_{i-1}. We consider the configuration σ^{v_1}. Without loss of generality, we assume $q_{v_0} = 0$ in σ^{v_1}. It implies $q_{v_1} = 2d - 2$ in σ^{v_1}.

Since the process v_{i+1} inherits the inheritance list from v_i $(0 \leq i \leq m-2)$, there exists the edge (v_{i+1}, v_i) in $G.\sigma^{v_i}$. Thus the following holds at σ^{v_i}:

$$(q_{v_i} = q_{v_{i+1}} \ \wedge \ v_i < v_{i+1}) \tag{1}$$
$$\vee \ (q_{v_i} = (q_{v_{i+1}} + 1) \ \mathrm{mod} \ 2d) \tag{2}$$

We observe the execution from σ^{v_i} to $\sigma^{v_{i+1}}$. Assume that $q_{v_i} = \lambda$ at σ^{v_i}. If the formula (1) is satisfied, exactly two rounds are spent between σ^{v_i} and $\sigma^{v_{i+1}}$ and $q_{v_{i+1}} = \lambda$ at $\sigma^{v_{i+1}}$. If the formula (2) is satisfied, exactly one round is spent and $q_{v_{i+1}} = \lambda - 1$ at $\sigma^{v_{i+1}}$.

From v_1 to v_{m-1}, let x be the number of pairs of processes that satisfy (1). Then, the number of pairs that satisfy (2) is $m-2-x$. Therefore $2x+(m-2-x) = x+m-2$ rounds are spent from σ^{v_1} to $\sigma^{v_{m-1}}$ and $q_{v_{m-1}} = 2d-2-(m-2-x) = 2d-m+x$ holds at $\sigma^{v_{m-1}}$. We assume that $q_v = 0$ at σ^{v_1}, so $0 \leq q_v \leq x+m-2$ holds at $\sigma^{v_{m-1}}$. Because of $m \leq d$, it follows that edge (v, v_{m-1}) does not exist in $G.\sigma^{v_{m-1}}$ (Neither formula (1) nor (2) are satisfied), and thus v cannot inherit the inheritance list from v_{m-1}.

This contradiction implies the length of any inheritance list is at most n. Since $\ell_i < \ell_{i+2}$ holds for any i, the synchronous execution starting from any configuration reaches a configuration within $2n$ rounds where there is no inheritance list. In that configuration, there is no head process and the configuration is ideal.   □

Lemma 7 leads the following theorem directly.

Theorem 3. *Let m be a positive integer. In any synchronous execution, each process of the alternator executes more than m actions within $2n+m$ rounds.*   □

Since the alternator is a LST protocol, we obtain the following theorem from Theorem 2 and Theorem 3.

Theorem 4. *Let m be a positive integer. In any execution, each process of the alternator executes more than m actions within $2n + m$ rounds.*   □

6   Conclusion

We presented a new method to derive efficiency of asynchronous protocols by observing their synchronous executions. The method is not universal and we defined LST protocols as a class of protocols to which the proposed method can be applied. It is worthwhile to say that several existing self-stabilizing protocols belong to the class. To show the effectiveness of the method, we applied the method for efficiency analysis of the alternator, a well-known self-stabilizing protocol for synchronization. This paper proves the possibility of a new approach to efficiency analysis of asynchronous protocols. One of our future works is to clarify the protocol class for which the proposed method can be applied to and to extend the method so that it can be applied to a wider class of protocols.

References

[1] M. G. Gouda, F. Haddix: The Alternator. In *Proc. Workshop on Self-Stabilizing System(WSS1999)*, 48–53. (1999) 142, 144, 148, 150

[2] M. G. Gouda, F. Haddix: The Linear Alternator. In *Proc. Workshop on Self-Stabilizing System(WSS1997)*, 31–47 (1997) 148

[3] T. Herman, T. Masuzawa: Self-stabilizing agent traversal. In *Proc. Workshop on Self-stabilizing Systems(WSS2001)*, 152–166. (2001) 144

[4] D. Kondou, H. Masuda, T. Masuzawa: A Self-stabilizing Protocol for Pipelined PIF. In *Proc. International Conference on Distributed Computing Systems(ICDCS2002)*, 181–190. (2002) 144

[5] B. Awerbuch: Complexity of network synchronization. *JACM*, 32, 4, 804–823. (1985) 144

[6] C. Johnen, L. O. Alima, A. K. Datta, S. Tixeuil: Self-stabilizing neighborhood synchronizer in tree networks. In *Proc. of the 19th ICDCS*, 487–494. (1999) 144

[7] C. Johnen, L. O. Alima, A. K. Datta, S. Tixeuil: Optimal snap-stabilizing neighborhood synchronizer in tree networks. *Parallel Processing Letters*, 12(3-4), 327–340. (2002) 144

[8] G. M. Brown, M. G. Gouda, C. L. Wu: A self-stabilizing token system. In *Proc. of the 20th Annual Hawaii International Conference on System Sciences*, 218–223. (1987) 144

[9] G. Tel: Introduction to Distributed Algorithms. Cambridge University Press (the second edition). (2000) 148

[10] S. Dolev: Self-stabilization. The MIT Press. (2000) 148

Time-Efficient Self-Stabilizing Algorithms through Hierarchical Structures

Felix C. Gärtner[1]* and Henning Pagnia[2]

[1] Swiss Federal Institute of Technology (EPFL), School of Computer and
Communication Sciences, Distributed Programming Laboratory, CH-1015 Lausanne,
Switzerland
fcg@acm.org
[2] University of Cooperative Education
D-68163 Mannheim, Germany, pagnia@computer.org

Abstract. We present a method of combining a self-stabilizing algorithm with a hierarchical structure to construct a self-stabilizing algorithm with improved stabilization time complexity and fault-containment
features. As a case study, a self-stabilizing spanning-tree algorithm is
presented which in favorable settings has logarithmic stabilization time
complexity.

1   Introduction

A common prejudice of the self-stabilization concept is that the notion is too
demanding to be of practical use. Self-stabilizing systems are required to recover
to a set of legal states starting from *any* initial configuration and in *every* execution [4]. Consequently, weaker notions of self-stabilization have been devised
such as *pseudo-stabilization* [2].

In this paper, we investigate another reason why self-stabilizing algorithms
may not be more common in practice. We characterize this reason with the term
true distribution which is borrowed from a seminal paper by Maekawa [11] in
the area of solving the distributed mutual exclusion problem. Intuitively, a protocol is truly distributed if no site participating in the protocol bears more
responsibility than another one. Usually, true distribution is a very desirable
property, since no site may become an availability or performance bottleneck.
Many self-stabilizing algorithms are (in this sense) truly distributed. However,
truly distributed algorithms are usually more costly in terms of execution time
or space than centralized or hierarchical solutions.

Algorithm designers often argue against sacrificing true distribution because
lack thereof makes algorithms less generally applicable and differing assumptions
must be made about individual network nodes, e.g., about their robustness. In
reality, however, the processing elements on which network protocols run are
far from homogeneous. The routers within the backbone of the Internet are

---

* Work was supported by Deutsche Forschungsgemeinschaft (DFG) as part of the
Emmy Noether programme.

highly specialized machines with mirrored disks, uninterruptible power supplies, skilled maintenance personnel, and no application load whereas, e.g., standard university workstations are often low-cost PCs with aged hardware and overfull, unbackuped disks. Even the hardware components which are directly concerned with handling network traffic (like switches and bridges) exist in many different forms. Moreover, real network structures are usually hierarchical (hosts attached to subnetworks which are attached to backbone networks) and not a "general graph" (as is assumed in many distributed algorithms). This fact can be exploited by real network protocols, e.g., by using hierarchies in DNS, NTP or employing hierarchical routing. However, true distribution is a conservative guideline for algorithm design: truly distributed algorithms will also run in heterogeneous environments. But truly distributed algorithms cannot exploit the characteristics of these environments to be more efficient.

What is needed are more flexible algorithms, i.e., algorithms which can be adapted or adapt themselves to different network settings. As a first step towards such algorithms, methods can help in which truly distributed algorithms can be adapted to heterogeneous network settings using additional structures. In this paper, we describe such a method for self-stabilizing algorithms in which true distribution can be sacrificed in favor of increased efficiency. Based on experiences in other areas [13, 8], we employ the concept of "adding logical structure" to the system to yield self-stabilizing algorithms with superior time efficiency and fault-containment properties. In particular, we apply this principle to the problem of self-stabilizing spanning tree construction.

Our approach can be briefly characterized as decomposing the entire network into a hierarchy of subnetworks and running individual instances of self-stabilizing spanning-tree algorithms within these subnetworks. The results of these algorithms are then combined in a wrapper algorithm which uses information about the hierarchy to yield a global self-stabilizing spanning tree algorithm with (in favorable settings) a logarithmic stabilization time complexity. We give formal conditions under which the composition is correct. We argue that our design principle makes self-stabilizing algorithms more practical by relating our findings to "real" Internet protocols.

We present the case study of self-stabilizing spanning-tree construction in Sect. 3 and discuss the generality and practical applicability of the approach in Sect. 4. However, in the following section we first provide a small toolbox of different self-stabilizing spanning-tree algorithms with which the general scheme of Sect. 3 may be instantiated.

2   A Toolbox of Self-Stabilizing Spanning Tree Algorithms

In this section we give examples of spanning-tree algorithms for different network settings. For references to more algorithms see the book by Dolev [5].

2.1   System Assumptions

The system is usually modeled as a graph of processing elements (processors, processes, nodes), where the edges between these elements model unidirectional or bidirectional communication links. In this paper, we denote by n the number of nodes in the system and by N an upper bound on n. Communication is usually restricted to the neighbors of a particular node. We denote by δ the diameter of the network (i.e., the length of the longest unique path between two nodes) and by Δ an upper bound on δ. A network is static if the communication topology remains fixed. It is dynamic if links and network nodes can go down and recover later. In the context of dynamic systems, self-stabilization refers to the time after the "final" link or node failure. The term "final failure" is typical for the literature on self-stabilization: Because stabilization is only guaranteed *eventually*, the assumption that faults eventually stop to occur is an approximation of the fact that there are no faults in the system "long enough" for the system to stabilize. It is assumed that the topology remains connected, i.e., there exists a path between any two network nodes even if a certain number of nodes and links may crash.

Algorithms are modeled as state machines performing a sequence of steps. A step consists of reading input and the local state, then performing a state transition and writing output. Communication can be performed by exchanging messages over the communication channels. But the more common model for communication is that of shared memory or shared registers [5]. It assumes that two neighboring nodes have access to a common data structure, variable or register which can store a certain amount of information. These variables can be distinguished between input and output variables (depending on which process can modify them). When executing a step, a process may read all its input variables, perform a state transition and write all its output variables in a single atomic operation. This is called *composite atomicity* [7]. A weaker notion of a step (called *read/write atomicity* [7]) also exists where a process can only either read or write its communication variables in one atomic step. A related characteristic of a system model is its execution semantics. In the literature on self-stabilization this is encapsulated within the notion of a *scheduler* (or *daemon*) [4]. Under a central daemon, at most one processing element is allowed to take a step at the same time.

The individual processes can be *anonymous*, meaning that they are indistinguishable and all run the same algorithm. Often, anonymous networks are called *uniform* networks [7]. A network is *semi-uniform* if there is one process (the root) which executes a different algorithm [7]. While there is no way to distinguish nodes, in uniform or semi-uniform algorithms nodes usually have a means of distinguishing their neighbors by ordering the incoming communication links. In the most general case it is assumed that processes have globally unique identifiers.

Two kinds of spanning trees may be distinguished: *breadth-first search* (BFS) trees result from a breadth-first traversal of the underlying network topology [10]. Similarly, *depth-first search* (DFS) trees are obtained from a depth-first traversal.

2.2 Lower Bounds

The usual time-complexity measure for self-stabilizing algorithms is that of *rounds* [9]. In synchronous models algorithms execute in rounds, i.e., processors execute steps at the same time and at a constant rate. Rounds can be defined in asynchronous models too, where the first round ends in a computation when every processor has executed at least one step. In general, the i-th round ends, when every processor has executed at least i steps so communication between any two processors in a particular system takes at least $\Omega(d)$ rounds. This is because it normally takes at least one round to propagate information between two adjacent processors. For the case of self-stabilizing spanning-tree construction and under certain assumptions, an arbitrary initial state may make it necessary to propagate information through the entire network. Therefore, a general lower bound of $\Omega(d)$ rounds can be assumed for self-stabilizing spanning-tree algorithms.

2.3 Two Basic Algorithms

The algorithm by Dolev, Israeli and Moran. One of the first papers to appear was by Dolev, Israeli and Moran [6, 7] in 1990. It contains a self-stabilizing BFS spanning-tree construction algorithm for semi-uniform systems with a central daemon under read/write atomicity. In the algorithm, every node maintains two variables: (1) a pointer to one if its incoming edges (this information is kept in a bit associated with each communication register), and (2) an integer measuring the distance in hops to the root of the tree. The distinguished node in the network acts as the root. The algorithm works as follows: The network nodes periodically exchange their distance value with each other. After reading the distance values of all neighbors, a network node chooses the neighbor with minimum distance *dist* as its new parent. It then writes its own distance into its output registers, which is *dist* + 1. The distinguished root node does not read the distance values of its neighbors and simply always sends a value of 0.

The algorithm stabilizes starting from the distinguished root node. After sufficient activations of the root, it has written 0 values into all of its output variables. These values will not change anymore. Note that without a distinguished root process the distance values in all nodes would grow without bound. More specifically, after reading all neighbors values for k times, the distance value of a process is at least $k + 1$. This means, that after the root has written its output registers, the direct neighbors of the root—after inspecting their input variables—will see that the root node has the minimum distance of all other nodes (the other nodes have distance at least 1). Hence, all direct neighbors of the root will select the root as their parent and update their distance correctly to 1. This line of reasoning can be continued incrementally for all other distances from the root. Hence, after $O(\delta)$ update cycles the entire tree will have stabilized.

The algorithm by Afek, Kutten and Yung. In the same year as Dolev, Israeli and Moran [6] published their algorithm, Afek, Kutten and Yung [1] presented an self-stabilizing algorithm for a slightly different setting. Their algorithm also constructs a BFS spanning-tree in the read/write atomicity model. However, they do not assume a distinguished root process. Instead they assume that all nodes have globally unique identifiers which can be totally ordered. The node with the largest identifier will eventually become the root of the tree.

The idea of the algorithm is as follows: Every node maintains a parent pointer and a distance variable like in the algorithm above, but it also stores the identifier of the root of the tree which it is supposed to be in. Periodically, nodes exchange this information. If a node notices that it has the maximum identifier in its neighborhood, it makes itself the root of its own tree. If it learns that there is a tree with a larger root identifier nearby, it joins this tree by sending a "join request" to the root of that tree and receiving a "grant" back. The subprotocol together with a combination of local consistency checks ensures that cycles and fake root identifiers are eventually detected and removed.

The algorithm stabilizes in $O(n^2)$ asynchronous rounds and needs $O(\log n)$ space per edge to store the process identifier. The authors argue this to be optimal since message communication buffers usually communicate "at least" the identifier.

2.4 Summary

This section has presented two self-stabilizing spanning tree construction algorithms. The one by Afek, Kutten and Yung [1] can be characterized as truly distributed. The semi-uniform algorithm of Dolev, Israeli and Moran [6, 7] takes a first step towards exploiting heterogeneity: it is therefore simpler than the other algorithm but must make additional robustness assumptions. Both algorithms can be used as building blocks for the method described in Sect. 3.

3 Adding Structure for Constructing Efficient Self-Stabilizing Spanning-Tree Algorithms

In this section we show how sacrificing full distribution can help to improve the efficiency of self-stabilizing algorithms. To demonstrate this, we perform a case study of applying the general principle of "introducing structure" to the area of self-stabilizing spanning-tree construction. By doing this, it is possible to transform an arbitrary self-stabilizing spanning-tree algorithm into one with increased efficiency and fault-containment properties.

3.1 System Assumptions and Base Algorithm Interface

We model a distributed system as a connected graph $G = (\Pi, E)$, where $\Pi = \{P_1, \ldots, P_n\}$ is the set of processing elements and $E \subseteq V \times V$ is the set of communication links between the processing elements. The starting point for the transformation is a set of self-stabilizing spanning-tree construction algorithms (e.g., those presented in Sect. 2). The remaining system assumptions (shared memory/message passing, distinguished identifiers/distinguished root, etc.) are the minimum assumptions necessary in order for the algorithms to work.

Within the transformation, we assume that there are multiple instances of the algorithm running concurrently throughout the network. We denote the set of all instances by $I = \{A, B, C, \ldots\}$. Each instance X of the algorithm consists of a set of local algorithm modules $x, x', \ldots$, one for each processing element which participates in the algorithm instance X. To simplify notation, x_i always denotes the local module of instance X running in P_i (e.g., the module of X running on P_3 is denoted x_3). There is at most one module of X running per processing element. Additionally, every processing element participates in at least one algorithm instance. We capture the distribution of algorithm instances to processing elements using a function $d : I \to 2^\Pi$ (where 2^Π denotes the powerset of Π, i.e., the set of all subsets of Π). We assume that the set of all algorithm instance names can be totally ordered (e.g., by using an alphabetic ordering).

Every algorithm instance running on a set of processing elements has a set of *possible roots*. For example, semi-uniform algorithms have only one preconfigured root. In other algorithms (like the one by Afek, Kutten and Yung [1]), the root will be the processing element with maximal identifier. In the case of process crashes, the processing element with the second highest identifier will eventually become root. Given the assumption that at most 1 process can fail by crashing within the protocol instance, it makes sense to select at least two processing elements, namely the ones with the highest identifiers, as possible roots for that algorithm instance. We capture the assignment of algorithm instances to possible roots using a function $r : I \to 2^\Pi$.

We assume that the individual instances of the algorithm do not interfere with each other during execution, i.e., each instance is able to execute as if it were the only algorithm running in the network. We assume that the communication topology needed by an algorithm instance respects the given communication topology, i.e., the communication graph of the algorithm instance is a subgraph of G.

We are not concerned how individual algorithm instances are created, we merely assume that they are up and running and that every processing element P_i has a means to access the interface of each algorithm module that is running on P_i. For example, bootstrapping of the algorithm can be performed off-line or on-line by an administrator who configures and starts the local algorithm modules as individual processes on the processing elements. Overall, we capture the deployment of algorithm instances in the definition of a *system*.

Definition 1 (System). *A system $S = (\Pi, I, d, r)$ consists of a set of processing elements $\Pi = \{P_1, \ldots, P_n\}$, a set of algorithm instances I, a function $d : I \to 2^\Pi$, and a function $r : I \to 2^\Pi$, such the following holds:*

1. *Every processing element participates in at least one algorithm instance, formally:*
$$\forall P \in \Pi : \exists X \in I : P \in d(X)$$

2. *A possible root P_i of an algorithm instance X always runs a local module x_i, formally:*

$$\forall X \in I : r(X) \subseteq d(X)$$

The basic interface of each module x_i of algorithm instance X consists of two methods:

- **boolean** *is_root*()
  This method returns **true** if and only if the processing element on which x_i runs is considered to be the root of the spanning tree which is maintained by algorithm instance X.
- **Neighbors** *parent*()
  If the processing element P on which x_i runs is not the root of the spanning tree which is maintained by algorithm instance X, then this method will return the identifier of the processing element P' which is considered to be the parent in that spanning tree. The identifier P' is guaranteed to be the identifier of a neighbor of P.

The algorithm interface is general enough to encapsulate any of the spanning-tree construction algorithms presented in Sect. 2.

As an example, consider the two system setups in Fig. 1. There are three instances A, B and C of the algorithm running on a network of five processing elements $P_1, \ldots, P_5$. For example, on the left side of Fig. 1 algorithm instance C runs on two processing elements P_3 and P_5 and consequently has two local modules called c_3 and c_5. Note that algorithm instances may overlap and that every processing element is covered by at least one algorithm instance.

An application running on some processing element P_i may access the interface of any algorithm module running on P_i. For example, an application running on P_3 may access b_3 and c_3.

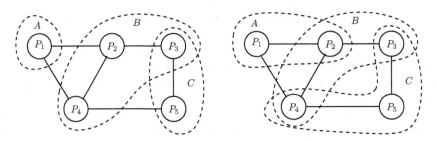

Fig. 1. Two simple system setups with three algorithm instances A, B, and C on a network of five processing elements $P_1, \ldots, P_5$

3.2   Introducing Structure

We now define an additional "overlay" structure $H = (I, \leftarrow)$ which is a rooted tree over I. The $\leftarrow$ relation is the "parent" relation over I, i.e., a child node always points to the parent node in ←. Additionally, H must satisfy two additional properties, *connectedness* and *consistency*. We first define connectedness.

Definition 2 (Connectedness). *A structure $H = (I, \leftarrow)$ is connected with respect to some system $S = (\Pi, I, d, r)$ if and only if the following holds: If $X \leftarrow Y$ in H then $d(X)$ and $d(Y)$ share a processing element in S, formally:*

$$\forall X, Y \in \Pi : X \leftarrow Y \Rightarrow d(X) \cap d(Y) \neq \emptyset$$

Basically, connectedness means that any pair of algorithm instances that are connected in H have a processing element in common. Sometimes it is impossible to find a connected structure for a system. This is the case for the system on the left side of Fig. 1 because A does not overlap with any other algorithm instance.

Fig. 2 gives examples and counterexamples of connected structures: (a) and (b) are connected structures with respect to the system on the left side of Fig. 2. The structure (c) however is not connected since $A \leftarrow C$ holds but A and C do not share a common processing element.

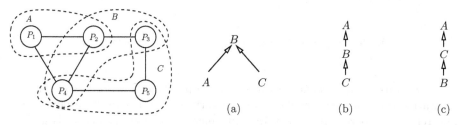

Fig. 2. Examples and counterexamples of connected structures for the example setting on the left: examples (a) and (b) satisfy the definition, (c) not

Definition 3 (Consistency). *A structure $H = (I, \leftarrow)$ is consistent with respect to a system $S = (\Pi, I, d, r)$ if and only if the following holds: If algorithm instance X is a parent of algorithm instance Y in H, then every possible root of Y must run a local algorithm module of X, formally:*

$$\forall X, Y \in I : X \leftarrow Y \Rightarrow r(Y) \subseteq d(X)$$

Intuitively, consistency means that it is possible to "go up" in the structure H at any root of a tree established in some algorithm instance. As an example, consider the left side of Fig. 2 and structure (a) and assume that the possible root of B is P_2 (i.e., $r(B) = \{P_2\}$). This setting is consistent, since $A \leftarrow B$ holds and every possible root of B is a node running a local module of instance A. On the other hand, if $r(B) = \{P_3\}$, then the structure would be inconsistent for the given system, since P_3 is not participating in algorithm instance A.

We assume that every processing element has means to access the structure H. In particular, a processing element can determine whether some algorithm instance is the root of H.

3.3   Deriving a Global Spanning Tree

Given the set of algorithm instances and the additional structure H, we now want to derive a self-stabilizing algorithm that constructs a spanning tree over the entire set of processing elements. Basically, we want to implement the spanning-tree interface given in Sect. 3.1 (i.e., the *is_root*() and the *parent*() methods).

First consider implementing the *is_root*() operation. Basically, the root of the entire spanning tree is the root of the top-level algorithm instance. Fig. 3 depicts the code of an implementation on a particular processing element P_i.

```
boolean is_root()
begin
    X := ⟨root element of H⟩
    if P_i ∈ d(X) then
        return x_i.is_root()
    else
        return false
    end
end
```

Fig. 3. Implementing *is_root*() on processing element P_i

Now, consider implementing the *parent*() operation. The idea of the implementation is to take the "smallest" level algorithm instance (with respect to H) and return the parent pointer of that instance. Note that "smallest" is not always well-defined since $\leftarrow$ is a partial order. In case there are two incomparable algorithm instances running on the same processing element, we use the assumed alphabetical order between instance names as a tie breaker. Along this line of reasoning, we now define a total order on the set of algorithm instances.

Definition 4. *Given a set I of algorithm instances and a structure $H = (I, \leftarrow)$. Let $\preceq$ denote the reflexive, transitive closure of $\leftarrow$. Define the relation $\leq$ over $I \times I$ as follows: $X \leq Y$ holds iff one of the following two cases is true:*

1. *either $X \preceq Y$,*
2. *or if $\neg X \preceq Y$ and $\neg Y \preceq X$, then X is "alphabetically smaller" than Y.*

Using $\leq$, we can implement *parent*() as shown in Fig. 4. We note that it is also possible to implement *parent*() by choosing the largest algorithm instance instead of the smallest (with respect to $\leq$) without compromising the correctness of our approach. If the largest instance is preferred, then the parent pointers of lower level algorithm instances dominate those of higher level instances and lower level structures are maintained in the combined tree rather than higher level structures. This might be preferable in some situations because it preserves a form of locality. If higher level pointers are preferred, then the three will generally be "less tall", i.e., the average distance to the root will be shorter.

Neighbors *parent*()
begin
    X := ⟨smallest algorithm instance with respect to $\leq$ running on P_i⟩
    return $x_i.parent$()
end

Fig. 4. Implementing *parent*() on processing element P_i

3.4 Examples

Fig. 5 shows an example system with a connected and consistent structure. The possible roots of the algorithm instances are also given in the figure. The overall spanning tree which is eventually constructed and emulated by our algorithm results from "overlaying" the individual spanning trees constructed within the algorithm instances.

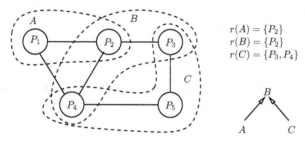

Fig. 5. Example system with a connected and consistent structure together with the possible roots of the algorithm instances

For example, algorithm instances A and B could be running with any (semi-uniform) self-stabilizing spanning tree algorithm which has P_2 pre-configured as the root. Instance C could be running an algorithm whose root eventually is the processing element with highest identifier. In this case, P_3 may have the highest identifier and P_4 the second highest. This makes sense if one of the two processes may crash. If P_3 crashes, the spanning tree constructed by instance C will stabilize to P_4 as root. Without a crash, the root will be P_3. The trees computed by the three algorithm instances are shown on the left side of Fig. 6. The "overlay" spanning tree computed by our combined algorithm is depicted on the right side of Fig. 6. Note that at processing element P_4 there are two parent pointers available (one in algorithm instance B and one in C). In such cases, the pointer of the "smaller" instance with respect to $\leq$ is chosen (i.e., B).

Fig. 7 (left) shows another example with nine processing elements and four algorithm instances with their local spanning trees. Instance B forms the "back-bone" of the network and is the top level instance. The resulting global spanning tree is depicted on the right side of Fig. 7. Note that the parent pointer of P_7

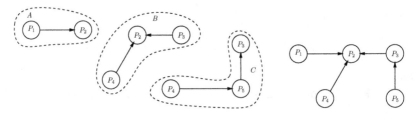

Fig. 6. Global spanning tree resulting from the example in Fig. 5: partial trees (left) and global tree (right)

in the global tree is the parent pointer from instance B and hence points to P_8 (and not the pointer of instance C because it ranks less according to $\leq$).

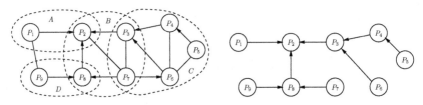

Fig. 7. Example with a "backbone" algorithm instance B and three "subnetwork" instances A, C, D (left) and resulting tree (right)

3.5   Correctness of the Transformed Algorithm

We now argue that the implementation of the spanning-tree operations given above in fact results in a self-stabilizing spanning-tree algorithm for the entire network provided the underlying algorithm instances are self-stabilizing and the structure is connected and consistent.

Assuming the underlying spanning-tree algorithm instances have all stabilized, we now give a mathematical definition of the ordering which is emulated by the implementation sketched above and show that it is in fact a rooted spanning tree.

Lemma 1. *Given a system* $S = (\Pi, I, d, r)$ *and a connected and consistent structure* $H = (I, \leftarrow)$. *If all algorithm instances* $X \in I$ *have stabilized to rooted spanning trees* $T_X = (d(X), \overset{X}{\leftarrow})$, *then the implementation given in Sect. 3.3 emulates the following rooted global spanning tree* $T = (\Pi, \leftarrow)$:

$$P_i \leftarrow P_j \Leftrightarrow \exists X \in I : [P_i, P_j \in d(X) \ \wedge \ P_i \overset{X}{\leftarrow} P_j \ \wedge \ [\forall Y \in I : X \leq Y]]$$

Proof. Basically, H determines the basic skeleton of T. The individual spanning trees of the algorithm instances yield the substructures of T. The property of consistency guarantees that the T is in fact a tree. The fact, that S is a system implies that every processing element is part of some instance in H. This together with the property of connectedness implies that every node is part of T.

It remains to be shown that the overall algorithm stabilizes, given that the underlying algorithm instances stabilize.

Lemma 2. *Given a system $S = (\Pi, I, d, r)$. Starting from an arbitrary initial state, if all algorithm instances $X \in I$ stabilize to a rooted spanning tree, then the overall algorithm will eventually stabilize to a rooted spanning tree.*

Proof. Since all algorithm instances do not interfere with each other, each algorithm instance will stabilize independently. Take the time t as the maximum stabilization time of any $X \in I$. After t, the overall algorithm will return a rooted spanning tree according to Lemma 1.

Theorem 1. *Given a system $S = (\Pi, I, d, r)$ and a connected and consistent structure $H = (I, \leftarrow)$. If all algorithm instances $X \in I$ run self-stabilizing spanning tree algorithms, then the implementation given in Sect. 3.3 emulates a global self-stabilizing spanning tree.*

3.6 Analysis

The composed algorithm has two main advantages. The first advantage is improved stabilization time. Consider the case where all algorithm instances employ a time-optimal self-stabilizing spanning tree algorithm (such as the one by Dolev, Israeli and Moran [7]). This algorithm stabilizes in $O(\delta)$ rounds where δ is the diameter of the network on which the algorithm runs. The point to note is that all algorithm instances run in parallel and that the diameters of the subnetworks in which the algorithm instances run can be considerably smaller than the overall diameter δ. Let $\delta_1, \ldots, \delta_k$ denote the diameters of the algorithm instances. Then the proof of Lemma 2 shows that the stabilization time is $O(\max_{1 \leq i \leq k} \delta_i)$. Note that this improvement is a result from the unique way in which self-stabilizing algorithms may be composed in parallel.

Consider a symmetric hierarchical decomposition of the network into subnetworks of equal size and a three level hierarchy as depicted in Fig. 8. The number of nodes in the network is $3^3 = 27$ and the network diameter is $\delta = 5$. But the overall algorithm will stabilize in steps proportional to the diameter of the largest instance network, which is 1. In general, an optimal decomposition into algorithm instances using such a hierarchic decomposition can improve the stabilization time in logarithmic scale. Decomposing n nodes into k levels yields a stabilization time in the order of $\log_k n$. Of course, this is not always feasible because it depends on the network topology, but at least sub-optimal results are achievable in practice since real networks like the Internet are often hierarchic and the diameter of the largest subnetwork is much smaller than the total diameter.

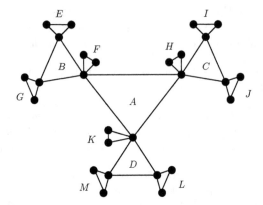

Fig. 8. Hierarchical decomposition of 27 nodes in a three layer hierarchy. The top layer consists of algorithm instance A, the middle layer of B, C and D, and the bottom layer of E, F, G (below B), H, I, J (below C) and K, L, M (below D)

The example shows that there are two extreme cases of the structure $H = (I, \leftarrow)$. The one case arises when I consists of just a single algorithm instance. In this case, adding structure does not have any benefit at all. The other case arises when I contains exactly one algorithm instance for every pair of neighboring nodes in H. In this case, the spanning tree is directly determined by H.

The second advantage of the composed algorithm is fault-containment. By adding the fixed structure, faults can only lead to perturbations within the algorithm instances in which they happen. This is in contrast to the case where a standard spanning-tree algorithm runs in the entire network: a single fault (e.g., of the root) can lead to a global reconfiguration. However, the level of fault-containment again depends on the distribution of algorithm instances to processing elements: if one processing element participates in all algorithm instances then a failure of this node may also cause global disruption.

4   Discussion

Many protocols running in the Internet like DNS or NTP sacrifice true distribution to gain efficiency, but still work rather robustly in practice. Their robustness stems from their ability to adapt their internal structures to the hierarchical and heterogeneous structure of the Internet. One particularly instructive example is the area of routing protocols.

When the Internet was a small network, routers used a truly distributed protocol to update their routing tables. Every router periodically broadcasted information to *all* other routers in the system and incorporated the received data into its own table (this was called *link-state routing* [12]). When the Internet evolved as an increasing collection of independent subnetworks (called *autonomous systems*) using a set of routers connected by high bandwidth communication links (the *backbone*), link-state routing was considered to be too inefficient for the entire network. The hierarchical nature of the Internet is exploited through modern routing protocols: within autonomous systems modern link-state routing strategies like OSPF [12] are applied (interior gateway routing). These are different from those running on the backbone (exterior gateway routing, e.g., BGP [14]).

Today, the standard approach to realize local area subnetworks, is to use switched Ethernets. In this case, it is also possible to increase the robustness by allowing for path redundancy between switches. In general, loops in the network topology of an Ethernet may cause data duplication and other forms of confusion. However, modern switches incorporate an adaptive spanning tree protocol to establish a unique path between all switches [3]. If a network segment becomes unreachable or network parameters are changed, the protocol automatically reconfigures the spanning-tree topology by activating a standby path.

The spanning-tree protocol employed in switches has striking similarities to some of the protocols described in Sect. 2. Initially, switches believe they are the root of the spanning tree but do not forward any frames. Governed by a timer, they regularly exchange status information. These messages contain (1) the identifier of the transmitting switch (usually a MAC address), (2) the identifier of the switch which is believed to be the root of the tree, and (3) the "cost" of the path towards the root. Using this information, a switch chooses the "shortest" path towards the root. If there are multiple possible roots, it selects the root with the smallest identifier (lowest MAC address). Links which are not included in the spanning tree are placed in blocking mode. Blocking links do not forward data frames but still transport status information.

The presentation above shows that the Internet maintains a set of protocols in a hierarchy to increase efficiency. Routing protocols contain spanning-tree construction, and so the hierarchical deployment is very similar to the approach sketched in Sect. 3. Algorithm instances can be replaced by self-stabilizing versions, so—apart from increasing efficiency—the hierarchical approach makes a transparent migration towards a wider deployment of self-stabilizing algorithms feasible.

5   Conclusions

We have presented a method to construct self-stabilizing algorithms with superior stabilization time and fault-containment properties from given solutions. The price we pay is sacrificing true distribution. We have argued that this is not a high price to pay in practice since real networks are not homogeneous. The only problem is to find flexible methods to map logical algorithm structures to physical network structures. We claim that our approach is one solution to this problem and hence may help to make self-stabilizing algorithms more practical.

The approach is general because it is applicable in almost the same way to many other important problems including the problem of self-stabilizing leader election and mutual exclusion. However, determining how to map the logical structures of these algorithms to existing network structures is a non-trivial design task and needs to be investigated further.

References

[1] Y. Afek, S. Kutten, and M. Yung. Memory-efficient self stabilizing protocols for general networks. In J. van Leeuwen and N. Santoro, editors, *Distributed Algorithms, 4th International Workshop*, volume 486 of *LNCS*, pages 15–28, Bari, Italy, 24–26 Sept. 1990. Springer, 1991. 157, 158, 159

[2] J. E. Burns, M. G. Gouda, and R. E. Miller. Stabilization and pseudo-stabilization. *Distributed Computing*, 7:35–42, 1993. 154

[3] Cisco Systems Inc. Using VlanDirector system documentation. Internet: http://www.cisco.com/univercd/cc/td/doc/product/rtrmgmt/sw_ntman/cwsimain/cwsi2/cwsiug2/vlan2/index.htm, 1998. 167

[4] E. W. Dijkstra. Self stabilizing systems in spite of distributed control. *Comm. of the ACM*, 17(11):643–644, 1974. 154, 156

[5] S. Dolev. *Self-Stabilization*. MIT Press, 2000. 155, 156

[6] S. Dolev, A. Israeli, and S. Moran. Self-stabilization of dynamic systems assuming only read/write atomicity. In C. Dwork, editor, *Proceedings of the 9th Annual ACM Symp. on Principles of Distribted Computing*, pages 103–118, Québec City, Québec, Canada, Aug. 1990. ACM Press. 157, 158

[7] S. Dolev, A. Israeli, and S. Moran. Self-stabilization of dynamic systems assuming only read/write atomicity. *Distributed Computing*, 7:3–16, 1993. 156, 157, 158, 165

[8] L. Fiege, M. Mezini, G. Mühl, and A. P. Buchmann. Engineering event-based systems with scopes. In B. Magnusson, editor, *Proc. European Conference on Object-Oriented Programming (ECOOP)*, volume 2374 of *LNCS*, pages 309–333, Malaga, Spain, June 2002. Springer. 155

[9] C. Génolini and S. Tixeuil. A lower bound on dynamic k-stabilization in asynchronous systems. In *Proc. 21st Symposium on Reliable Distributed Systems (SRDS 2002), IEEE Computer Society Press*, pages 211–221, 2002. 157

[10] D. E. Knuth. *The Art of Computer Programming*, volume III (Sorting and Searching). Addison-Wesley, Reading, MA, second edition, 1997. 156

[11] M. Maekawa. A $\sqrt{N}$ algorithm for mutual exclusion in decentralized systems. *ACM Trans. on Computer Systems*, 3(2):145–159, 1985. 154

[12] J. Moy. OSPF version 2. Internet: RFC 1583, Mar. 1994. 166, 167

[13] H. Pagnia and O. Theel. Sacrificing true distribution for gaining access efficiency of replicated objects. In *Proc. 31st IEEE Hawaii Intl. Conference on System Sciences (HICSS-31)*, Big Island, HI, USA, 1998. 155

[14] Y. Rekhter. A border gateway protocol 4 (BGP-4). Internet: RFC 1771, Mar. 1995. 167

A Stabilizing Solution
to the Stable Path Problem

Jorge A. Cobb[1], Mohamed G. Gouda[2], and Ravi Musunuri[1]

[1] Department of Computer Science, The University of Texas at Dallas
Richardson, TX 75083-0688
{cobb,musunuri}@utdallas.edu
[2] Department of Computer Science, The University of Texas at Austin
1 University Station C0500, Austin, TX 78712-0233
gouda@cs.utexas.edu

Abstract. The stable path problem is an abstraction of the basic functionality of the Internet's BGP routing protocol. This abstraction has received considerable attention, due to the instabilities observed in BGP. In this abstraction, each process informs its neighboring processes of its current path to the destination. From the paths received from its neighbors, each process chooses the best path according to some locally chosen routing policy. However, since routing policies are chosen locally, conflicts may occur between processes, resulting in unstable behavior. Current solutions either require expensive path histories, or prevent processes from locally choosing their routing policy. In this paper, we present a solution with small overhead, and furthermore, each process has the freedom to choose any routing policy. However, to avoid instabilities, each process is restricted to choose a path that is consistent with the current paths of its descendants on the routing tree. This is enforced through diffusing computations. Furthermore, our solution is stabilizing, and thus, recovers automatically from transient faults.

1 Introduction

The Border Gateway Protocol (BGP) [14] has become the de-facto standard for exchanging routing information between Internet Service Providers (ISPs). Generally, ISPs choose a path to each destination based on a locally chosen routing policy. Furthermore, ISPs are unwilling to share their local policies with other ISPs. Due to this lack of coordination between ISPs, Varadhan et al. showed that BGP exhibits unstable behavior, i.e., the chosen path to each destination may continuously oscillate [16]. Furthermore, simple techniques like route-flap-damping [17] do not eliminate these oscillations, but simply increase the oscillation period. Furthermore, route-flap-damping may also significantly increase the convergence times of stable routes [13].

To study the problem formally, Griffin et al. proposed an abstract model of BGP routing behavior [9]. In this abstraction, the network consists of a set of processes interconnected by channels. Each process informs its neighboring

S.-T. Huang and T. Herman (Eds.): SSS 2003, LNCS 2704, pp. 169–183, 2003.

processes of its current path to the destination. From the paths received from its neighbors, each process chooses the best path according to some local routing policy. Conflicts between local routing policies result in unstable behavior.

Three solutions to this problem have been proposed. The first approach analyzes the local routing policies of all processes, and decides whether the routing policy is "safe", that is, whether the network is guaranteed to converge to a stable configuration. However, this approach has two disadvantages. First, ISPs are often unwilling to share their local policies. Second, Griffin and Wilfong [9] proved that deciding the safety of a routing policy is an NP-complete problem.

The second approach maintains path histories during run-time to determine if the network is oscillating and thus failing to converge. This approach was proposed by Griffin et al. in their safe path-vector protocol [10]. Oscillations are detected through loops in the path histories, and selected paths are removed to ensure convergence. However, the removed paths may be of later use as the network topology changes. Furthermore, the existence of a loop in the path history is necessary but not sufficient for divergence. Finally, maintaining path histories significantly increases the memory and message overhead.

The third approach, proposed by Gao and Rexford [3] [4] restricts the routing policy to a hierarchical structure. Therefore, no routing conflicts occur, and the network is guaranteed to reach a stable state. However, this severely restricts the choice of routing policies, and the desired property of locally choosing a routing policy is lost.

The solution we present in this paper introduces a small overhead, and furthermore, each process has the freedom to choose its individual routing policy. However, to avoid instabilities, each process is restricted to choose a path that is consistent with the current paths of its descendants on the routing tree. This is enforced through diffusing computations. Furthermore, our solution is stabilizing [15][12], and thus, it recovers automatically from transient faults.

2   Notation

We begin with an overview of our process notation. A similar notation may be found in [6]. A network consists of a set of processes interconnected via communication channels. Each channel transmits a sequence of messages between two processes. The channel from a process p to a neighboring process q is denoted $ch(p, q)$. A single message type, *path*, is used in our protocols. The number of *path* messages in channel $ch(p, q)$ is denoted $\#ch(p, q)$.

Channels have the following properties. For every pair of processes p and q, if there is a channel from p to q, then there is also a channel from q to p. For simplicity, even though channels may fail, we assume the network remains connected. In addition, channels may lose and reorder messages. Finally, each channel has a known bound on its message lifetime.

A process consists of a set of inputs, a set of variables, a parameter, and a set of actions. The inputs declared in a process can be read, but not written, by the actions of that process. The variables declared in a process can be read and written by the actions of that process. The parameter is discussed further below.

Every action is of the form: $<$guard$> \rightarrow <$command$>$. The $<$guard$>$ can be of three types: local, receiving, and timeout. A local guard is a boolean expression over the inputs, variables, and parameter declared in the process. An action with a local guard is said to be enabled if its guard evaluates to true. A receiving guard at process p is of the form

rcv *path* **from** q

where q is a neighbor of p. An action with this guard is enabled iff there is a message of type *path* in channel $ch(q, p)$. Furthermore, if this action is chosen for execution, then this message is removed from channel $ch(q, p)$. Finally, a timeout guard at process p is of the form

timeout $\#ch(p, q) = 0 \ \land \ \#ch(q, p) = 0$

where q is a neighbor of p. An action with this guard is enabled iff there are no *path* messages in either channel $ch(p, q)$ or channel $ch(q, p)$[1].

The $<$command$>$ in an action is a sequence of conditional statements or sends statements. Conditional statements are of the following form.

$<$variable$> := <$expression$>$ **if** $<$boolean$>$

If $<$boolean$>$ is true before the conditional statement is executed, then $<$variable$>$ is assigned the current value of $<$expression$>$. If $<$boolean$>$ is false, then $<$variable$>$ remains unchanged. If the phrase **if** $<$boolean$>$ is not present, then the value of $<$expression$>$ is assigned to $<$variable$>$ unconditionally. A send statement in process p is of the form **send** *path* **to** q, where q is a neighbor of p.

The parameter declared in a process is used to write a set of actions as a single action, with one action for each possible value of the parameter. For example, if we have the following parameter definition,

par g : **element of** $\{r, s\}$

then the following action

rcv *path* **from** $g \rightarrow$ **send** *path* **to** g

is a shorthand notation for the following two actions.

rcv *path* **from** $r \rightarrow$ **send** *path* **to** r

⫿

rcv *path* **from** $s \rightarrow$ **send** *path* **to** s

An execution step of a protocol consists of choosing an enabled action out of all the actions of all processes, and executing the command of this action. An execution of a protocol consists of a sequence of execution steps, which either never ends, or ends in a state where all actions are disabled. We assume all executions of a protocol are weakly fair, that is, an action whose guard is continuously true must be eventually executed.

---

[1] This form of timeout can be easily implemented using timers, as shown in [6].

3   Ordered Paths

As a prelude to the stable path problem, we formally define the routing policy of a process to be an ordering on all paths originating at the process. In addition, we present a greedy protocol where each process attempts to improve the order of its path without regard for other processes. We begin with some notation.

Definition 1. *A* path *is a sequence of processes. Paths have the following properties:*

- $|P|$ *denotes the number of processes in the path.*
- λ *denotes the empty path.*
- P_i *denotes the ith process in path P. P_1 and $P_{|P|}$ are the first and last processes in P, respectively.*
- $p{:}P$ *denotes the concatenation of process p with path P.*
- *Process* root *is a distinguished process. A path is* rooted *iff it is simple and its last process is* root.
- *A path is a* network *path iff, for every pair of consecutive processes p and q along the path, p and q are neighbors.*

Each process p attempts to find a network path from itself to *root*. However, paths must be consistent between neighbors: if P and Q are the paths chosen by p and q, respectively, and if $q = P_2$, then $p{:}Q = P$.

We assume that rooted paths are ordered, and that processes are greedy. That is, each process chooses the path with highest order among the paths offered by its neighbors. We next formalize the ordering of paths.

Definition 2. *A* path ordering *is a tuple $\langle V, \preceq \rangle$, where:*

- *V is a set of processes, and $\preceq$ is a transitive relation on paths from V,*
- *for every pair of rooted paths P and Q,*

$$(P_1 = Q_1) \Rightarrow (P \preceq Q \;\; \vee \;\; Q \preceq P)$$
$$(P \prec Q) \equiv (P \preceq Q \;\; \wedge \;\; Q \not\preceq P)$$

- *for every path P, $P \preceq root$.*
- *for every rooted path P, $\lambda \prec P$.*

Intuitively, if $p = P_1 = P_1'$, then $P \prec P'$ indicates that p prefers path P' over path P, i.e., P' has a higher order than P.

We next present the *greedy protocol*. In this protocol, each process chooses the highest ordered path from those offered by its neighbors. To do so, each pair of neighboring processes exchange a single *path* message between them. This message contains the current rooted path chosen by the process.

The specification consists of two processes: process *root* and a non-root process p. These processes store in variable P their current rooted path. Process *root* simply stores *root* in its variable since the highest ordered rooted path from *root* to itself is just itself. The greedy protocol is specified as follows:

process p
inp N : **set of neighbors**
var P : **path**,   // path of p //
           G : **path**   // path from neighbor g //
par g : **element of** N // any neighbor //
begin
~ **rcv** $path(G)$ **from** g →
           $P := p{:}G$ **if** $P \prec p{:}G$ ∨ $g = P_2$;
           $P := \lambda$ **if** $\neg sound(P)$;
           send $path(P)$ **to** g

▯
~ **timeout** $\#ch(p,g) = 0$ ∧ $\#ch(g,p) = 0$ →
           send $path(P)$ **to** g **if** $p < g$
end

process $root$
inp N : **set of neighbors**
var P : **path**   // path of $root$ //
           G : **path**   // path from neighbor g //
par g : **element of** N // any neighbor //
begin
~ **rcv** $path(G)$ **from** g →
           $P := root$; **send** $path(P)$ **to** g

▯
~ **timeout** $\#ch(root,g) = 0$ ∧ $\#ch(g,root) = 0$ →
           send $path(P)$ **to** g **if** $root < g$
end

Both processes contain two actions: a timeout action and a receive action. The timeout action retransmits the *path* message if it is lost, and is similar in both processes. The receive action is different between both processes.

In process p, upon receiving a *path* message from g, P is updated by concatenating p to the path given by g, i.e., process p chooses g as the next process along its path to *root*. This update is performed only under the following two conditions. First, if g is already the next process along the path of p, i.e., $g = P_2$. In this case, any change in the path of g must be reflected in the path of p. Second, if the path through g has a higher order than P. In this case, to improve the order of its path, p chooses the path through g. After updating its path, p performs a sanity check to see if its path P is sound, where $sound(P)$ is defined as follows:

$$sound(P) \equiv (P_1 = p \ \wedge \ P_2 \in N \ \wedge \ rooted(P)).$$

If the path is not sound, then the empty path is chosen. After the sanity check, p returns the *path* message to g containing the updated path P.

The receive action in process $root$ simply returns the *path* message to g with $root$ as the path, because this path has the highest order in the network.

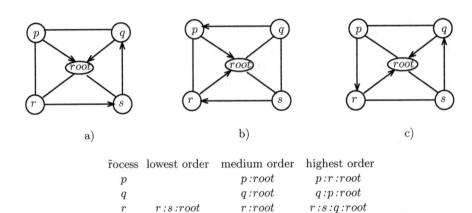

Process	lowest order	medium order	highest order
p		p :root	p :r :root
q		q :root	q :p :root
r	r :s :root	r :root	r :s :q :root
s	s :root	s :r :root	s :q :root

Fig. 1. Unstable path selection

4   Stable Path Problem

Conflicts between the routing policies of neighbors may cause the greedy protocol to never achieve a stable configuration. An example[2] of these conflicts is shown in Figure 1. Arrows indicate the current path taken by each process, and the ordering of paths at each process is given in a table at the bottom of the figure. Paths not included in the table are assumed to have the lowest order.

Figure 1(a) shows the initial choice of each process. Process q notices that the path through p is ordered higher than its current path, and changes its path to q :p :root. Next, s notices that the path through q is ordered lower than the path directly to root, and updates its path accordingly. Then, r notices that the path directly to root is ordered higher than the new path through s, and changes its path to r :root. Finally, s notices that the path through r is ordered higher than its current path directly to root, and changes its path to s :r :root. The resulting configuration is shown in Figure 1(b). Similarly, Figure 1(c) is derived from Figure 1(b) after processes p, q, and s, in this order, change their paths. Finally, Figure 1(a) is obtained from Figure 1(c) after processes r and p change their paths. Thus, a stable configuration is never reached.

Given the path ordering, the stable path problem consists of deciding if the greedy protocol will always reach a stable configuration. However, as shown in [11], this problem is NP-complete. Therefore, we propose to strengthen the greedy protocol to ensure it always reaches a stable configuration. In our enhanced protocol, any path ordering may be used, and path histories are unnecessary. However, to ensure convergence, a process is prevented from choosing a path with higher order if by doing so it causes a conflict with other processes.

---

[2] This is the classical "bad gadget" example first introduced in [8].

5   Monotonic Path Orderings

In [8] [9], it is shown that if the path ordering is consistent with a cost function, then a stable configuration is always achieved. Below, we give a more general result based on path monotonicity[3]. Path monotonicity formalizes the notion of consistency in a path ordering.

Definition 3. *A path ordering* $\langle V, \preceq \rangle$ *is* monotonic *if and only if, for every pair of processes p and q, and for every pair of rooted paths Q and Q' originating at q, such that $p \notin Q$ and $p \notin Q'$,*

$$Q \preceq Q' \Rightarrow p{:}Q \preceq p{:}Q'$$

If a path ordering is monotonic, and q is the next process along the path of p, then any change of path performed by q to improve the order of its path results in an increase in the order of the path of p. That is, q is consistent with p.

Theorem 1. *If* $\langle V, \preceq \rangle$ *is a monotonic path ordering, then the greedy protocol always converges to a stable configuration. Furthermore, at this stable configuration, the path chosen by each process is the highest-ordered rooted network path originating at that process.*

From above, if a network has a monotonic path ordering, then a stable state is guaranteed to be reached. However, path orderings are chosen independent at each process, and thus, they cannot be guaranteed to be monotonic. Below, we show how we can modify the greedy protocol to ensure that even if the path ordering is not monotonic, the network is guaranteed to reach a stable state.

6   Enforcing Monotonic Path Orderings

If a path ordering is monotonic, then the order of the paths chosen by each process is nondecreasing. To see this, consider a process p and the next process q along the path of p. If q chooses a new path whose order is at least the order of its previous path, then the order of the new path of p is at least the order of its previous path. Thus, stability is assured.

Since we have chosen to allow any path ordering, we strengthen the protocol to ensure that the order of the chosen path at each process is non-decreasing. We refer to this restriction as the *monotonic ordering property*.

Note that it is not sufficient for each process to choose a new path whose order is greater than the order of its previous path. This is because, when a process p changes its path, each process q whose path includes p must update its path to reflect the new path of p. The new path of q may have a lower order than its original path, violating the monotonic ordering property.

The above violation is prevented as follows. Before p adopts a new path, p asks q if this change of path will cause the order of the path of q to decrease. If this is the case, p refrains from adopting the new path.

---

[3] Path monotonicity is similar to the monotonicity of routing metrics presented in [7].

The coordination between p and q is performed via a diffusing computation [5] along the *routing tree*. The routing tree is defined as follows. For every process p and its next-hop neighbor q along its path, consider the directed edge (p, q). The union of all these edges over all processes form a routing tree. In addition, if edge (p, q) is on the routing tree, then p is a *child* of q and q is the *parent* of p. Similarly, if there is a path from p to q along the routing tree, then p is a *descendant* of q (denoted $desc(p, q)$), and q is an *ancestor* of p (denoted $anc(q, p)$). In particular, every process is its own ancestor and descendant.

Diffusing computations are performed along the subtree of the process desiring a new path. When process p desires a new path, p propagates its new path along its subtree. When process q in the subtree of p receives the path of p, it determines if this new path, along with the network path from q to p, has a lower order than its current path. If so, q rejects the new path, and p is prevented from adopting the new path. Otherwise, q continues the propagation of the new path of p down the subtree. If all processes in the subtree allow the new path, a positive feedback is sent to p, and p adopts the new path.

Process p maintains two path variables, P and P^*, that store the current path of p and the tentative path of p, respectively. In addition, p maintains a set, called *clean*, where it stores the identifiers of neighboring processes that have allowed p to proceed with the tentative path P^*.

Neighboring processes periodically exchange a single message between them, called *path*. This message contains three fields: the current path of the process, the tentative path of the process, and a boolean bit indicating if all neighbors have allowed the process to adopt its tentative path, that is, if *clean* contains all neighbors of the process.

As an example, consider Figure 2. The current path from p to *root* is P, and the tentative path from p to *root* is P^*. Before p adopts the new path P^*, it must consult with all descendants in its subtree. To do so, p includes P^* in the next *path* message it sends to its neighbors[4]. This is depicted in Figure 2(a).

When q and r receive this message, they check if the order of the new path is at least the order of their current path. If so, their tentative paths are set to $q:P^*$ and $r:P^*$, respectively, and these tentative paths are included in the *path* messages they send to their neighbors. Similarly, s and t receive the tentative path $q:P^*$ from q, and u and v receive the tentative path $r:P^*$ from r.

Since $s, t, u,$ and v are childless, they return *true* bit of the next *path* message to q and r. This is shown in Figure 2(b). Note that q and r reply *true* to each other since neither is a child of the other. Thus, q and r receive a positive reply from each neighbor, and thus, each replies a *true* bit to p.

The final step is shown in Figure 2(c). Process p assigns P^* to P, effectively adopting P^* as its current path. Then, the updated path P is propagated to all descendants of p. Each process along the way appends its own identifier to the path, ensuring that each process receives the entire path to *root*.

---

[4] Process p also includes two other fields in this message. However, only the necessary fields at each step in the figure will be shown.

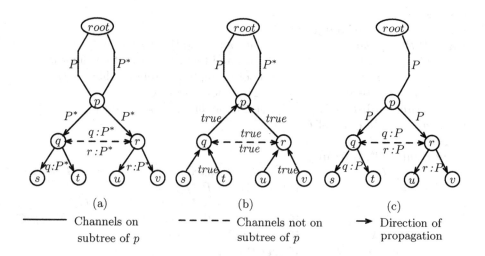

Fig. 2. Diffusing computation example

7   Monotonic Paths Protocol

In this section, we present the specification of the monotonic paths protocol that was briefly described in the previous section. Each process p maintains variables P, P^* and *clean*, described earlier. In addition, it maintains a set of neighbor id's, named *wait*. If $g \in wait$, then p ignores the next *path* message from g when deciding if the diffusing computation ended along the subtree of g. The reason for this is explained below.

The specifications of process *root* and of a non-root process p are given below.

process *root*
inp N : **set of neighbors**
var P, P^* : **path,**   // path and tentative path of *root* //
          G, G^* : **path,**   // path and tentative path of neighbor g //
          b : **boolean,**   // boolean reply bit from neighbor g //
          wait : **subset of** N,   // ignore next message //
          clean : **subset of** N // neighbors in agreement with *root* //
par g : **element of** G
begin
~ **rcv** $path(G, G^*, b)$ **from** g $\rightarrow$
        $P, P^*, wait, clean := root, root, \emptyset, N;$
        send $path(P, P^*, true)$ **to** g

⫿
~ **timeout** $\#ch(root, g) = 0$ $\land$ $\#ch(root, p) = 0$ $\rightarrow$

$\qquad$ **send** $path(P, P^*, true)$ **to** g **if** $p < g$
end

process p
inp N : **set of neighbors**
var P, P^* : **path**,   // path and tentative path of p //
 $\qquad$ G, G^* : **path**,   // path and tentative path of neighbor g //
 $\qquad$ b : **boolean**,   // boolean reply bit from neighbor g //
 $\qquad$ $wait$: **subset of** N, // ignore next message //
 $\qquad$ $clean$: **subset of** N // neighbors in agreement with p //
par g : **element of** G
begin
$\tilde{}$ **rcv** $path(G, G^*, b)$ **from** g $\rightarrow$
 $\qquad$ $P := p{:}G$ $\qquad\qquad\qquad$ **if** $g = P_2$ $\vee$ $(clean = N$ $\wedge$ $P^* = p{:}G$ $\wedge$ $G = G^*$
 $\qquad$ $P^* := P$ $\qquad\qquad\qquad$ **if** $(g = P_2^*$ $\wedge$ $P^* \neq p{:}G^*)$ $\vee$
 $\qquad\qquad\qquad\qquad\qquad\qquad$ $(p = G_2$ $\wedge$ $G^* \neq g{:}P^*$ $\wedge$ $G = G^*$ $\wedge$ $g \notin wait$
 $\qquad$ $P^* := G^*$ $\qquad\qquad\qquad$ **if** $P = P^*$ $\wedge$ $P \preceq p{:}G^*$ $\wedge$ $(g \neq P_2 \Rightarrow P \prec p{:}G^*)$;
 $\qquad$ $P, P^* := \lambda, \lambda$ $\qquad\qquad$ **if** $\neg sound(P)$ $\vee$ $\neg sound(P)$;
 $\qquad$ $wait, clean := N, \emptyset$ $\qquad$ **if** $new(P, P^*)$;
 $\qquad$ $wait := wait - \{g\}$;
 $\qquad$ $clean := clean \bigcup \{g\}$ **if** $p \neq G_2$ $\vee$ $(G = g{:}P$ $\wedge$ $G^* = g{:}P^*$ $\wedge$ $b)$;
 $\qquad$ **send** $path(P, P^*, clean = N)$ **to** g
$\rrbracket$
$\tilde{}$ **timeout** $\#ch(p, g) = 0$ $\wedge$ $\#ch(g, p) = 0$ $\rightarrow$
 $\qquad$ **send** $path(P, P^*, clean = N)$ **to** g **if** $p < g$
end

Each process consists of two actions: a timeout action to retransmit the *path* message, and a receive action to receive the *path* message from a neighbor g.

Process *root* has only minor changes. Thus, consider process p, and consider first the receive action. Upon receiving a *path* message from g, p must decide whether or not to perform each of the following steps:

- Process p may update its path P to follow the path G of neighbor g, that is, P is assigned $p{:}G$, and g becomes the parent of p.
- Process p may choose to abort its current diffusing computation. This is represented by assigning its current path P to its tentative path P^*.
- Process p may choose to start a new diffusing computation to propagate the tentative path G^* of g, in an attempt to gain approval for this path from the descendants of p. Thus, P^* is assigned $p{:}G^*$.

These three steps are performed by the first three assignment statements of the receive action.

Consider the first step of choosing g as the parent of p by updating P from G. This is performed under two conditions. First, if g is the parent of p (i.e., $g = P_2$), then p must update P from G, as described in Section 3. Second, p may have started a diffusing computation using the tentative path from a neighbor g

who is not current parent of p. If so, p chooses g as its new parent provided all descendants agreed (i.e., $clean = N$), the path offered by g is the desired path (i.e., $P^* = p{:}G$), and g is not involved in a diffusing computation (i.e., $G = G^*$).

Next, consider when p aborts its diffusing computation by assigning P to P^*. This is done in two occasions. One occasion is when g is the tentative parent of p and the path being propagated by g is not the desired path (i.e., $g = P_2^* \wedge P^* \neq p{:}G^*$). The other occasion is when g is a child of p (i.e., $p = G_2$), g has not adopted the tentative path of p (i.e., $G^* \neq g{:}P^*$), and the diffusing computation along g has finished (i.e., $G = G^*$). This indicates that g rejected the tentative path. The last conjunct, $g \notin wait$, is explained below.

Consider the third step of initiating a new diffusing computation. This is performed when p is currently not involved in a diffusing computation, and the tentative path offered by g has an order at least that of the current path of p (i.e., $P = P^* \wedge P \preceq p{:}G^*$). Also, if g is not the parent of p, then the order of the tentative path must be strictly greater than the order of the current path (i.e., $g \neq P_2 \Rightarrow P \prec p{:}G^*$). This is necessary to ensure the network reaches a stable configuration, rather than alternating between paths of the same order.

Next, process p checks if either P or P^* have changed (i.e., $new(P, P^*)$). If either of these changed, then $clean$ is assigned the empty set, because the paths of the descendants of p may no longer be consistent with the paths of p.

Assume that the paths of p did change, and subsequently, p receives a $path$ message from a child g, where $G = G^* \neq P^*$. In this case, p cannot determine whether g is rejecting the diffusing computation, or simply g has not yet received the new paths from p. The neighbor set $wait$ aids in distinguishing between these two cases. Whenever the paths of p change, $wait$ is assigned the entire set of neighbors, indicating that the next message from each neighbor should not be considered to determine if the diffusing computation has terminated. When the next message is received from g, g is removed from $wait$.

Before propagating the newly obtained paths to its neighbors, p checks if these paths are sound. If they are not, both are set to the empty path.

Finally, before sending a $path$ message to g, p checks whether the diffusing computation has finished along the subtree of g. This is true if either g is not a child of p (i.e., $p \neq G_2$), or g has the desired paths and reports all of its descendants as consistent (i.e., $G = p{:}P \wedge G^* = p{:}P^* \wedge b = true$).

The timeout action of p is similar to the timeout action in the greedy protocol, except that both P and P^* are included in the message, plus a bit indicating if all descendants agree with p (i.e., $clean = N$).

8   Stabilization

A protocol is said to be stabilizing iff, when started from an arbitrary initial state, it converges to a state contained in a set of legitimate states, and the set of legitimate states is closed under execution [15, 12]. In this section, we perform a slight modification to the monotonic paths protocol to ensure it is stabilizing. We refer to this final protocol as the stabilizing monotonic paths protocol.

To distinguish between variables with the same name but in different processes, we prefix variables with the name of their process.

The following relationship is crucial for the correct behavior of the monotonic paths protocol: for every p and q, where $desc(p,q) \ \wedge \ q.P \neq q.P^* \ \wedge \ q.clean = q.N$:

$$p.P = rt(p,q):q.P \ \wedge \ p.P^* = rt(p,q):q.P^* \ \wedge \ p.clean = p.N$$

where $rt(p,q)$ corresponds the path in the routing tree from p to q.

This relationship, however, is not restored automatically, for the following reason. Assume q propagates its current and tentative paths to a descendant p. Although p is required to adopt the current path of q, it is *not* required to adopt the tentative path of q, because its order may be lower than the current path of p. In this case, p is free to reject the tentative path of q.

We solve this problem by removing p from the routing tree whenever this relationship does not hold. That is, p assigns the empty path to both its current and tentative paths. In addition, to enforce monotonicity, we must ensure that $P \preceq P^*$. Note that this is violated only in faulty states, and it can be restored by assigning an empty path to both P and P^*.

Both requirements above are accomplished by weakening the **if** condition on the fourth assignment statement in the receive action to the following:

$$P, P^* := \lambda, \lambda \quad \textbf{if} \ \neg sound(P) \ \vee \ \neg sound(P^*) \ \vee \ P \npreceq P^* \ \vee$$
$$(g = P_2 \ \wedge \ G \neq G^* \ \wedge \ b) \nRightarrow (P = p{:}G \ \wedge \ P^* = p{:}G^* \ \wedge \ clean = N)$$

9   Correctness Proof

We next present an outline of the correctness proof of the stabilizing monotonic paths protocol. Due to space constraints, the detailed proofs are found in [2].

Given that our network is based on message passing, and to ensure stabilization, we make some assumptions about the timing of sending and receiving events. Specifically, each process must receive and handle incoming messages faster than its neighbors can send messages to it. This is easily implemented by placing an upper limit on the rate at which each process can send a new *path* message, and by placing a lower limit on the rate at which incoming messages are handled. Assuming each channel can only store a finite number of messages, then, eventually, for every pair of neighboring processes, only a single path message circulates between them.

Lemma 1. *Starting from an arbitrary state, eventually the following hold and continue to hold.*

- *For every pair of neighboring processes p and q, $\#ch(p,q) + \#ch(q,p) \leq 0$.*
- *All path variables of all processes and all path values in all path messages are either sound or are equal to the empty path.*
- *For every process p, $p.P \preceq p.P^*$, and for every message $path(G, G^*, b)$ in any channel, $G \preceq G^*$.*

Our proofs are based on induction over the number of hops between a process and its descendants. We define $hops(p, q)$ to be the number of hops from p to q along the routing tree. Furthermore, for all p, $hops(p, p) = 0$. In addition, we refer to the values contained in a *path* message using the following notation. The first field of the *path* message in the channel from p to q is referred to as $path(p, q).P$, while the second and third fields of the same message are referred to as $path(p, q).P^*$ and $path(p, q).b$, respectively.

Lemma 2. *From any arbitrary state, the network reaches a state where both of the following hold and continue to hold.*

- *For every process p and neighbor g of p, if $p.P \neq p.P^* \;\wedge\; g \in p.clean \;\wedge\; \#ch(p, g) > 0$, then:*

$$path(p, g).P = p.P \;\wedge\; path(p, g).P^* = p.P^*$$

- *For every process p and neighbor g of p, such that*

$$\#ch(p, g) > 0 \;\wedge\; path(p, g).P \neq path(p, g).P^* \;\wedge\; path(p, g).b$$

   we have

$$p.P_1 \neq g \;\vee\; (p.P = path(p, g).P \;\wedge\; p.P^* = path(p, g).P^* \;\wedge\; p.clean = p.N)$$

We define $Diffusing(k)$, where $k \geq 1$, as follows: for every process p and every neighbor g of p, such that $p.P \neq p.P^* \;\wedge\; g \in p.clean$, and for every descendant q of g, such that $hops(q, p) \leq k$, and for every neighbor r of q,

$$q.P = rt(q, g){:}p.P \;\wedge\; q.P^* = rt(q, g){:}p.P^* \;\wedge\; q.clean = q.N \;\wedge$$
$$(\#ch(q, r) > 0 \Rightarrow (path(q, r).P = q.P \;\wedge\; path(q, r).P^* = q.P^* \;\wedge\; path(q, r).b))$$

Lemma 2 serves as a base case for an induction proof of $Diffusing(k)$, resulting in the following theorem.

Theorem 2. *For every k, $k \geq 1$, starting from an arbitrary state, eventually $Diffusing(k)$ holds and continues to hold.*

Theorem 2 shows that eventually the values indicating the successful completion of a diffusing computation may be trusted. Its proof is similar to the proofs of diffusing computations presented in [1].

Although $Diffusing(k)$ holds for all k, this does not imply, however, that all processes are part of the routing tree. In particular, to reestablish $Diffusing(k)$ some processes may choose an empty path. We must show that this eventually stops, and all processes obtain and retain a rooted path.

As an additional notation, for a network rooted path R, $R_{j,root}$ denotes the path along the routing tree from R_j to root.

We define $SoundPath(R)$, where R is a rooted network path, as follows. There exists a k, $0 \leq k \leq |R| - 1$, such that both of the following hold.

– for every j, $k < j < |R|$,

$$R_j.P = R_{j,root} \ \wedge \ (\#ch(R_{j+1}, R_j) > 0 \Rightarrow path(R_{j+1}, R_j).P = R_{j+1,root})$$

and for every neighbor r of R_j,

$$\#ch(R_j, r) > 0 \Rightarrow (path(R_j, r).P = R_{j,root} \ \vee$$
$$path(R_j, r).P \neq path(R_j, r).P^* = R_{j,root})$$

– if $0 < k$, then

$$R_k.P \neq R_k.P^* = R_{k,root} \ \wedge \ R_k.clean = R_k.N \ \wedge$$
$$\#ch(R_k, R_{k+1}) > 0 \Rightarrow (path(R_k, R_{k+1}).b \ \wedge$$
$$path(R_k, R_{k+1}).P \neq path(R_k, R_{k+1}).P^*)$$

Predicate $SoundPath(R)$ indicates that the processes along the rooted path are in agreement with each other. That is, the path can be divided into two segments. In the first segment, from R_{k+1} to $root$, all processes have in variable P the current path along the routing tree to $root$. In the second segment, from R_1 up to R_k, each process has a value for variable P that is different from the path along the routing tree, but the process is expecting to receive the routing-tree path in the final step of the diffusing computation.

Theorem 3. *From an arbitrary initial state, the following eventually holds and continues to hold:*

(for every R, where R is a network and rooted path, $SoundPath(R)$)

Finally, since all paths along the routing tree are in agreement, eventually all processes take part in the routing tree.

Theorem 4. *Starting from an arbitrary initial state, all of the following eventually hold and continue to hold.*

– *Every process is located in the routing tree.*
– *For every process p, $p.P$ ceases to change value, and is equal to the path along the routing tree from p to root.*
– *If the path ordering is monotonic, then for every process p, $p.P$ is the highest ordered network path from p to root.*

10   Concluding Remarks

We have assumed throughout the paper that although a process may prefer some paths over others, it will not reject paths, that is, it will always choose one of the paths being offered by its neighbors. However, as mentioned in [8][9], it is possible for a process to maintain a list of unacceptable paths. If all its neighbors offer only paths from this list of unacceptable paths, then the process will choose the empty path, and disconnect itself from the routing tree. In a future paper, we will enhance our model and protocols to handle lists of unacceptable paths.

References

[1] Cobb, J. A., Gouda, M. G., "Stabilization of General Loop-Free Routing", *Journal of Parallel and Distributed Computing*, Vol. 62, No. 5, May, 2002. 181

[2] Cobb, J. A., Gouda, M. G., Musuburi, R., "A Stabilizing Solution to The Stable Path Problem", Tech. Report, Dept. of Comp. Science, Univ. of Texas at Dallas. 180

[3] Gao, L., Rexford, J., "Stable Internet Routing Without Global Coordination", *IEEE/ACM Transactions on Networking*, Vol. 9, No. 6, Dec. 2001. 170

[4] Gao, L., Rexford, J., "Stable Internet Routing Without Global Coordination", *Proc. of the ACM SIGMETRICS*, June 2000. 170

[5] Garcia-Lunes-Aceves, J. J., "Loop-Free Routing Using Diffusing Computations", *IEEE/ACM Transactions on Networking*, Volume 1, No. 1, Feb., 1993. 176

[6] Gouda, M. G., *Elements of Network Protocol Design*, John Wiley & Sons, 1998. 170, 171

[7] Gouda, M. G., Schneider, M., "Maximizable Routing Metrics", *Proc. of the IEEE International Conference on Network Protocols*, 1998. 175

[8] Griffin, T. G., Shepherd, F. B., Wilfong, G., "Policy Disputes in Path Vector Protocols", *Proc. of the IEEE Int'l Conf. on Net. Protocols*, Oct., 1999. 174, 175, 182

[9] Griffin, T. G., Shepherd, F. B., Wilfong, G., "The Stable Paths Problem and Interdomain Routing", *IEEE/ACM Tran. on Networking*, Vol. 10, No. 2, Apr. 2002. 169, 170, 175, 182

[10] Griffin, T. G., Wilfong, G., "A Safe Path Vector Protocol", *Proc. of the INFOCOM Conference*, 2000. 170

[11] Griffin, T. G., Wilfong, G., "An Analysis of BGP Convergence Properties", *Proc. of the ACM SIGCOMM Conf.*, 1999. 174

[12] Herman, T., "A Comprehensive Bibliography on Self-Stabilization", *Chicago Journal of Theoretical Computer Science*, working paper, 2002. 170, 179

[13] Mao, Z. M., Govindan, R., Varghese, G., and Katz, R., "Route Flap Damping Exacerbates Internet Routing Convergence", *ACM SIGCOMM Conf.*, Aug., 2002. 169

[14] Rekhtar, Y., Li, T., "A Border Gateway Protocol" RFC1771, 1995. 169

[15] Schneider, M., "Self-Stabilization", *ACM Computing Surveys*, Vol. 25, No. 1, 1993. 170, 179

[16] Varadhan, K., Govindan, R., Estrin, D., "Persistent Route Oscillations in Inter-Domain Routing", *Computer Networks*, Jan. 2000. 169

[17] Villamizar, C., Chandra, R., Govindan, R., "BGP Route Flap Damping", RFC 2439, 1998. 169

Route Preserving Stabilization[*]

Colette Johnen[1] and Sébastien Tixeuil[1,2]

[1] Laboratoire de Recherche en Informatique, CNRS UMR 8623,
Université Paris-Sud XI, F-91405 Orsay cedex, France
[2] INRIA Futurs, Équipe Grand Large

Abstract. A distributed system is *self-stabilizing* if it returns to a legitimate state in a finite number of steps regardless of the initial state,
and the system remains in a legitimate state until another fault occurs.
A routing algorithm is *loop-free* if, a path being constructed between two
processors p and q, any edges cost change induces a modification of the
routing tables in such a way that at any time, there always exists a path
from p to q.
We present a self-stabilizing loop-free routing algorithm that is also *route
preserving*. This last property means that, a tree being constructed, any
message sent to the root is received in a bounded amount of time, even in
the presence of continuous edge cost changes. Also, and unlike previous
approaches, we do not require that a bound on the network diameter is
known to the processors that perform the routing algorithm. We guarantee self-stabilization for many metrics (such as minimum distance, shortest path, best transmitter, depth first search metrics, etc.), by reusing
previous results on r-operators.

1 Introduction

In 1974, Dijkstra pioneered the concept of self-stabilization in a distributed network [5]. A distributed system is self-stabilizing if it returns to a *legitimate* state
in a finite number of steps regardless of the initial state, and the system remains
in a legitimate state until another fault occurs. Thus, a self-stabilizing algorithm
tolerates transient processor faults. These transient faults include variable corruption, program counter corruption (which temporarily cause a processor to
execute its code from any point), and communication channel corruption.

In the context of computer networks, resuming correct behavior after a fault
occurs can be very costly [13]: the whole network may have to be shut down
and globally reset in a good initial state. While this approach is feasible for
small networks, it is far from practical in large networks such as the Internet.
Self-stabilization provides a way to recover from faults without the cost and
inconvenience of a generalized human intervention: after a fault is diagnosed,
one simply has to remove, repair, or reinitialize the faulty components, and the
system, by itself, will return to a good global state within a relatively short
amount of time.

---

[*] This work was supported in part by the French projects STAR and DYNAMO.

S.-T. Huang and T. Herman (Eds.): SSS 2003, LNCS 2704, pp. 184–198, 2003.
© Springer-Verlag Berlin Heidelberg 2003

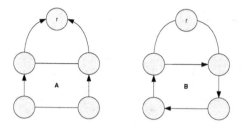

Fig. 1. Example of self-stabilizing routing

In the context of the communication networks, [15] showed that crash and restart failures may lead the distributed systems into an arbitrary configurations, highlighting the need for algorithms that are resilient to those failures (such as self-stabilizing algorithms). Fault-tolerance is an important issue in the design of network routing protocols since the topology changes due to the link/node failures and repairs. Many existing routing protocols are self-stabilizing (for example [13] reports that RIP and OSPF have been proved self-stabilizing by Nancy Lynch).

Related works The primary task of a routing protocol is to generate and maintain a routing table with the appropriate desirable property. This property is usually stated in terms of maximizing a particular *routing metric*. In [6] is presented a self-stabilizing routing protocols on Breath-first path metric (shortest path metric where all edge weighs are 1). An optimal self-stabilizing algorithm for the shortest path metric is presented in [2]. In [11], a general self-stabilizing protocol that computes routing table for several routing metrics (for instance shortest path, maximal bandwidth path) on id-based networks is presented. In [9, 10], another approach for routing is taken by means of r-operators (for minimum distance, shortest path, best transmitter, depth first search metrics). A common drawback of these algorithms (and those in RIP/OSPF) is that they are not *loop-free*: assume that a tree is initially present in the network, then if edge costs change, the self-stabilization property of the algorithm makes it return to a configuration where a tree is built. However, in the reconfiguration phase, it is possible that a cycle appears (see Figure 1). If a message is sent during this phase, it may loop in the network.

To circumvent this problem, self-stabilizing loop-free algorithms were developed. Assume that there exists a path between two nodes p and q. After any edges cost change, the loop-free protocol modifies its routing tables to compute the new optimal path. During this re-building phase, they always exists a path from p to q. In [1] are presented two self-stabilizing routing protocols with shortest path metric. One of these protocols is loop-free, but requires unbounded memory per processor. In [4], a general self-stabilizing loop-free protocol is presented (using the formalism of [11]). The known self-stabilizing loop-free protocols (such as [1, 4]) suffer from two drawbacks: *(i)* they require that an upper bound on the diameter of the network is known to make them stabilizing, and

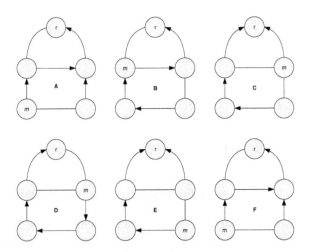

Fig. 2. Example of self-stabilizing loop-free routing

(ii) if edge costs change often, it is possible that messages sent actually loop in the network. For example, in Figure 2, at each step there is a tree towards r that is constructed, yet message m does not reach r during configurations **A** to **F**. Since configurations **A** and **F** are the same, it is possible that m loops forever in the network if edge costs continue changing.

Our contribution We present a self-stabilizing loop-free routing algorithm that is also *route preserving*. Our solution is self-stabilizing so that it can recover from any transient failure once faults cease to occur; it is loop-free so that, a tree being constructed, a tree remains forever in the network even with continuous edge cost changes; it is route preserving so that, a tree being constructed, any message sent to the root is received within a bounded amount of time, even in the presence of continuous edge cost changes. This last feature is by providing a *routing policy* that permits to interleave consistently routing table updates and message forwarding actions. Figure 3 captures that our system recovers from transient faults (denoted by dotted lines in the figure) by eventually reaching a shortest path configuration provided that no new faults occur. In addition, edge cost changes (dashed lines in the figure) preserve the route preserving predicate in the sense that only route preserving configurations can be reached (denoted by grayed circles in the figure).

Also, and unlike [1] and [4], we do not require that a bound on the network diameter is known to all processors in the network. This makes our solution more adaptive to network changes. As in [4], we guarantee self-stabilization for many metrics (such as minimum distance, shortest path, best transmitter, depth first search metrics, etc.). Since our approach is based on r-operators (see [9]), the set of metrics that we support is distinct from that of [4] (usual metrics however, such as shortest path tree, are common to both approaches).

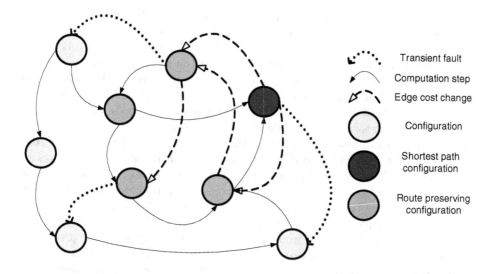

Fig. 3. Properties of route-preserving stabilization

Outline of the paper The remaining of the paper is organized as follows. In Section 2, we present the underlying model for self-stabilizing distributed systems. For sake of clarity, in Section 3, we present a first version of our algorithm using the intuitive shortest path metric, and prove the self-stabilizing route preserving property of this algorithm in Section 4. Section 5 provides the generic version of our algorithm, that supports as many metrics as r-operators. Concluding remarks are given in Section 6.

2   Model

Distributed systems A distributed system S is modeled as a collection of processors linked with communication media allowing them to exchange information. A distributed system is a connected graph $G = (V, E)$, where V is the set of nodes ($|V| = n$) and E is the set of links or edges. Each node $i \in V$ represents a processor, P_i. (For the sake of simplicity, we will use i and P_i interchangeably to represent the processor.) Each edge, denoted by a pair $(i, j) \in E$, represents a communication link between P_i and P_j, where P_i and P_j are called *neighbors*. Any ordered tuple of successive links $((i, k), (k, s), .., (l, j))$, represents a *path* $p_{i,j}$ between P_i and P_j. If two nodes P_i and P_j are connected by some path $p_{i,j}$ (note that $p_{i,i}$ is a path), P_j is said to be *reachable* from P_i.

The processors asynchronously execute their programs consisting of a set of variables and a finite set of rules. The variables are part of the shared register which is used to communicate with the neighbors. A processor can write only into its own shared register and can read only from the shared registers, owned by the neighboring processors or itself. So, variables of a processor can be accessed by the processor and its neighbors. The program for a protocol consists of a sequence of rules: $< rule > \cdots < rule >$. Each *rule* is the form: $< guard > \longrightarrow < action >$. A *guard* is a boolean expression over the variables of a node and its neighborhood. An *action* is allowed to update the variables of the node only. Any rule whose guard is *true* is said to be *enabled*. A node with one or more enabled rules is said to be *privileged* and may make a *move* executing the action corresponding to the chosen enabled rule. We do not make any assumption on the policy adopted by a node when more than one rule guards are satisfied.

The *state* of a processor is defined by the values of its local variables. A *configuration* of a distributed system $G = (V, E)$ is an instance of the states of its processors. The set of configurations of G is denoted as $\mathcal{C}$. Processor actions change the global system configuration. Moreover, several processor actions may occur at the same time. A *computation* e of a system G is defined as a *weakly fair, maximal* sequence of configurations $c_1, c_2, \ldots$ such that for $i = 1, 2, \ldots$, the configuration c_{i+1} is reached from c_i by a single step of at least one processor. During a computation step, one or more processors execute a step and a processor may take at most one step. *Weak fairness* of the sequence means that if any action in G is continuously enabled along the sequence, it is eventually chosen for execution. *Maximality* means that the sequence is either infinite, or it is finite and no action of G is enabled in the final global state.

Let $\mathcal{C}$ be the set of possible configurations and $\mathcal{E}$ be the set of all possible computations of a system G. Then the set of computations of G starting with a particular *initial configuration* $c_1 \in \mathcal{C}$ will be denoted by $\mathcal{E}_{c_1}$. Every computation $e \in \mathcal{E}_{c_1}$ is of the form $c_1, c_2, \ldots$ The set of computations of $\mathcal{E}$ whose initial configurations are all elements of $B \subseteq \mathcal{C}$ is denoted as $\mathcal{E}_B$. Thus, $\mathcal{E} = \mathcal{E}_{\mathcal{C}}$.

We introduce the concept of an *attractor* to define self-stabilization. Intuitively, an attractor is a set of configurations of a system G that "attracts" another set of configurations of G for any computation of G.

Definition 1 (Attractor). *Let B_1 and B_2 be subsets of $\mathcal{C}$. Then B_1 is an attractor for B_2 if and only if $\forall e \in \mathcal{E}_{B_2}, (e = c_1, c_2, \ldots), \exists i \geq 1 : c_i \in B_1$.*

The shortest path maintenance is a static (or *silent*, see [7]) problem. The set of configurations that matches the specification of static problems is called the set of *legitimate* configurations, denoted as $\mathcal{L}$. The remainder $\mathcal{C} \setminus \mathcal{L}$ denotes the set of *illegitimate* configurations.

Definition 2 (Self-Stabilization). *A distributed system $\mathcal{S}$ is called self-stabilizing if and only if there exists a non-empty set $\mathcal{L} \subseteq \mathcal{C}$ such that the following conditions hold: (i)$\forall e \in \mathcal{E}_{\mathcal{L}}, (e = c_1, c_2, \ldots), \forall i \geq 1, c_i \in \mathcal{L}$ (closure). (ii) $\mathcal{L}$ is an attractor for $\mathcal{C}$ (convergence).*

3 The Route Preserving Self-Stabilizing Shortest Path Algorithm

3.1 Problem to Be Solved

In this section, we present the problem to be solved by our algorithm. The purpose of our contribution is threefold: we wish to build a shortest path tree rooted at r (the shortest path problem), we wish to be able to recover from any transient fault (the self-stabilization requirement), and we want that when routes are constructed, messages can be routed during changes of edge costs (the route preserving requirement).

The Shortest Path Problem We associate to each link (i, j) of $G = (V, E)$ a positive integer $c_{i,j}$ that denotes the cost of a communication through this link in both directions (*i.e.* from i to j and from j to i). Each processor i has the following inputs: $\mathcal{N}_i$ is the locally ordered set of neighbors of i, and $c_{i,j}$ is the cost of edge between processors i and j.

On each processor i, the following variables are available: p_i is a pointer to a particular neighbor of i, that is equal to the next processor $j \in \mathcal{N}_i$ on the current path from i to r, and w_i is an integer variable that is equal to the cost of the current path from i to r.

Given a source r, the shortest path problem consists in finding for each processor i a path from i to r (or from r to i) whose overall cost is minimal. Each path is induced by the p variables at all nodes $i \neq r$. We denote by $\dot{w}_i$ the cost of the shortest path from i to r (note that $\dot{w}_r = 0$). In a shortest path from i to r, $\dot{w}_i$ is equal to the minimum of the costs at a neighbor j of i plus the cost from j to i for any possible neighbor j of i. Formally, $\forall i \neq r$, $\dot{w}_i = Min_{j \in \mathcal{N}_i}(\dot{w}_j + c_{i,j})$. We now define a shortest path configuration (that must be eventually reached by any algorithm that wishes to solve the shortest path problem):

Definition 3 (Shortest-Path Configuration). *Let $\mathcal{SP}$ be the following predicate on system configurations: $\mathcal{SP} \equiv \{\forall i \in V, w_i = \dot{w}_i\}$. A shortest path configuration is a configuration that satisfies $\mathcal{SP}$.*

The self-stabilization requirement Not only our algorithm eventually provides a shortest path configuration, it also ensures that the initial state can be arbitrary. Once the system is stabilized, the set of p pointers should induce a shortest path tree rooted at r.

Due to the self-stabilization property of our algorithm, it computes for each processor $i \neq r$ a shortest path to r from any initial configuration under any weakly fair scheduler. Our algorithm does not make any assumption about the initial value of w_i or p_i on any processor i. We now define the legitimate configurations for our purpose using a *legitimate predicate* $\mathcal{LP}$.

Definition 4 (Legitimate Configuration). *Let $\mathcal{LP}$ be the following predicate on system configurations: $\mathcal{LP} \equiv \{(\forall i \neq r, (w_i = \dot{w}_i) \wedge (w_i = w_{p_i} + c_{i,p_i})) \wedge (w_r = 0)\}$. A legitimate configuration is a configuration that satisfies $\mathcal{LP}$.*

The route preserving requirement We wish to preserve a route towards the root r once a path is constructed, even if edge costs are modified. For that purpose, we define so that the stabilizing algorithm wishes to change node variables.

Definition 5 (Task Preservation under Input Change). *Let TS be a task specification, let TC be a set of changes of inputs in the system. A distributed system S preserves TS under TC if and only if there exists a non-empty set of configurations $C \subseteq \mathcal{C}$ such that the following conditions hold: (i) C is closed, (ii) C is closed under any change in TC, and (iii) every computation starting from $c \in C$ eventually satisfies TS.*

For our purpose, the task to be solved (TS) is to be able to route a message for any node i to the root r, while the set of changes of inputs (TC) is the set of possible variation of edge costs.

3.2 Description

Each processor i performs several kinds of actions with different objectives:

Route Finding i wishes to reach a configuration where every node maintains a route towards r (so that messages can be sent to r). This goal is achieved by having the weight of each node (the w_i variable) set to a value that is strictly greater than that of its parent (denoted by the w_{p_i} variable).

Route Preserving The rules of the algorithms that are executed *after* a route is present towards r from every node i have to preserve a route towards r from every node i. Also, arbitrary changes of edge costs must not break the such defined routes (for the route preserving requirement).

Shortest Path Finding i wishes to reach a shortest path configuration.

Self-Stabilization i wishes to reach a legitimate configuration (for the self-stabilization requirement). For that purpose, if $i = r$, then i updates w_i so that $w_i = 0$, and if $i \neq r$, i updates p_i and w_i so that $w_i = Min_{j \in \mathcal{N}_i}(w_j + c_{i,j})$.

Formal Description Each processor i (except the root) has the following variables: rw_i (the current value broadcast in i's sub-tree) is an integer, and p_i (the parent of i) is a pointer to a neighbor of i. Each processor i (including the root) has the following variables: w_i (the weight of i) is an integer, and st_i (the status of i) takes value in $\{P, N\}$. Intuitively, a status of P as st_i denotes that i is currently **P**ropagating its value to its sub-tree, while a value of N denotes that i is currently **N**eutral relatively to sub-tree broadcasting, *i.e.* all node in i's sub-tree acknowledged the last broadcasted value).

All processors have the following local macro: $\hat{w}_i$ is the best possible value of w_i according to the current configuration (see table below). Let j be a child of i ($p_j = i$). j is called a *descendant* of i iff $w_j > w_i$. Each processor (except the root) has the following local macros: $\mathcal{D}_i$ is the set of the descendants of i in the tree, $\hat{p}_i$ is the best possible parent i according to the current configuration if such a neighbor exists otherwise the value of $\hat{p}$ is $\perp$ (the best parent j should have the neutral status and should have a weight that minimizes the new weight value of i: $\hat{w}_j + c_{i,j}$), and ubw_i is the upper bound of w_i (that i might take and still preserve convergence towards a legitimate state) in the current configuration (see table below).

$$\hat{w}_i \quad \equiv \quad \begin{cases} \min_{j \in \mathcal{N}_i}(w_j + c_{i,j}) & \text{if } i \neq r \\ 0 & \text{otherwise} \end{cases}$$

$$\hat{p}_i \quad \equiv \quad \begin{cases} \min_{j \in \mathcal{N}_i}(j :: (w_j = \hat{w}_i - c_{i,j}) \wedge (st_j = \mathsf{N})) & \text{if there exists } j \in \mathcal{N}_i :: \\ & \quad (w_j = \hat{w}_i - c_{i,j}) \wedge (st_j = \mathsf{N}) \\ \bot & \text{otherwise} \end{cases}$$

$$\mathcal{D}_i \quad \equiv \quad \{ j \in \mathcal{N}_i :: p_j = i \wedge w_j > w_i \}$$

$$ubw_i \equiv \begin{cases} \min_{j \in \mathcal{D}_i}(w_j - c_{i,j}) & \text{if } \mathcal{D}_i \neq \emptyset \\ \infty & \text{otherwise} \end{cases}$$

Each processor (except the root) has the following local predicates: End_PIF is used to avoid that a processor increases its weight (i.e. to perform R_3 action) simultaneously with one of its descendants, $Safe\_MOVE$ is used to avoid that a processor i takes the status P (i.e. to perform R_2 action) when it could change its parent, and $Safe\_INC$ is verified by i when it needs to increase its weight (see table below). Intuitively, End_PIF_i is satisfied when i's sub-tree has received the value broadcasted by i, $Safe\_MOVE_i$ is satisfied when i is allowed to choose a new parent (i.e. change its p_i variable) without compromising the loop-free and route preserving properties of the routing algorithm, and $Safe\_Inc_i$ is satisfied when i is can safely increment its current broadcast value (i.e. rw_i).

$$End\_PIF_i \quad \equiv \quad (\forall j \in \mathcal{D}_i, st_j = \mathsf{N})$$

$$Safe\_MOVE_i \equiv \left(\begin{array}{l} ((\hat{w}_i < w_i) \vee ((w_i = \hat{w}_i) \wedge (\hat{p}_i \neq p_i))) \\ \wedge (\hat{p}_i \neq \bot) \end{array} \right)$$

$$Safe\_INC_i \quad \equiv \quad \left(\begin{array}{l} ((w_i < rw_{p_i} + c_{p_i,i}) \wedge (st_{p_i} = \mathsf{P})) \\ \vee (w_i < w_{p_i} + c_{p_i,i}) \end{array} \right)$$

The rules of our algorithm are the following:

1. On the root r processor:
   - $R_0 :: (w_r \neq 0) \vee (st_p \neq \mathsf{N}) \rightarrow$
     $w_r := 0; st_r := \mathsf{N}$
2. On any other processor i:
   - $R_1 :: (st_i = \mathsf{N}) \wedge Safe\_MOVE_i \rightarrow$
     $w_i := \hat{w}_i; \ rw_p := w_i; \ p_i := \hat{p}_i$
   - $R_2 :: (st_i = \mathsf{N}) \wedge \neg Safe\_MOVE_i \wedge Safe\_INC_i \rightarrow$
     $rw_i := rw_{p_i} + c_{p_i,i}; \ st_i := \mathsf{P}$

- $R_3 :: (st_i = \mathsf{P}) \wedge End\_PIF_i \wedge (ubw_i \geq rw_i) \rightarrow$
  $w_i := rw_i;\ st := \mathsf{N}$
- $R_4 :: (rw_i < w_i) \rightarrow rw_i := w_i$

The R_0 and R_4 rules are designed to ensure that eventually the variable values on a processor are locally correct. The R_1 action allows a processor to get the best value for its w and p variables according to the state of its neighbor. The R_2 action is executed when i needs to increase its weight, while the actual increase is achieved by executing the R_3 action.

Observation 1 *The weight of a processor increases only after that this processor has performed the rule R_3. Actions R_1, R_2 and R_3 are mutually exclusive: a processor cannot simultaneously verify two rule guards of R_1, R_2 or R_3. Rule R_0 is performed at most once. After any action on i, we have $w_i \leq rw_i$ therefore the action R_4 is performed at most once by any processor.*

Lemma 1. *When a processor i performs R_3, none of its descendants and parent can perform R_3 simultaneously with i.*

Proof. When the R_3 guard holds, i's descendants and parent have Status N. They cannot satisfy the R_3 guard.

4   Proof of Correctness

In this section, we show that our algorithm is self-stabilizing for the shortest path tree problem. We also prove that there exists a *route preserving* set of configurations $\mathcal{RP}$ that ensure routing of messages towards the root r and that is preserved for any change of edge cost.

4.1   Route Preserving Proof

We wish to find a non-empty set of configurations $\mathcal{RP}$ that verifies the following properties: *(i)* $\mathcal{RP}$ is not empty, *(ii)* $\mathcal{RP}$ is closed (any action of any processor executing our algorithm preserves $\mathcal{RP}$), *(iii)* $\mathcal{RP}$ is closed under any edge cost changes, and *(iv)* every computation starting from a configuration in $\mathcal{RP}$ is guaranteed to deliver the message at r after finite time. Once $\mathcal{RP}$ is verified, any message sent to r reaches it. Therefore, once $\mathcal{RP}$ is verified, our algorithm guarantees that *(i)* any message towards r reaches its destination, even when the edge costs vary, and *(ii)* routes to r are eventually the costless ones. We define $\mathcal{RP}$ as the set of configurations where Predicates $\Pr_i^{\mathcal{RP}_1}$ and $\Pr_i^{\mathcal{RP}_2}$ hold at each $i \in V$. Those predicates are defined as follows:

Definition 6. *Let $\Pr_i^{\mathcal{RP}_1}$ be the following predicate on processor state:*

$$\Pr_i^{\mathcal{RP}_1} \equiv \begin{cases} rw_i \geq w_i & if\ i \neq r \\ w_r = 0 \wedge st_r = \mathsf{N} & otherwise \end{cases}$$

Definition 7. *Let* $\Pr_i^{\mathcal{RP}_2}$ *be the following predicate on processor state:*

$$\Pr_i^{\mathcal{RP}_2} \equiv \begin{cases} w_{p_i} < w_i \ if \ i \neq r \\ w_r = 0 \quad otherwise \end{cases}$$

Our algorithm ensures that increasing a weight is safe: *(i)* i cannot gain a new child while performing its weight increase action, *(ii)* all descendants j of i still satisfy Predicate $\Pr_j^{\mathcal{RP}_2}$ after any action of i, and *(iii)* i changing its p_i variable also preserves Predicate $\Pr_i^{\mathcal{RP}_2}$. In our algorithm, the st_i variable at processor i helps to guarantee Properties *(i)* and *(iii)*. The rw_i variable of i represents the maximal value that i can take and its descendants still satisfy Predicate $\Pr_i^{\mathcal{RP}_2}$ predicate. We now prove that the preserving predicate $\Pr_i^{\mathcal{RP}_1} \wedge \Pr_i^{\mathcal{RP}_2}$ is closed.

Lemma 2. $A^{\mathcal{RP}} \equiv \{\forall i \in V, \Pr_i^{\mathcal{RP}_1} \ holds\}$ *is an attractor for* true.

Proof. A processor i that does not verify $\Pr_i^{\mathcal{RP}_1}$ verifies forever R_0 or R_4 guard. By the weak fairness hypothesis, every enabled processor i executes an action. After this action, we have $rw_i \geq w_i$ (observation 1).

Observation 2 *In* $A^{\mathcal{RP}}$, *no processor performs the actions* R_0 *and* R_4.

Lemma 3. *In* $A^{\mathcal{RP}}$, *on any processor* i, $\Pr_i^{\mathcal{RP}_2}$ *is closed.*

Proof. Predicate $\Pr_i^{\mathcal{RP}_2}$ may not be satisfied after that either: *(i)* i executes R_1 or, *(ii)* p_i executes R_3.
Just before i executes R_1 to choose j as its parent, j has status N. Therefore j cannot increase it weight (i.e. perform action R_3) simultaneously with i's action. Thus, we have $w_i \geq w_j + c_{i,j}$, after i's action. Let us now study the predicate value on i when its parent j performs the action R_3. When j performs the action R_3, Its descendants (i.e. children of j that verify the $\Pr^{\mathcal{RP}_2}$ predicate) cannot perform the action R_3 (lemma 1). A descendant of j still verifies $\Pr^{\mathcal{RP}_2}$ after the action of j ($w_j < w_i$ where $i \in \mathcal{D}_j$). During the j action, j cannot gain a new descendant via action R_1 because j has the status P.

Lemma 4. $\mathcal{RP}$ *is not empty and is closed.*

Any configuration of $\mathcal{LP}$ (the non-empty set of legitimate configurations) is in $\mathcal{RP}$, so $\mathcal{RP}$ is not empty. By lemmas 2 and 3, $\mathcal{RP}$ is closed.

Lemma 5. $\mathcal{RP}$ *is closed under any edge cost change.*

Proof. Predicate $\Pr^{\mathcal{RP}_1}$ only involves local variables of a processor i (it does not involve the local variables of i's neighbors and edge cost values). Predicate $\Pr^{\mathcal{RP}_2}$ only involves local variables of a processor i and the local variables of i's neighbors. Therefore, the $\mathcal{RP}$ set of configuration is independent of edge cost values.

There remains to show that every computation starting from a configuration in $\mathcal{RP}$ is guaranteed to deliver the message at r after finite time. For that purpose we distinguish the two aspects of routing: *(i)* maintaining the routing tables accurate, and *(ii)* using the routing tables to actually deliver messages (using a *routing policy*). Our algorithm typically updates the routing tables at each processor; we now consider a possible scheme for the message delivery problem. We consider the following *routing policy* (denoted by RP) for every message: *(i)* a message to r from a processor $i \neq r$ is sent to p_i, *(ii)* on a processor i, R_3 is performed only when i does not have any message to send to r.

Lemma 6. *There exists a routing policy RP such that once a configuration in $\mathcal{RP}$ is reached, there exists a bound on the number of hops for any message sent towards r.*

Proof. The current weight of a message m on a processor i is the weight of i. According to the definition of $\mathcal{RP}$ and RP, the two following assertions hold: *(i)* the weight of a message decreases each time the message is transmitted to the next processor on the path, and *(ii)* the weight of a message m is 0 if and only if m has reached r.

Indeed, the weight of m on processor i can only increase when i performs action R_3 (R_3 is the only action that may increase the weight of a processor). The routing policy RP guarantees that a processor does not have any waiting message to r when it performs R_3. The weight of message never increases, therefore, the weight of a message is an upper bound on the number of processors that are traversed before reaching r.

We now consider a new routing policy RP' that ensures fairness of rules execution and message forwarding. Point *(ii)* of routing policy RP is changed as follows. A processor i holding the R_3 guard executes the following actions *(i)* i sends a message to its descendants and to its application layer to have them keep any message to r; *(ii)* i sends to p_i any waiting message to r in its buffer and its incoming channels from its descendants, *(iii)* i performs R_3, and *(iv)* i authorizes its children to continue routing of their own user messages.

With the routing policy RP', a processor i that prevents the R_3 rule from executing is eventually message free (and can then execute R_3). As expected, configurations in $\mathcal{RP}$ are secured under any series of modifications of edge costs. Moreover, any computation starting from a configuration in $\mathcal{RP}$ guarantees that any message sent to r reaches r in a bounded number of hops (this bound is the weight of the sender processor at the sending time).

4.2   Self-Stabilization Proof

From now onwards, we consider that the initial configuration is a configuration in $A^{\mathcal{RP}}$. Such a configuration is eventually reached by Lemma 2. Also, we assume that edge costs remain constant. This does not break the route preserving requirement, since when $A^{\mathcal{RP}}$ hold, routing can always be performed. However, self-stabilization towards a shortest path tree is only guaranteed if edge costs remain constant for a sufficiently long period of time.

The overview of our proof is as follows. First, we show that starting from a configuration in $A^{\mathcal{RP}}$, the weight of each processor eventually gets lower bounded by the weight of its parent plus the cost of the link. Then, we show that whenever a processors initiates a propagation of information to its subtree, this propagation eventually gets back to it (a processor with Status P eventually gets Status N). Then, we prove that the weight of each processor eventually gets greater or equal to the optimal weight of this processor (when the shortest path tree is constructed). Finally, we prove that the algorithm converges to a configuration where a shortest path tree is built, and where local consistency also holds, which makes the configuration legitimate. The complete proof is presented in [12].

5   The Generic Algorithm

r-operators Following work of Tel concerning wave algorithms (see [14]), an *infimum* $\oplus$ (hereby called an *s-operator*) over a set $\mathbb{S}$ is an associative, commutative and idempotent (*i.e.* $x \oplus x = x$) binary operator. Such an operator defines a partial order relation $\leq_\oplus$ over the set $\mathbb{S}$ by: $x \leq_\oplus y$ if and only if $x \oplus y = x$. We denote by $e_\oplus$ a greatest element on $\mathbb{S}$, that verifies $x \leq_\oplus e_\oplus$ for every $x \in \mathbb{S} \cup \{e_\oplus\}$. Hence, the $(\mathbb{S} \cup \{e_\oplus\}, \oplus)$structure is an *Abelian idempotent semi-group*[1] (see [3]) with $e_\oplus$ as identity element.

In [8], a distorted algebra — the r-algebra — is proposed. This algebra generalizes the Abelian idempotent semi-group, and still allows convergence to terminal configuration of wave-like algorithms.

Definition 8 (r-Operator). *The binary operator $\lhd$ on $\mathbb{S} \cup \{e_\oplus\}$ is an r-operator if there exists a surjective mapping r called r-mapping, such that it verifies the following conditions: (i) r-associativity: $(x \lhd y) \lhd r(z) = x \lhd (y \lhd z)$; (ii) r-commutativity: $r(x) \lhd y = r(y) \lhd x$; (iii) r-idempotency: $r(x) \lhd x = r(x)$ and (iv) right identity element: $\exists e_\lhd \in \mathbb{S} \cup \{e_\oplus\}, x \lhd e_\lhd = x$.*

Definition 9 (Strict Idempotency). *An r-operator $\lhd$ based on the s-operator $\oplus$ is strictly idempotent if, for any $x \in \mathbb{S} \setminus \{e_\oplus\}$, $x <_\oplus r(x)$ (i.e. $x \leq_\oplus r(x)$ and $r(x) \neq x$).*

For example, the operator $\min_1(x, y) = \min(x, y + 1)$ is a strictly idempotent r-operator on $\mathbb{N} \cup \{+\infty\}$, with $+\infty$ as its identity element. It is based on the s-operator min and on the surjective r-mapping $r(x) = x + 1$. Note that although the set $\mathbb{N} \cup \{+\infty\}$ has a greatest element, it is an infinite set, and its greatest element can not be used as an upper bound for a particular algorithm (such as in the works of [1, 4]).

In [9], it is proved that if a strictly idempotent r-operator is executed at every processor in the network, then the system is self-stabilizing for the operation

---

[1] The prefix *semi* means that the structure cannot be completed to obtain a group, since the law is idempotent.

defined by the r-operator. The r-operators defined in [9] provide solutions for minimum distance tree and forest, shortest path tree and forest, best transmitters tree and forest, etc. For example, the operator $\min_1$ stabilizes to a minimum distance tree when a single node has 0 as the first term of every $\min_1$ computation and every other node has $e_{\min_1} = +\infty$ as the first term of every $\min_1$ computation.

The algorithm that we provide is self-stabilizing for every r-operator defined in [9], yet preserves routes for every message sent to the root when the r-functions of the system are modified after a tree is constructed.

The generic algorithm It is parameterized by an n-ary r-operator $\lhd$. A mapping $\lhd$ from $\mathbb{S} \cup \{e_\oplus\}^n$ into $\mathbb{S} \cup \{e_\oplus\}$ is an *n-ary r-operator* if there exists an *s-operator* $\oplus$ on $\mathbb{S} \cup \{e_\oplus\}$ and $n - 1$ homomorphisms (called *r-mappings*) $r_1, \ldots, r_{n-1}$ of $(\mathbb{S} \cup \{e_\oplus\}, \oplus)$ such that $\lhd(x_0, \ldots, x_{n-1}) = x_0 \oplus r_1(x_1) \oplus \cdots \oplus r_{n-1}(x_{n-1})$ for any $x_0, \ldots, x_{n-1}$ in $\mathbb{S} \cup \{e_\oplus\}$.

For our purpose, we associate to each link (i, j) of $G = (V, E)$ a bijective r-function $r_{i,j}$ that is strictly idempotent. Each processor i has the following inputs: *(i)* $\mathcal{N}_i$ is the locally ordered set of neighbors of i, and *(ii)* $r_{i,j}$ is the bijective r-function associated to the edge between processors i and j. Each processor i (except the root) has the following variables: *(i)* $rw_i^\oplus$ (the current value broadcast in i's sub-tree) is an integer, and *(ii)* p_i (the parent of i) is a pointer to a neighbor of i. Each processor i (including the root) has the following variables: *(i)* $w_i^\oplus$ (the weight of i, in the sense of $\oplus$) is an integer, and *(ii)* st_i (the status of i) takes value in $\{\mathsf{P}, \mathsf{N}\}$. Note that $w_i^\oplus$ and $rw_i^\oplus$ are elements of $\mathbb{S} \cup \{e_\oplus\}$.

All processors have the following local macro: $\hat{w}_i^\oplus$ is the best possible value of $w_i^\oplus$ according to the current configuration. Let j be a child of i ($p_j = i$). j is called a *descendant* of i iff $w_i^\oplus <_\oplus w_j^\oplus$. Each processor (except the root) has the following local macro: $\hat{p}_i$ is the best possible parent i according to the current configuration if a such neighbor exists otherwise the value of $\hat{p}$ is $\bot$. $r_{i,j}^{-1}$ is the reverse function of $r_{i,j}$ (since $r_{i,j}$ is bijective, $r_{i,j}^{-1}$ is always defined, and the best parent j should have the neutral status and should have a weight equal to $r_{i,j}^{-1}(\hat{w}_i^\oplus)$), $\mathcal{D}_i$ is the set of the descendants of i in the tree, and $ubw_i^\oplus$ is the upper bound of w_i (in the sense of $\oplus$) in the current configuration (see table below).

Each processor (except the root) has the following local predicates: End_PIF_i is used to avoid that a processor increases its weight (i.e. to perform R_3 action) simultaneously with one of its descendants, $Safe\_MOVE_i$ is used to avoid that a processor i takes the status P (i.e. to perform R_2 action) when it could change its parent, and $Safe\_INC_i$ is verified by i when it needs to increase its weight (see table below).

$$\hat{w}_i^\oplus \equiv \begin{cases} \oplus_{j \in \mathcal{N}_i}(r_{i,j}(w_j^\oplus)) & \text{if } i \neq r \\ 0 & \text{otherwise} \end{cases}$$

$$\hat{p}_i \equiv \begin{cases} \oplus_{j \in \mathcal{N}_i}(j :: (w_j^\oplus = r_{i,j}^{-1}(\hat{w}_i^\oplus)) \wedge (st_j = \mathsf{N})) \text{ if there exists } j \in \mathcal{N}_i :: \\ \qquad\qquad\qquad\qquad\qquad\qquad (w_j^\oplus = r_{i,j}^{-1}(\hat{w}_i^\oplus)) \wedge (st_j = \mathsf{N}) \\ \bot \qquad\qquad\qquad\qquad\qquad\qquad\qquad \text{otherwise} \end{cases}$$

$$\mathcal{D}_i \equiv \{j \in \mathcal{N}_i :: p_j = i \wedge w_i^\oplus <_\oplus w_j^\oplus\}$$

$$ubw_i^\oplus \equiv \begin{cases} \oplus_{j \in \mathcal{D}_i} r_{i,j}^{-1}(w_j^\oplus) \text{ if } \mathcal{D}_i \neq \emptyset \\ \infty \qquad\qquad\quad \text{otherwise} \end{cases}$$

The local predicates of our generic algorithm are the following:

$$End\_PIF_i \equiv (\forall j \in \mathcal{D}_i, st_j = \mathsf{N})$$

$$Safe\_MOVE_i \equiv \begin{pmatrix} ((\hat{w}_i^\oplus <_\oplus w_i^\oplus) \vee ((w_i^\oplus = \hat{w}_i^\oplus) \wedge (\hat{p}_i \neq p_i))) \\ \wedge (\hat{p}_i \neq \bot) \end{pmatrix}$$

$$Safe\_INC_i \equiv \begin{pmatrix} ((w_i <_\oplus r_{p_i,i}(rw_{p_i}^\oplus)) \wedge (st_{p_i} = \mathsf{P})) \\ \vee (w_i <_\oplus r_{p_i,i}(w_{p_i}^\oplus)) \end{pmatrix}$$

The rules of our generic algorithm are the following:

1. On the root r processor:
   - $R_0 :: (w_r^\oplus \neq 0) \vee (st_p \neq \mathsf{N}) \rightarrow$
     $w_r := 0; st_r := \mathsf{N}$
2. On any other processor i:
   - $R_1 :: (st_i = \mathsf{N}) \wedge Safe\_MOVE_i \rightarrow$
     $w_i^\oplus := \hat{w}_i^\oplus; \ rw_p^\oplus := w_i^\oplus; \ p_i := \hat{p}_i$
   - $R_2 :: (st_i = \mathsf{N}) \wedge \neg Safe\_MOVE_i \wedge Safe\_INC_i \rightarrow$
     $rw_i^\oplus := r_{p_i,i}(rw_{p_i}^\oplus); \ st_i := \mathsf{P}$
   - $R_3 :: (st_i = \mathsf{P}) \wedge End\_PIF_i \wedge (rw_i^\oplus \leq_\oplus ubw_i^\oplus) \rightarrow$
     $w_i^\oplus := rw_i^\oplus; \ st := \mathsf{N}$
   - $R_4 :: (rw_i^\oplus <_\oplus w_i^\oplus) \rightarrow rw_i^\oplus := w_i^\oplus$

We now quickly sketch two possible applications of the generic algorithm. The interested reader can refer to [9, 10] for more details. First, to solve the shortest path problem with r-operators, it is sufficient to consider $\mathbb{N}$ as $\mathbb{S}$, $+\infty$ as $e_\oplus$, min as $\oplus$, and $x \mapsto x + c_{i,j}$ as r_i^j. Second, in a telecommunication network where some terminals must chose their "best" transmitter, distance is not always the relevant criterium, and it can be interesting to know the transmitter from where there exists a least failure rate path, and to know the path itself. If we consider $[0,1] \cap \mathbb{R}$ as $\mathbb{S}$, 0 as $e_\oplus$, max as $\oplus$, and $x \mapsto x \times \tau_i^j$ as r_i^j (where τ_i^j is the reliability rate – $0 < \tau_i^j < 1$ – of the edge between i and j) our parameterized algorithm ensures that a best transmitter tree is maintained despite transient failures (in a self-stabilizing way) and that once a coherent tree is constructed towards a transmitter, a coherent tree remains even if edge rates continue changing.

6   Conclusion

In this paper, we presented a self-stabilizing loop-free routing algorithm that is also *route preserving*. This algorithm also does not require that a bound on the network diameter is known to all processors in the network. These two key properties make our approach suitable for mobile *ad-hoc* networks, where nodes move often (inducing changes in the diameter of the system and in the edge costs). Unlike previous approaches on self-stabilizing routing and mobile networks, we specifically address the message delivery issue, even in an environment where dynamic changes occur all the time.

References

[1] A Arora, MG Gouda, and T Herman. Composite routing protocols. In *Proceedings of the 2nd IEEE Symposium on Parallel and Distributed Processing*, pages 70–78, 1990. 185, 186, 195

[2] B Awerbuch, S Kutten, Y Mansour, B Patt-Shamir, and G Varghese. Time optimal self-stabilizing synchronization. In *STOC93 Proceedings of the 25th Annual ACM Symposium on Theory of Computing*, pages 652–661, 1993. 185

[3] F Baccelli, G Cohen, G Olsder, and JP Quadrat. Synchronization and linearity, an algebra for discrete event systems. *Series in Probability and Mathematical Statistics*, 1992. 195

[4] JA Cobb and MG Gouda. Stabilization of general loop-free routing. *Journal of Parallel and Distributed Computing*, 62(5):922–944, 2002. 185, 186, 195

[5] EW Dijkstra. Self stabilizing systems in spite of distributed control. *Communications of the Association of the Computing Machinery*, 17(11):643–644, 1974. 184

[6] S Dolev. Self-stabilizing routing and related protocols. *Journal of Parallel and Distributed Computing*, 42(2):122–127, 1997. 185

[7] S Dolev, MG Gouda, and M Schneider. Memory requirements for silent stabilization. *Acta Informatica*, 36(6):447–462, 1999. 188

[8] B Ducourthial. New operators for computing with associative nets. In *Proceedings of the Fifth International Colloquium on Structural Information and Communication Complexity (SIROCCO'98), Amalfi, Italia*, pages 51–65, 1998. 195

[9] B Ducourthial and S Tixeuil. Self-stabilization with r-operators. *Distributed Computing*, 14(3):147–162, 2001. 185, 186, 195, 196, 197

[10] B Ducourthial and S Tixeuil. Self-stabilization with path algebra. *Theoretical Computer Science*, 293(1):219–236, 2003. 185, 197

[11] MG Gouda and M Schneider. Stabilization of maximal metric trees. In *Proceedings of the Fourth Workshop on Self-Stabilizing Systems (published in association with ICDCS99 The 19th IEEE International Conference on Distributed Computing Systems)*, pages 10–17. IEEE Computer Society, 1999. 185

[12] C Johnen and S Tixeuil. Route preserving stabilization. Technical Report 1353, LRI, Université Paris-Sud XI, 2003. 195

[13] R Perlman. *Interconnexion Networks*. Addison Wesley, 2000. 184, 185

[14] G Tel. *Introduction to Distributed Algorithms*. Cambridge University Press, 1994. 195

[15] G Varghese and M Jayaram. The fault span of crash failures. *Journal of the Association of the Computing Machinery*, 47(2):244–293, 2000. 185

An Improved Snap-Stabilizing PIF Algorithm

Lélia Blin, Alain Cournier, and Vincent Villain

LaRIA, Université de Picardie Jules Verne, France
5, rue du Moulin Neuf, 80000 Amiens, France
{blin,cournier,villain}@laria.u-picardie.fr

Abstract. A *snap-stabilizing protocol*, starting from any arbitrary initial configuration, always behaves according to its specification. In [10], Cournier and al. present the first snap-stabilizing Propagation of Information with Feedback (PIF) protocol in arbitrary networks. But, in order to achieve the desirable property of snap-stabilization, the algorithm needs the knowledge of the exact size of the network. This drawback prevents the protocol from working on dynamical systems. In this paper, we propose an original protocol which solves this drawback.

Keywords: Fault-tolerance, propagation of information with feedback, reset protocols, self-stabilization, snap-stabilization, wave algorithms.

1   Introduction

Chang [8] and Segall [18] defined the concept of *Propagation of Information with Feedback* (PIF) (also called *wave propagation*). A processor p initiates the first phase of the wave: the propagation or broadcast phase. Every processor, upon receiving the first broadcast message, chooses the sender of this message as its parent in the PIF wave, and forwards the wave to its neighbors except its parent. When a processor receives a feedback (acknowledgment) message from all its children with respect to the current PIF wave, it sends a feedback message to its parent. So, eventually, the feedback phase ends at p. Broadcast with feedback scheme has been used extensively in distributed computing to solve a wide class of problems, e.g., spanning tree construction, distributed infimum function computations, snapshot, termination detection, and synchronization (see [17, 19, 16] for details). So, designing efficient fault-tolerant wave algorithms is an important task in the distributed computing research.

The concept of *self-stabilization* [12] is the most general technique to design a system to tolerate arbitrary transient faults. A self-stabilizing system, regardless of the initial states of the processors and initial messages in the links, is guaranteed to converge to the intended behavior in finite time. *Snap-stabilization* was introduced in [7]. A *snap-stabilizing* algorithm guarantees that it always behaves according to its specification. In other words, a snap-stabilizing algorithm is also a self-stabilizing algorithm which stabilizes in 0 steps. Obviously, a *snap-stabilizing* protocol is optimal in stabilization time.

S.-T. Huang and T. Herman (Eds.): SSS 2003, LNCS 2704, pp. 199–214, 2003.
© Springer-Verlag Berlin Heidelberg 2003

Related Work. PIF algorithms have been proposed in the area of self-stabilization, e.g., [7, 13, 15] for tree networks, and [9, 10, 20] for arbitrary networks. The self-stabilizing PIF protocols have also been used in the area of self-stabilizing synchronizers [2, 4, 6]. The most general method to "repair" the system is to reset the entire system after a transient fault is detected. Reset protocols are also PIF-based algorithms. Several reset protocols exist in the self-stabilizing literature (see [1, 3, 4, 5, 20]). Self-stabilizing snapshot algorithms [14, 20] are also based on the PIF scheme. The first snap-stabilizing PIF algorithm for arbitrary networks has been presented in [10].

Contribution. In [10], the system needs the knowledge of the exact size of the network (i.e., the number of processors). So this size must be constant and the protocol cannot work on dynamical networks. In this paper, we solve this drawback by the composition of three protocols. The first one is the actual PIF protocol, the second one allows the processors to execute the feedback phase, and the role of the third one is to deal with the processors having an abnormal state.

Outline of the paper. In the next section (Section 2), we describe the distributed system and the model in which our PIF scheme is written. In the same section, we also state what it means for a protocol to be snap-stabilizing and give a formal statement of the problem solved in this paper. The PIF algorithm is presented in Section 3. We then prove the correctness of the algorithm in Section 4, followed by the complexity analysis. Finally, we make some concluding remarks in Section 5.

2   Preliminaries

Distributed System. We consider an asynchronous network of N processors connected by bidirectional communication links according to an arbitrary topology. We consider networks which are *asynchronous*. $Neig_p$ denotes the set of neighbors of processor p ($Neig_p$ is shown as an input from the system). We consider the local shared memory model of communication. The program of every processor consists of a set of *shared variables* (henceforth, referred to as variables) and a finite set of actions. A processor can only write to its own variables, and read its own variables and variables owned by the neighboring processors.

Each action is of the following form: $< label >::< guard > \longrightarrow < statement >$. The guard of an action in the program of p is a boolean expression involving the variables of p and its neighbors. The statement of an action of p updates one or more variables of p. An action can be executed only if its guard evaluates to true. We assume that the actions are atomically executed, meaning, the evaluation of a guard and the execution of the corresponding statement of an action, if executed, are done in one atomic step.

The *state* of a processor is defined by the value of its variables. The *state* of a system is the product of the states of all processors ($\in V$). We will refer to the state of a processor and system as a (*local*) *state* and (*global*) *configuration*, respectively. Let a distributed protocol $\mathcal{P}$ be a collection of binary transition relations denoted by $\mapsto$, on $\mathcal{C}$, the set of all possible configurations of the system. A *computation* of a protocol $\mathcal{P}$ is a *maximal* sequence of configurations $e = \gamma_0, \gamma_1, \ldots, \gamma_i, \gamma_{i+1}, \ldots$, such that for $i \geq 0, \gamma_i \mapsto \gamma_{i+1}$ (a single *computation step*) if γ_{i+1} exists, or γ_i is a terminal configuration. *Maximality* means that the sequence is either infinite, or it is finite and no action of $\mathcal{P}$ is enabled in the final configuration. All computations considered in this paper are assumed to be maximal. The set of all possible computations of $\mathcal{P}$ in system S is denoted as $\mathcal{E}$. A processor p is said to be *enabled* in γ ($\gamma \in \mathcal{C}$) if there exists an action A such that the guard of A is true in γ. We consider that any processor p executed a *disable action* in the computation step $\gamma_i \mapsto \gamma_{i+1}$ if p was enabled in γ_i and not enabled in γ_{i+1}, but did not execute any action between these two configurations. (The disable action represents the following situation: At least one neighbor of p changed its state between γ_i and γ_{i+1}, and this change effectively made the guard of all actions of p false.) Similarly, an action A is said to be enabled (in γ) at p if the guard of A is true at p (in γ).

We assume a *weakly fair and distributed daemon*. The *weak fairness* means that if a processor p is continuously enabled, then p will be eventually chosen by the daemon to execute an action. The *distributed* daemon implies that during a computation step, if one or more processors are enabled, then the daemon chooses at least one (possibly more) of these enabled processors to execute an action.

In order to make our algorithm more readable, we designed it as a *composition* of three algorithms. In this composition, if a processor p is enabled for k of the combined protocols, then, if the daemon chooses it, p executes an enabled action of each of the k protocols, in the same step. Variables, predicates, or macros of an algorithm A used by an algorithm B are shown as inputs in Algorithm B.

In order to compute the time complexity measure, we use the definition of *round* [13]. This definition captures the execution rate of the slowest processor in any computation. Given a computation e ($e \in \mathcal{E}$), the *first round* of e (let us call it e') is the minimal prefix of e containing the execution of one action (an action of the protocol or the disable action) of every continuously enabled processor from the first configuration. Let e'' be the suffix of e, i.e., $e = e'e''$. The *second round* of e is the first round of e'', and so on.

Snap-Stabilization. Let $\mathcal{X}$ be a set. $x \vdash P$ means that an element $x \in \mathcal{X}$ satisfies the predicate P defined on the set $\mathcal{X}$.

Definition 1 (Snap-Stabilization). *Let T be a task, and $\mathcal{SP}_T$ a specification of T. The protocol $\mathcal{P}$ is snap-stabilizing for the specification $\mathcal{SP}_T$ on $\mathcal{E}$ if and only if the following condition holds:* $\forall e \in \mathcal{E} :: e \vdash \mathcal{SP}_T$.

The Problem To Be Solved. Any processor can be an initiator in a PIF protocol, and several PIF protocols may run simultaneously. We consider the problem in this paper in a general setting of the PIF scheme where we assume that the PIF is initiated by a processor, called the *root*. We denote the root processor by r.

Specification 1 (PIF Cycle)   *A finite computation* $e = \gamma_0, \ldots, \gamma_i, \gamma_{i+1}, \ldots,$
$\gamma_t \in \mathcal{E}$ *is called a PIF Cycle, if and only if the following condition is true:*
If Processor r broadcasts a message m in the computation step $\gamma_0 \mapsto \gamma_1$, *then:*

[PIF1] *For each* $p \neq r$, *there exists a unique* $i \in [1, t-1]$ *such that p receives m*
       in $\gamma_i \mapsto \gamma_{i+1}$, *and*
[PIF2] *In* γ_t, *r receives an acknowledgment of the receipt of m from every pro-*
       cessor $p \neq r$.

Remark 1. So in practice, to prove that a PIF algorithm is snap-stabilizing we
have to show that every execution of the algorithm satisfies the following two
conditions: 1. if r has a message m to broadcast, then it will be able to start
the broadcast in a finite time, and 2. starting from any configuration where r is
ready to broadcast, the system satisfies Specification 1.

3   Algorithm

The snap-stabilizing PIF algorithm we proposed is divided in three parts: PIF
Algorithm (Algorithms 1 and 2), Question Algorithm (Algorithms 3 and 4), and
Error Algorithm (Algorithms 5 and 6). PIF Algorithm is the main algorithm.
It works in three phases: the broadcast phase, the feedback phase following the
broadcast phase, and the cleaning phase which cleans the trace of the feedback
phase so that the root is ready to broadcast a new message. Question Algorithm
controls that the processors do not execute the feedback phase too early. Error
Algorithm cleans the processors which do not have a normal configuration.

   We first present the normal behavior of the PIF algorithm. We then explain
the method of error correction.

3.1   Normal Behavior

Consider the configuration where $\forall p, Pif_p = C$. We refer to this configuration
as the *normal starting configuration*. In this configuration, the root is the only
enabled processor. The root broadcasts a message m and switches to the broadcast phase by executing $Pif_r = B$ (*B-action*). When a processor p (such that
$Pif_p = C$) waiting for a message finds one of its neighbors q in the broadcast
phase, p receives the message from q. Then, p sets its variable Pif_p to B, points
to q using the variable Par_p, and sets its level L_p to $L_q + 1$ (*B-action*). Typically, L_p contains the length of the path followed by the broadcast message
from the root r to p. (Since r never receives a broadcast message from any of
its neighbor, r does not have any variable Par and L_r is shown as a **constant**
in the algorithm.) Processor p is now in the broadcast phase ($Pif_p = B$) and
is supposed to broadcast the message to its neighbors (except Par_p). So, step
by step, a spanning tree (w.r.t. the variable Par) rooted at r is dynamically
built during the broadcast phase. Let us call this tree the $B\text{-}tree_r$. Each time
a processor broadcast m, it also executes $Que_p := Q$ (*QB-action* in Question

Algorithm). When its neighbors (with variable $Pif \neq C$) have taken p's question in account by setting Que to R (QR-action), p can also execute QR-action, meaning that it send a request to r: "Do you authorize me to feedback?". Eventually, some processors in B-tree$_r$ cannot broadcast the message because all its neighbors have received the message from some other neighbor. The processors which are not able to broadcast the message further are the leaves of B-tree$_r$. In this case the leaves execute $Que_p := W$ (QW-action), meaning that now they are waiting for an answer from r. This action is propagated toward the root if possible. (p propagates it if all its children in B-tree$_r$ have setted their Que variable to W and no neighbor has still $Pif_p = C$.) With similar conditions, r executes its QA-action: it sends an answer to its children (QA-action) meaning that they are authorized to feedback. When a leaf receives this answer, it can execute the feedback phase (F-action). So, step by step, every processor p propagates the feedback phase towards the root in B-tree$_r$ by executing F-action. The feedback phase eventually reaches the root r. Finally, the leaf processors in B-tree$_r$ initiate the third phase, called the *cleaning phase*. The aim of this phase is to erase the trace of the last PIF cycle (the broadcast phase followed by the feedback phase) initiated by the root, i.e., to bring the system in the normal starting configuration again ($\forall p, Pif_p = C$). A leaf processor p in B-tree$_r$ initiates the cleaning phase by setting Pif_p to C when each of its neighbors q is either in the feedback phase ($Pif_q = F$) or in the cleaning phase ($Pif_q = C$). So, the cleaning phase works in parallel and follows the feedback phase. Once all neighbors of the root change to the cleaning phase, the root also participates in the cleaning phase.

3.2 Error Correction

During the normal behavior, the processors must maintain some properties based on the value of their variables and that of their parent. For the processors p which are not the root ($p \neq r$), we list some of those conditions below:

1. If p is in the broadcast phase, then its parent is also in the broadcast phase. Also, if p is in the feedback phase, then its parent is either in the broadcast or feedback phase (Predicate $GoodPif$ in PIF Algorithm).
2. If p is involved in the PIF Cycle ($Pif_p \neq C$), then its level L_p must be equal to one plus the level of its parent (Predicate $GoodLevel$ in PIF Algorithm).
3. If p is involved in the PIF Cycle it must satisfy (1) and (2) (Predicate $\neg AbRoot$ in PIF Algorithm).

Starting now from any configuration, a processor p may satisfy $AbRoot$. In this case, we cannot simply set Pif_p to C. Assume that $Pif_p = B$. Since p satisfies $AbRoot$, that means that some processors in the broadcast phase can be in the abnormal tree rooted in p (B-tree$_p$). If we simply set Pif_p to C, p can participate again to the broadcast of the tree of which it was the root. Since we do not assume the knowledge of any bound on the L values (we may assume that the maximum value of L is any upper bound of N), this scheme can progress infinitely often (respectively, too many times), and the system contains an abnormal tree which can prevent (respectively, dramaticaly slow down) the progression of the tree of the normal broadcast phase (B-$tree_r$). Error Algorithm solves this problem by paralyzing the progress of any abnormal tree before to remove it. A processor p can broadcast a message from a neighbor q only if q satisfies $Pif_q = B$ and $FreeError(q)$, i.e., $E_q = C$ (see *Potential* and *Pre_Potential* in PIF Algorithm). So, if p is an abnormal root, it sets its variable E_p to B and broadcasts this value in its tree (and only in its tree). When p receives an aknowledgment of all its children (value F of variable E), it knows that all the processors q of its tree have $E_q = F$ and no processor can now participate in the broadcast of q. Then p can leave its tree and it will not try to broadcast a message of one of the processors q before q broadcasts a message of another tree. By this process, all abnormal trees eventually disappear, and B-$tree_r$ will be able to grow until it reaches all the processors of the network.

Question Algorithm has now to deal with abnormal trees meaning that some processor p broadcasting the message from r can execute the B-*action* while q, one of its neighbors, belongs to an abnormal tree. Then, to prevent q to set Que_q to A, p is waiting for q to set Que_q to R (QR-*action*). This value will erase all A values in the path from q to the abnormal root. Since only r can generate a A value, q will never receives any A and will eventually leave the abnormal tree as described above.

Algorithm 1 $\mathcal{PIF}$ for the root ($p = r$).

Input:
    $Neig_p$: set of (locally) ordered neighbors of p
    $AnswerOK()$: predicate from Question Algorithm
Constant:
    $L_p = 0$
Variables:
    $Pif_p \in \{B, F, C\}$
Predicates:
    $Leaf(p) \equiv (\forall q \in Neig_p :: (Pif_q \neq C) \Rightarrow (Par_q \neq p))$;
  $Broadcast(p) \equiv (Pif_p = C) \wedge Leaf(p)$;
    $CFree(p) \equiv (\forall q \in Neig_p :: (Pif_q \neq C))$;
    $BLeaf(p) \equiv (Pif_p = B) \wedge (\forall q \in Neig_p :: (Par_q = p) \Rightarrow (Pif_q = F))$;
  $Feedback(p) \equiv BLeaf(p) \wedge CFree(p) \wedge AnswerOK(p)$;
  $Cleaning(p) \equiv (Pif_p = F) \wedge Leaf(p) \wedge (\forall q \in Neig_p :: Pif_q \neq B)$;
Actions:
B-*action* :: $Broadcast(p) \rightarrow Pif_p := B$;
F-*action* :: $Feedback(p) \rightarrow Pif_p := F$
C-*action* :: $Cleaning(p) \rightarrow Pif_p := C$

Algorithm 2 $\mathcal{PIF}$ for $p \neq r$.

Input:
  $Neig_p$: set of (locally) ordered neighbors of p
  $AnswerOK()$: predicate from Question Algorithm
  $FreeError()$, $CError()$: predicates from Error Algorithm
Variables:
  $Pif_p \in \{B, F, C\}$
  L_p : integer
  $Par_p \in Neig_p$
Macros:
$Pre\_Potential_p = \{q \in Neig_p :: (Pif_q = B) \wedge (Par_q \neq p) \wedge FreeError(q)\};$
  $Potential_p = \{q \in Pre\_Potential :: \forall q' \in Pre\_Potential, L_q \leq L_{q'}\};$
    $Child_p \equiv \{q \in Neig_p :: (Pif_q \in \{B, F\}) \wedge (Par_q = p)$
        $\wedge[(Pif_p \neq Pif_q) \Rightarrow (Pif_p = B)] \wedge (L_q = L_p + 1)\};$
Predicates:
    $Leaf(p) \equiv (\forall q \in Neig_p :: (Pif_q \neq C) \Rightarrow (Par_q \neq p));$
$Broadcast(p) \equiv (Pif_p = C) \wedge Leaf(p) \wedge (Potential_p \neq \emptyset);$
    $CFree(p) \equiv (\forall q \in Neig_p :: (Pif_q \neq C);$
      $BF(p) \equiv (Pif_p = B) \vee (Pif_p = F);$
  $GoodPif(p) \equiv BF(p) \Rightarrow ((Pif_{Par_p} \neq Pif_p) \Rightarrow (Pif_{Par_p} = B));$
$GoodLevel(p) \equiv BF(p) \Rightarrow (L_p = L_{Par_p} + 1);$
    $AbRoot(p) \equiv \neg GoodPif(p) \vee \neg GoodLevel(p);$
    $Normal(p) \equiv \neg AbRoot(p) \wedge FreeError(p);$
    $BLeaf(p) \equiv (Pif_p = B) \wedge (\forall q \in Neig_p :: (Par_q = p) \Rightarrow (Pif_q = F));$
  $Feedback(p) \equiv BLeaf(p) \wedge Normal(p) \wedge CFree(p) \wedge AnswerOK(p);$
  $Cleaning(p) \equiv (Pif_p = F) \wedge Normal(p) \wedge Leaf(p) \wedge (\forall q \in Neig_p :: Pif_q \neq B));$
Actions:
$B\text{-}action :: Broadcast(p) \rightarrow Pif_p := B; Par_p := min_{\prec p}(Potential_p); L_p := L_{Par_p} + 1;$
$F\text{-}action :: Feedback(p) \rightarrow Pif_p := F$
$C\text{-}action :: Cleaning(p) \rightarrow Pif_p := C$
$E\text{-}action :: CError(p) \rightarrow Pif_p := C$

---

4   Proof of Correctness

As the system can start in an arbitrary (including an undesirable) configuration, we need to show that the algorithm can deal with all the possible errors. To characterize these erroneous configurations, in Subsection 4.1, we define some terms to distinguish these configurations. Moreover, we must show that despite these erroneous configurations, the system always behaves according to its specifications, i.e., is snap-stabilizing.

4.1   Some Definitions

Definition 2 (E-Trace). *Let Y be a t-uple of processors ($Y = (p_0, p_1, \ldots, p_k)$).* $E - trace(Y) = E_0 E_1 \ldots E_k$ *is the sequence of the values of Variable E on processors p_i ($i = 0 \ldots k$).*

Algorithm 3   Question Algorithm for the root $(p = r)$.

Input:
  $Neig_p$: set of (locally) ordered neighbors of p
  Par_q, Pif_p, Pif_q: variables from $\mathcal{PIF}$
  $CFree()$, $Broadcast()$: predicate from $\mathcal{PIF}$
Variables: $Que_p \in \{Q, R, A\}$

the protocol below concerns only p such that $Pif_p \in \{B, F\}$

Predicates:
  $Require(p) \equiv ([[(Que_p = Q) \wedge (\forall q \in Neig_p :: (Que_q \in \{Q, R\})]$
  $\qquad\qquad \vee [(Que_q \in \{W, A\})$
  $\qquad\qquad\qquad \wedge (\exists q \in Neig_p :: (Que_q = Q) \vee ((Par_q = p) \wedge (Que_q = R)))]])$;
  $Answer(p) \equiv (Que_p = R) \wedge CFree(p)$
  $\qquad\qquad \wedge (\forall q \in Neig_p :: (Pif_q \neq C) \Rightarrow [((Par_q = p) \wedge (Que_q = W))$
  $\qquad\qquad\qquad\qquad\qquad\qquad \vee ((Par_q \neq p) \wedge (Que_q \in \{W, A\}))]])$;
  $AnswerOK(p) \equiv (Que_p = A) \wedge (\forall q \in Neig_p :: (Pif_p \neq C) \Rightarrow (Que_q = A))$;
Actions:
  $QB\text{-}action :: Broadcast(p) \rightarrow Que_p := Q$
  $QR\text{-}action :: Require(p) \quad\rightarrow Que_p := R$
  $QA\text{-}action :: Answer(p) \quad\rightarrow Que_p := A$

Example: Let p and q be two processors such that $E_p = C$ and $E_q = B$. Then $E - Trace(p, q) = CB$.

Definition 3 (E-Prohibited Pairs). *Let p and q such that $Pif_p \neq C$ and $Pif_q \neq C$, and $Par_q = p$. The $E - trace(p, q)$ of type $\{CB, CF, FC, FB\}$ are called E-prohibited pairs. In this case, we also say that $E - trace(p, q)$ is E-prohibited.*

Remark 2. Let p and q such that $Pif_p \neq C$ and $Pif_q \neq C$, and $Par_q = p$. $E - trace(p, q)$ is E-prohibited if and only if $(FCorrection(p) \wedge E_q \neq F) \vee BCorrection(q) \vee (FCorrection(q) \wedge E_p = C)$.

Definition 4 (Path). *The sequence of processors $p_0, p_1, p_2, \ldots p_k$ is called a path if $\forall i, 1 \leq i \leq k$, $p_i \in Neig_{i-1}$. The path is referred to as an elementary path if $\forall i, j, 0 \leq i < j \leq k$, $p_i \neq p_j$. The processors p_0 and p_k are termed as the extremities of the path.*

Definition 5 (ParentPath). *For any processor p such that $BF(p)$, a unique path $p_0, p_1, p_2, \ldots p_k = p$, called $ParentPath(p)$, exists if and only if the following conditions are true: 1. $\forall i, 1 \leq i \leq k$, $Par_{p_i} = p_{i-1}$. 2. $\forall i, 1 \leq i \leq k$, $BF(p_i) \wedge \neg AbRoot(p_i) \wedge (E - Trace(p_{i-1}, p)$ is not E-prohibited). 3. $p_0 = r$ or $AbRoot(p_0)$ or $E - Trace(Par_{p_0}, p_0)$ is E-prohibited.*

Definition 6 (Tree). *For any processor p such that $p = r$ or p is an abnormal processor, we define a set $Tree(p)$ of processors as follows: For any processor q, $q \in Tree(p)$ if and only if p is the first extremity of $ParentPath(q)$.*

Algorithm 4   Question Algorithm for $p \neq r$.

Input:
   $Neig_p$: set of (locally) ordered neighbors of p
   Par_p, Par_q, Pif_p, Pif_q: variables from $\mathcal{PIF}$
   $CFree()$, $Broadcast()$: predicate from $\mathcal{PIF}$
Variables: $Que_p \in \{Q, R, W, A\}$

the protocol below concerns only p such that $Pif_p \in \{B, F\}$

Predicates:
$Require(p) \equiv \neg AbRoot(p)$
$\qquad \wedge ([[(Que_p = Q) \wedge (\forall q \in Neig_p :: (Que_q \in \{Q, R\})]$
$\qquad\qquad \vee [(Que_q \in \{W, A\}) \wedge (\exists q \in Neig_p :: (Que_q = Q)$
$\qquad\qquad\qquad\qquad \vee ((Par_q = p) \wedge (Que_q = R)))]]);$
$Wait(p) \equiv \neg AbRoot(p) \wedge (Que_p = R) \wedge (Que_{Par_p} = R) \wedge CFree(p)$
$\qquad \wedge (\forall q \in Neig_p :: (Que_q \neq Q) \wedge ((Par_q = p) \Rightarrow (Que_q = W)));$
$Answer(p) \equiv \neg AbRoot(p) \wedge (Que_p = W) \wedge (Que_{Par_p} = A)$
$\qquad \wedge (\forall q \in Neig_p :: (Pif_q \neq C) \Rightarrow [((Par_q = p) \wedge (Que_q = W))$
$\qquad\qquad\qquad\qquad \vee ((Par_q \neq p) \wedge (Que_q \in \{W, A\}))]);$
$AnswerOK(p) \equiv (Que_p = A) \wedge (\forall q \in Neig_p :: (Pif_p \neq C) \Rightarrow (Que_q = A));$
Actions:
$QB\text{-}action :: Broadcast(p) \rightarrow Que_p := Q$
$QR\text{-}action :: Require(p) \quad \rightarrow Que_p := R$
$QW\text{-}action :: Wait(p) \quad\;\; \rightarrow Que_p := W$
$QA\text{-}action :: Answer(p) \quad \rightarrow Que_p := A$

Algorithm 5   Error Algorithm for the root $(p = r)$.

Constant:
   $E_p = C$

Definition 7 (NormalTree). *A tree containing only processors p such that $Normal(p) \vee p = r$ is called a NormalTree. Obviously, the system contains only one NormalTree: this tree is rooted by r. A tree rooted by another processor than r is called an AbnormalTree.*

Definition 8 (Alive). *A tree T satisfies $Alive(T)$ (or is called Alive) if and only if: $\exists p \in T$ such that $(Pif_p = B) \wedge (E_p = C)$.*

Definition 9 (Dead). *A tree T satisfies $Dead(T)$ (or is called Dead) if and only if $\neg Alive(T)$.*

Remark 3. No processor can hook a Dead tree.

Definition 10 (Alive AbNormal Root: AAR). *A processor p is called AAR if and only if $AbRoot(p) \wedge Alive(Tree(p))$.*

Definition 11 (Falldown Alive AbNormal Root: FAAR). *A processor p is called FAAR if and only if $CError(p) \wedge AAR(p)$.*

Algorithm 6   Error Algorithm for $p \neq r$.

Input:
  Par_p, Pif_p: variables from $\mathcal{PIF}$
  $Child_p$: macro from $\mathcal{PIF}$
  $AbRoot()$, $BF()$: predicates from $\mathcal{PIF}$
Variables:
  $E_p \in \{B, F, C\}$
General Predicate:
$FreeError(p) \equiv BF(p) \Rightarrow (E_p = C)$;

the action below concerns only p such that $Pif_p = C$

Action:
$EB\text{-}init :: Broadcast(p) \rightarrow E_p := C$

the protocol below concerns only p such that $Pif_p \in \{B, F\}$

Predicates:
  $BError(p) \equiv (E_p = C) \wedge (AbRoot(p) \vee (E_{Par_p} = B)) \wedge (\forall q \in Child_p :: E_q = C)$;
  $FError(p) \equiv (E_p = B) \wedge (AbRoot(p) \vee (E_{Par_p} = B)) \wedge (\forall q \in Child_p :: E_q = F)$;
  $FAbRoot(p) \equiv (E_p = F) \wedge AbRoot(p)$;
$BCorrection(p) \equiv [(E_p = B) \wedge (\neg AbRoot(p)) \wedge (E_{par_p} \neq B)]$;
$FCorrection(p) \equiv (E_p = F) \wedge [(\neg AbRoot(p) \wedge E_{par_p} = C) \vee (\exists q \in Child_p :: E_q \neq F)]$;
  $CError(p) \equiv FAbRoot(p) \vee BCorrection(p) \vee FCorrection(p)$;
Actions:
$EB\text{-}action :: BError(p) \rightarrow E_p := B$
$EF\text{-}action :: FError(p) \rightarrow E_p := F$
$EC\text{-}action :: CError(p) \rightarrow E_p := C$

Definition 12 (Potential Falldown Alive AbNormal Root:PFAAR).
A processor p is called PFAAR in γ_0 if and only if $\exists e : \gamma_0 \gamma_1 \ldots \gamma_i \ldots$ such that $\exists i \geq 0$, p is FAAR in γ_i.

4.2   Abnormal Processors

In this subsection, we show that the network contains no abnormal processor in at most $3N - 2$ rounds. We first deduce from the algorithm and Remark 2 the following lemma.

Lemma 1. *Any p in the $NormalTree$ satisfies $E - Trace(ParentPath(p)) \in C^+$, and any p in an $AbnormalTree$ satisfies $E - Trace(ParentPath(p)) \in B^*C^* \cup B^*F^*$.*

Lemma 2. *Error Algorithm never generates E-prohibited pairs.*

Proof. Let p and q such that $Par_q = p$. By checking all the non E-prohibited pairs ($Pif_p = C$, $Pif_q = C$, or $E - trace(p, q) \in \{BB, BC, BF, CC, FF\}$) and the actions of Error Algorithm, it is easy to see that we cannot create any E-prohibited pair.

By checking the actions of PIF and Error Algorithms and by Lemma 2, we can deduce the following result.

Lemma 3. *After the first round the system cannot contain any E-prohibited pair.*

Proof. Let p and q be two processors such that $E - trace(p, q)$ is E-prohibited at the first configuration ($Par_q = p$, $Pif_p \neq C$, $Pif_q \neq C$, and $E - trace(p, q) \in \{CB, CF, FC, FB\}$).

1. Assume that $E - Trace(p, q) = CB$. The only actions of $\mathcal{PIF}$ or Error Algorithm q can execute are E-action and EC-action, respectively, since $BCorrection(q) \Rightarrow CError(q)$. Until q moves, no action of p can change the value of E_p or set Pif_p to C. So q is continuously enabled and, since the daemon is weakly fair, q will execute the E-action and EC-action during the first round. After this move, $E - Trace(p, q)$ is never more an E-prohibited pair.
2. Assume that $E - Trace(p, q) = CF$. The case is similar to the previous one.
3. Assume that $E - Trace(p, q) = FC$. The only actions of $\mathcal{PIF}$ or Error Algorithm p can execute are E-action and EC-action, respectively, since $FCorrection(p) \Rightarrow CError(p)$. If q is not enabled or does not move before p, p will execute E-action and EC-action during the first round. After this move, $E - Trace(p, q)$ is never more an E-prohibited pair. Assume now that q is enabled and moves before p. Depending on Pif_p and Pif_q, q can satisfy $Feedback(q)$ or $Cleaning(q)$.
   (a) If q satisfies $Feedback(q)$ (in this case $Pif_p = Pif_q = B$), it executes Now q cannot be enabled for $\mathcal{PIF}$ until p moves. Since p is still enabled, the system is still executing the first round, and , as previously, p eventually executes execute the E-action and EC-action during the first round. After this move, $E - Trace(p, q)$ is never more an E-prohibited pair.
   (b) If q satisfies $Cleaning(q)$ (in this case $Pif_p = Pif_q = F$), executes C-action. Now $Pif_q = C$ and $E - Trace(p, q)$ is never more an E-prohibited pair.
4. Assume that $E - Trace(p, q) = FB$. Both p and q satisfy $CError()$. When one of them (or both of them) executes the E-action and EC-action, $E - Trace(p, q)$ is never more an E-prohibited pair.

By Lemma 2, Error Algorithm never generates E-prohibited pairs. Since we just showed that the initial E-prohibited pairs disappear in one round, the lemma is proved.

Corollary 1. *After the first round, the predicates $BCorrection(p)$ and $FCorrection(p)$ will be never more satisfied. The only two ways for a processor p to change Pif_p to C are: p satisfies $FAbRoot(p)$, therefore it satisfies $AbRoot(p)$, or p satisfies $Leaf(p)$.*

Lemma 4. *After the first round the root of an abnormal tree can leave it only if the tree is dead.*

Proof. Let ar be the root of an abnormal tree. From Lemma 1, for all p in $Tree(ar)$, $E - Trace(ParentPath(p)) \in B^*C^* \cup B^*F^*$. By Error Algorithm, ar cannot leave the tree until $E_{ar} = F$. So, when ar executes E-*action* and EC-*action*, $E - Trace(ParentPath(p)) \in F^+$ for all p in $Tree(ar)$. By Definition 9 , $Tree(ar)$ is dead.

Lemma 5. *Every processor p such that $PIF_p = C$ in γ satisfies $\neg PFAAR(p)$.*

Proof. If p never moves then the lemma holds. Assume now that p executes B-*action*. Let q be the parent of p, q is in an abnormal tree. $E_p = C$ after p moves. So by Lemma 4, the root of the abnormal tree will leave the tree only when the tree is dead. When p becomes the root of a part of the initial tree, $Tree(p)$ is still dead and the lemma holds.

Lemma 6. *After the first round, every processor p satisfies $\neg PFAAR(p)$.*

Proof. We check the three possible cases after the first round.

(1) If p verifies $Pif_p = C$, by Lemma 5, p satisfies $\neg PFAAR(p)$.

(2) If p is in the normal tree then it must execute C-*action* before to be able to hook on to an abnormal tree. After p executes C-*action*, $Pif_p = C$. Lemma 5 implies that p satisfies $\neg PFAAR(p)$.

(3) If p is in an abnormal tree then Lemma 4 implies that p leaves the tree only if $Tree(p)$ is dead. So, when p leaves the tree, it does not verify $FAAR(p)$, since after this move, p verifies $Pif_p = C$, by the same reasoning as previously, p satisfies $\neg PFAAR(p)$.

Lemma 7. *After the first round all abnormal trees become dead in at most $N-1$ rounds.*

Proof. Corollary 1 implies that after the first round, the root p of an abnormal tree cannot leave it before $E_p = F$. The worst case is obtained when any processor in the tree has the C value in Variable E. So, it is necessary to propagate the B value from the root to the leaves. Then, $h + 1$ rounds are necessary to propagate this value where h is the maximum height of the tree. All the processors different from the root can be in the abnormal tree, this implies that the maximum height is $N - 2$, thus the system needs at most $N - 1$ rounds to propagate B in the tree.

Lemma 8. *In at most $3N - 2$ rounds, the system does not contain any abnormal tree.*

Proof. From Lemma 6, after the first round, no processor can leave an abnormal tree and hook on to it again. So any abnormal tree can only contain any processor at most once, and then, disappear once the successive abnormal roots leave it (see Lemma 1). As in proof of Lemma 7, it is necessary to have $N - 1$ rounds to propagate the value F up, and $N-1$ rounds to apply $C-action$ and $EC-action$. After that, all the dead trees have disappear and the system does not contain any abnormal tree in at most $3N - 2$ rounds.

4.3   Proof of Snap-Stabilisation

Lemma 9. *From any initial configuration containing no abnormal tree, the root executes the B-action in at most 5N rounds.*

Proof. From these configurations, the worst case is the following: The root has $Pif_r = B$ and all the other processors have their Pif variable equal to C. In this case, the system has to perform a quite complete PIF cycle (a complete cycle except the first step: B-*action* of r). According to the algorithm, B-*action* is propagated to all processors in at most $N - 1$ rounds. One extra round is necessary for the leaf processors of the broadcast to set their Que variable to R. The time used by the QW-*action* is bounded by the maximum length of the tree, $N - 1$ rounds. By a similar reasoning taking in account that r also executes the respective actions, it is obvious that QA-*action*, F-*action*, and C-*action* need at most N rounds. Furthermore the total time is $5N - 1$ rounds, and the root can execute B-*action* during the next round.

By Lemmas 8 and 9, we can claim the following result.

Theorem 1. *From any initial configuration, the root can execute B-action in at most 8N − 2 rounds.*

Lemma 10. *Let p be a processor in an abnormal tree such that $Que_p \in \{Q, R\}$. While p does not leave the tree, $Que_p \neq A$.*

Proof. If p also satisfies $AbRoot(p)$, then p cannot execute QA-*action* before it leaves the tree. Otherwise, if there exists an A value on ParentPath(p), the Q and R values are a barrier for the A. So while p does not leave the tree, it will never receive any A value.

Theorem 2. *From any configuration such that the root executes B-action, the execution satisfies PIF specification.*

Proof. 1. Assume that there exist some processors which never receive the message m sent by r. Then there exists a processor p which never receives m but one of its neighbor (q) does. When q receives m (in configuration γ), it executes the B-*action*. Then, if $Pif_q \neq C$ and $Que_p \in \{W, A\}$, (Pif_q, Que_p) will stay equal to (B, Q) while Que_p equals R, so p eventually executes the QR-*action*. We can remark in this case, that p is in an abnormal tree, since it never receives m. From Lemma 10, $Que_p \neq A$ while p does not leave the tree. While p does not leave the tree, q cannot execute the F-*action*. (q does not satisfy $AnswerOK(q)$ because p). From Lemma 8, p eventually leaves the tree and we reach a configuration where $Pif_p = C$.
While $Pif_p = C$, q cannot execute the F-*action*. From Lemma 8, the system does not contain any abnormal tree in a finite time, so $\forall p'$ neighbor of p, $Par_{p'} \neq p$. So p satisfies $Broadcast(p)$ forever and eventually receives m. (it executes the B-*action*.) We obtain a contradiction.

2. Assume that there exists a processor p, which receives the message m at least twice. p executed the B-, F-, and C-actions for m before it satisfies again $Broadcast(p)$ for m. Let P_1 be $ParentPath(p)$ (respectively, P_2) corresponding to the first (respectively, second) reception of m by p. It is clear that Pif_r always equals B while some processor is still in B in the network. So, at least a processor of P_1 has still its Pif variable equal to F. Then $P_2 \neq P_1$. So there exists a path (P_1) from r to p such that $Pif - Trace(P_1) \in B^+F^+C^+$ and there exists a path (P_2) such that the $Pif - Trace(P_2) \in B^+C^+$. In this case, the contradiction is that p was not able to execute B-action for the first reception of m, since at least its neighbor in P_2 had its Pif variable equal to C.

We proved that every processor receives m exactly once. (Property [PIF1] of Specification 1.) We now show Property [PIF2]. Assume that a processor p is such that $Pif_p = B$. Then, it is clear that every processor in ParentPath(p) have their Pif variable equal to B. So, when r executes the F-action, the other processors executed F-action before and their Pif variable is in $\{C, F\}$.

The execution satisfies PIF specification.

From Remark 1 and Theorems 1 and 2, the following theorem is obvious.

Theorem 3. *The composition of $\mathcal{PIF}$, Question, and Error Algorithms is snap-stabilizing for Specification 1.*

4.4   Complexity Analysis

From Theorem 1 and Lemma 9, we can deduce the following result.

Lemma 11. *From any initial configuration, a complete PIF cycle is executed in at most $13N - 2$ rounds.*

The performances described by Theorem 1 and Lemmas 9 and 11 are the same as those of the previous snap-stabilizing PIF algorithm ([10]) up to a small constant.

5   Conclusion

We presented a new snap-stabilizing PIF algorithm on an arbitrary network. The algorithm does not use a pre-constructed spanning tree. The snap-stabilizing property guarantees that when a processor p initiates the broadcast wave, the broadcast message will reach every processor in the network. Moreover, all the feedback messages correspond to the broadcast message and will be received by p. The snap-stabilizing PIF algorithm presented in this paper improved the solution presented in [10] because it does not need the knowledge of the exact size of the network. So our protocol can be used on dynamic networks. This protocol is a bold step in the comparison of power of self-stabilization and snap-stabilization. It has been proved in [11] that, in the local shared memory model of communication, any static protocol that can be self-stabilized by the extensions of [14] can also be snap-stabilized by extensions using the snap-stabilizing PIF of [10]. With this new PIF algorithm, we conjecture that this result can be extended for dynamic protocols.

References

[1] Y Afek, S Kutten, and M Yung. Memory-efficient self-stabilization on general networks. In *WDAG90 Distributed Algorithms 4th International Workshop Proceedings, Springer-Verlag LNCS:486*, pages 15–28, 1990. 200

[2] L. O. Alima, J. Beauquier, A. K. Datta, and S. Tixeuil. Self-stabilization with global rooted synchronizers. In *ICDCS98 Proceedings of the 18th International Conference on Distributed Computing Systems*, pages 102–109, 1998. 200

[3] A Arora and MG Gouda. Distributed reset. *IEEE Transactions on Computers*, 43:1026–1038, 1994. 200

[4] B Awerbuch, S Kutten, Y Mansour, B Patt-Shamir, and G Varghese. Time optimal self-stabilizing synchronization. In *STOC93 Proceedings of the 25th Annual ACM Symposium on Theory of Computing*, pages 652–661, 1993. 200

[5] B Awerbuch, B Patt-Shamir, and G Varghese. Self-stabilization by local checking and correction. In *FOCS91 Proceedings of the 31st Annual IEEE Symposium on Foundations of Computer Science*, pages 268–277, 1991. 200

[6] B Awerbuch and G Varghese. Distributed program checking: a paradigm for building self-stabilizing distributed protocols. In *FOCS91 Proceedings of the 31st Annual IEEE Symposium on Foundations of Computer Science*, pages 258–267, 1991. 200

[7] A Bui, AK Datta, F Petit, and V Villain. State-optimal snap-stabilizing PIF in tree networks. In *Proceedings of the Forth Workshop on Self-Stabilizing Systems*, pages 78–85. IEEE Computer Society Press, 1999. 199, 200

[8] EJH Chang. Echo algorithms: depth parallel operations on general graphs. *IEEE Transactions on Software Engineering*, SE-8:391–401, 1982. 199

[9] A Cournier, AK Datta, F Petit, and V Villain. Self-stabilizing PIF algorithm in arbitrary rooted networks. In *21st International Conference on Distributed Computing Systems (ICDCS-21)*, pages 91–98. IEEE Computer Society Press, 2001. 200

[10] A Cournier, AK Datta, F Petit, and V Villain. Snap-stabilizing PIF algorithm in arbitrary rooted networks. In *22st International Conference on Distributed Computing Systems (ICDCS-22)*, pages 199–206. IEEE Computer Society Press, 2002. 199, 200, 212, 213

[11] A Cournier, AK Datta, F Petit, and V Villain. Enabling snap-stabilization. In *23rd International Conference on Distributed Computing Systems (ICDCS-23)*. To appear, 2003. 212

[12] EW Dijkstra. Self stabilizing systems in spite of distributed control. *Communications of the Association of the Computing Machinery*, 17:643–644, 1974. 199

[13] S Dolev, A Israeli, and S Moran. Uniform dynamic self-stabilizing leader election. *IEEE Transactions on Parallel and Distributed Systems*, 8(4):424–440, 1997. 200, 201

[14] S Katz and KJ Perry. Self-stabilizing extensions for message-passing systems. *Distributed Computing*, 7:17–26, 1993. 200, 213

[15] HSM Kruijer. Self-stabilization (in spite of distributed control) in tree-structured systems. *Information Processing Letters*, 8:91–95, 1979. 200

[16] N Lynch. *Distributed algorithms*. Morgan Kaufmann, 1996. 199

[17] M Raynal and JM Helary. *Synchronization and Control of Distributed Systems and Programs*. John Wiley and Sons, Chichester, UK, 1990. 199

[18] A Segall. Distributed network protocols. *IEEE Transactions on Information Theory*, IT-29:23–35, 1983. 199

[19] G Tel. *Introduction to distributed algorithms*. Cambridge University Press, 1994. 199

[20] G Varghese. Self-stabilization by local checking and correction (Ph.D. thesis). Technical Report MIT/LCS/TR-583, MIT, 1993. 200

Author Index